Learning Together and Alone

Learning Together and Alone

Cooperative, Competitive, and Individualistic Learning

FIFTH EDITION

David W. Johnson
University of Minnesota

Roger T. Johnson
University of Minnesota

Allyn and Bacon
Boston   London   Toronto   Sydney   Tokyo   Singapore

Vice President and Editor-in-Chief, Social Sciences and Education: Sean W. Wakely
Editorial Assistant: Jessica J. Barnard
Marketing Manager: Brad Parkins
Composition and Prepress Buyer: Linda Cox
Manufacturing Buyer: Megan Cochran
Cover Administrator: Jenny Hart
Photo Director: Susan Duane
Production Administrator: Deborah Brown
Editorial-Production Service: P. M. Gordon Associates

Library of Congress Cataloging-in-Publication Data

Johnson, David W., 1940–
    Learning together and alone : cooperative, competitive, and
individualistic learning / David W. Johnson, Roger T. Johnson. —
5th ed.
        p.   cm.
    Includes bibliographical references and index.
    ISBN 0–205–28771–9
    1. Group work in education.   2. Individualized instruction.
3. Interaction analysis in education.   4. Lesson planning.
I. Johnson, Roger T., 1938–   . II. Title
LB1032.J595   1999
371.102—dc21   98–25026
                                                      CIP

Photo Credits: P. xii, Will Faller; p. 12, Robert Harbison (top), Will Faller (bottom); p. 48,
Will Hart (top and bottom); p. 58, Will Hart (top), Brian Smith (bottom); p. 68, Brian
Smith (top), Will Hart (bottom); p. 90, Will Faller; p. 102, Will Hart (top), Will Faller
(bottom); p. 124, Tony Neste; p. 150, Will Hart (top), Brian Smith (bottom); p. 162, Will
Faller (top), Robert Harbison (middle and bottom); p. 168, Will Hart (top and bottom).

Printed in the United States of America
10   9   8   03

Contents

Preface

As you may have surmised, we are brothers, and as such we are very familiar with competition. Growing up, we raced to see who would get through a door first, measured to see who got more cake (or more of anything), and argued to see who would sit by the window in the car. One incident we both remember vividly is the corncob fight. For a few years while growing up in Indiana, we lived (and worked!) on a farm. We regularly practiced our throwing accuracy with corncobs, and more than occasionally we practiced on each other. In one of these desperate battles, we each had gathered a large feed sack full of cobs and were flinging and dodging our way through the barn. When the older brother gained the upper hand, as he usually did, the younger brother scampered up the ladder into the hayloft, taking a well-aimed cob in the seat of his pants. The hayloft advantage provided a problem for the older brother as he was nipped a couple of times without even coming close to his opponent. So taking his sack of corncobs between his teeth, he started up the ladder (the only way to the loft). As he got about halfway up, he realized he was getting pelted with more cobs than could be thrown at one time and looked up to see the younger brother standing at the top of the ladder shaking out his bag of corncobs and enjoying himself immensely. The tables turned, however, when the older brother reached the top of the ladder and the younger brother discovered he was out of ammunition. Then it was the younger brother's turn to be pelted as he crouched in the hay while the older brother let him have it—one by one. We still argue about who got the most out of the battle, the younger brother releasing the waterfall of cobs down the ladder or the brother delivering the one-by-one pelting in the hayloft.

We are sure that people who knew us then are surprised to see us cooperating on this book and in the related teacher workshops we conduct. It should be no surprise; the ideas presented here on how to recognize appropriate and inappropriate competitive, individualistic, and cooperative efforts are important enough for even two brothers to cooperate. We are also accidentally, but admirably, suited to work together on this topic. David struggled through graduate school at Columbia University, gaining the skills of an academic social psychologist, while Roger, after teaching for several years at the elementary school level, took the easy route through the University of California as a part-time staff member in teacher education. With the years of classroom teaching experience and the research and writing in social psychology represented by our combined backgrounds, and brought together at the University of Minnesota, we readily recognized the potential of this conceptual scheme—structuring learning in ways consistent with instructional aims.

We believe that all three goals structures—competitive, individualistic, and cooperative–can be used productively and integrated into the same lesson. We believe that all students should be able to compete for fun and enjoyment, work autonomously on their own, and cooperate effectively with others. Just as important, students should know *when* to compete, *when* to work on their own, and *when* to cooperate. While all three goal structures may be effective under certain conditions, competitive and individualistic efforts are effective only when used in the context of a larger framework of cooperation. Carefully planned cooperation becomes the framework within which competitive and individualistic efforts take place. The different types of cooperative learning (formal cooperative learning, informal cooperative learning, and cooperative base groups), furthermore, may be used in an integrated way to maximize the success of any class session.

In our work with teachers in workshops and in our own classes at the University of Minnesota, we have found a few obstacles that hinder implementation. First, teachers often do not realize the potential that implementing appropriate goal structures has for their classroom. The research is clear (see Appendix A). Achievement will go up, relationships will become more positive, and psychological health will improve when goal structures are used appropriately. After all, goal structures concentrate on what is the most powerful variable in the learning situation—the interaction patterns and interdependencies of the students as they work toward a goal. The second obstacle to recognizing the importance of using cooperative as well as competitive and individualized activities is the powerful mythology that surrounds competition. How many times have you heard a version of social Darwinism that suggests "it's a dog-eat-dog world" or "a survival-of-the-fittest society" or that "students need to learn how to compete so they can survive in the business world?" Even the business world does not believe that the world is savagely competitive. As a social psychologist with management training, David could spend much of his time teaching people in business and industry how to reduce inappropriate competition and increase cooperation in their companies. Society cannot be described as competitive; it is by definition cooperative. Within the cooperative framework of society, however, there *is* competition, sometimes too much.

Another obstacle we have observed is the "I'm-already-doing-that" feeling many teachers have when we describe cooperation. If you really are doing it as well as it can be done, much of this book will not be useful. Yet frequently we find that teachers who say (or think) they are using goal structures appropriately are surprised by certain aspects of each when these goal structures are carefully described from a social psychological point of view and when the steps for implementing and monitoring them are explained. Finally, the educational history of many students and teachers is such that they find cooperating within the school rather strange and difficult. Our own students seem relieved when they find that they are not going to have to compete against each other, and a sigh of relief seems to go through the classroom when the cooperative approach is announced. Students, however, are usually somewhat reluctant at first to cooperate with each other and tend to work individualistically when they should be cooperating. It takes some relationship building and trust development before they are able to share ideas and help each other effectively to produce a true group effort. Your students may have some of the same attitudes (so may the teachers in your school), and if they do, you may need to teach and encourage the skills needed to work together.

We wish we could be with you as you implement appropriate goal structures in your instructional program. We would like to help. For most of you, this book and the ideas shared here are the best we can do. We assume your classes will blossom as our own have and as those of teachers near us have. One thing is certain: for those of you who want to match the appropriate student interaction patterns with instructional goals and want to move to a predominantly cooperative classroom, the rationale for doing so is here, and you will be able to discuss goal structuring fluently with anyone. We hope that enough of the strategies have been given, but implementing ideas is your profession and if something is left out, we trust you to find and include it. Above all, enjoy the process. Practice your own skills as you encourage them in your students. You may even try a little cooperating with fellow teachers! In fact, we suggest that the best way to work with the ideas in this book is to approach the task cooperatively with a friend and fellow teacher with whom to share thoughts and successes. Enjoy yourself, persevere, and accept any resulting success with some modesty.

Thanks are due to many people for their help in writing this book and preparing the manuscript. Credit must be given to Edythe Johnson Holubec, our sister, who's always there to lend a hand cheerfully when it's needed; and Linda Johnson, who is so often called on to assemble the whole from bits and pieces. We also owe much to many social psychologists who have conducted research and formulated theory in this area. We owe much to the teachers who have listened to our bridge building and given us help in reconstructing when we needed it. We owe much to our students, who have been patient with our enthusiasm and helpful in challenging and implementing our ideas. Finally, we owe much to our wives and children for making our lives truly cooperative.

David W. Johnson
Roger T. Johnson

1

Cooperative, Competitive, and Individualistic Learning

Once, in the remote past, a tribe of people after years of wandering generally in a southern direction, decided to settle in a valley in a remote part of what is now the United States. They faced the challenges of building shelter, ensuring an adequate supply of water and food the year round, providing for their defense, and creating a good life for themselves and their children. To achieve these goals, they had a choice among three ways of organizing themselves:

1. The tribe could emphasize competition among its members to determine who was best. It is important to place the best and the brightest in charge of the tribe. For each task, members would compete to see who could do it better and faster than anyone else. Those who won were placed in positions of authority and were given the most food and the most comfortable caves. Those who were last were considered of no real importance and were given very little food and the coldest and least secure caves. In this way, the tribe believed they would flourish by constantly ensuring that the strongest, quickest, and most successful members of the tribe benefited the most.

2. The tribe could emphasize working alone, individualistically on one's own. Each tribe member would do each task alone, separate and apart from all others. When a person was hungry, it was up to him or her to hunt or grow food. When danger threatened, each would be responsible for his or her safety. Each person was expected to be an extreme individualist.

3. The tribe could emphasize working together, cooperatively. For each task, tribe members would create a division of labor in which everyone had a part and all contributed. All benefited, sharing equally in the results. Some would hunt, some would grow food, some would take care of and educate the children, and some would build and repair

the houses. Each would assist the others. Because everyone contributed in some way, the tribe members worked on improving communication, leadership, decision making, and ways conflicts were managed. They also became a very friendly tribe and had lots of parties and fun.

Exercise 1.1   *What Is Your Preference?*

Which way would you organize the civilization? In Table 1.1, rank the three alternatives from most preferred ("1") to least preferred ("3") and explain why you ranked the alternative as you did. Find a partner. Share your ranking and reasons. Listen to his or her ranking and reasons. Come to consensus as to how the civilization should be organized.

TABLE 1.1

RANK	INTERDEPENDENCE	REASONS
_____	Competition	
_____	Individualistic Efforts	
_____	Cooperation	

For any task, humans can organize their efforts in these three ways: competitively,[1] individualistically, or cooperatively. Each has its advocates and critics. The truth may be that humans are good at all three. We compete for fun and excitement, we take satisfaction from our individual and autonomous accomplishments, and we cooperate with great focus and determination. Each may be effective under certain conditions. Each time we interact with another human being, we make a choice about the balance of these three ways in the relationship.

In order to make an informed choice among these three alternatives, educators must be able to answer the following questions (see also Figure 1.1):

1. What are cooperative, competitive, and individualistic efforts?
2. What are the expected outcomes of cooperative, competitive, and individualistic efforts?
3. What are the conditions under which cooperative, competitive, and individualistic efforts may be used effectively?
4. How do you structure lessons cooperatively, competitively, or individualistically?
5. How do you use cooperative, competitive, and individualistic learning in an integrated way?

---

1. For a heart-rending but true-life story of the misery of having to live with rabid competition among children, readers may write to our mother, Mrs. Frances W. Johnson, 7208 Cornelia Drive, Edina, Minnesota 55435.

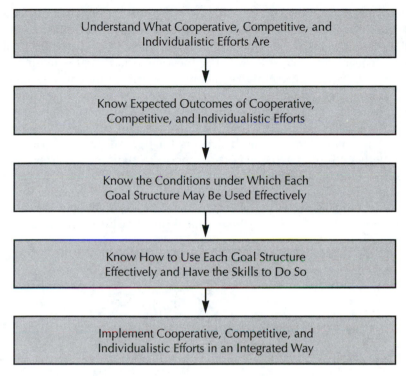

FIGURE 1.1   Using Goal Structures Appropriately

STRUCTURING LEARNING GOALS

In your classroom you (the teacher) have the same choice that the tribe did. You may structure lessons so that students

1. Engage in a win–lose struggle to see who is best in completing the assignment.
2. Work independently to complete the assignment.
3. Work together in small groups, ensuring that all members complete the assignment.

Students' learning goals may be structured to promote cooperative, competitive, or individualistic efforts. In every classroom, instructional activities are aimed at accomplishing goals and are conducted under a goal structure. A **learning goal** is a desired future state of demonstrating competence or mastery in the subject area being studied. The **goal structure** specifies the ways in which students will interact with each other and the teacher to achieve the goal. Students may interact to promote each other's success or obstruct each other's success. Students may also avoid interaction and thereby have no effect on the success or failure of others. Whenever people strive to achieve a goal, they may engage in cooperative, competitive, or individualistic efforts.

Each goal structure has its place (Johnson & Johnson, 1989). In the ideal classroom, all students would learn how to work cooperatively with others, compete for fun and enjoyment, and work autonomously. The teacher decides which goal structure to implement within each lesson. The most important goal structure, and the one that should be used the majority of the time in learning situations, is cooperation.

Social interdependence exists continually. It is one of the most fundamental and ubiquitous aspects of being human and it affects all aspects of our lives including our productivity, the quality of our relationships, and our psychological health. Nothing is more basic to humans than being for, against, or indifferent to other people. Whether it is quite personal or so impersonal that we are barely aware of it, every lesson contains social interdependence. In order to decide which goal structure, or combination of goal structures to use in a lesson, teachers must understand the nature of cooperative, competitive, and individualistic efforts, the conditions under which each is effective, and the teacher's role in using each goal structure.

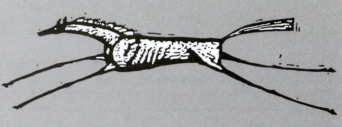

Our horse, Maude, could give a fantastic ride! She did not like leaving the barn. The four oldest of us, Frank, Helen, Roger, and David, would have to drag her away from the barn, trying to get far enough for a long ride. Then we would all jump on her back and wait for the inevitable. First she would try to scrape us off on fences as we tried to ride her away from the barn. Once she got turned in the barn's direction, we got the ride of our lives. She would race full speed to the barn (the younger author never seemed to remember to duck as Maude flew through the barn door). The point is that Maude was not committed to leaving the barn, but she had a strong commitment to return to it. All teachers have seen the difference between students who are committed to learning goals and those who are not. If students are not committed to instructional goals, they are like Maude going away from the barn. If students are committed to instructional goals, they are like Maude returning to the barn. Take the advice of the younger author and duck at the barn door when you successfully "turn on" your students.

Exercise 1.2   Definitions Exercise

Table 1.2 gives three concepts and three definitions taken from Deutsch (1962) and Johnson and Johnson (1989). Match each definition with the correct concept. Find a partner and (a) compare answers and (b) explain your reasoning for each answer.

TABLE 1.2

_____	1. Competitive Efforts	a. Exists when there is positive interdependence among students' goal attainments; students perceive that they can reach their goals if and only if the other students in the group also reach their goals.

	2. Individualistic Efforts	b. Exists when there is negative interdependence among goal achievements; students perceive that they can obtain their goals if and only if the other students in the class fail to obtain their goals.
	3. Cooperative Efforts	c. Exists when there is no interdependence among goal achievements; students perceive that the achievement of their goals is unrelated to what other students do.

COOPERATIVE EFFORTS

Ua dullah maa al-jamaa (God's hand is with the group).
Arabic saying

The human species seems to have a **cooperation imperative:** We desire and seek out opportunities to operate jointly with others to achieve mutual goals. Cooperation is an inescapable fact of life. From cradle to grave we cooperate with others in family, work, leisure, and community by working jointly to achieve mutual goals. Throughout history, people have come together to (a) accomplish feats that any one of them could not achieve alone and (b) share their joys and sorrows. From conceiving a child to sending a rocket to the moon, our successes require cooperation among individuals.

Cooperation is working together to accomplish shared goals. Within cooperative situations, individuals seek outcomes that are beneficial to themselves *and* beneficial to all other group members. **Cooperative learning** is the instructional use of small groups so that students work together to maximize their own and each other's learning (see Table 1.3). Students perceive that they can reach their learning goals if and only if the other students in the learning group also reach their goals (Deutsch, 1962; Johnson & Johnson, 1989). Three types of cooperative learning exist: formal cooperative learning, informal cooperative learning, and cooperative base groups (Chapter 3). Not all grouping, however, is cooperative. A number of basic elements must be implemented if grouping is to be truly cooperative (see Chapter 5). The teacher's role is centered around implementing the basic elements in cooperative lessons.

Cooperative efforts result in participants recognizing that all group members share a common fate (*We all sink or swim together*), strive for mutual benefit so that all group members gain from each other's efforts (*Your efforts benefit me and my efforts benefit you*), recognize that one's performance is mutually caused by oneself and one's colleagues (*United we stand, divided we fall*), empower each other (*Together we can achieve anything*), and feel proud and celebrate jointly when a group member is recognized for achievement (*You got an A! That is terrific!*).

During the past fifty years, cooperative learning has been the least used goal structure in instructional situations. The use of cooperative learning has both its advocates and its critics. The disagreement may be resolved by (a) examining the

TABLE 1.3   Aspects of Cooperation

Goal	Class members are assigned to small groups (often heterogeneous) and instructed to (a) learn the assigned material and (b) ensure all other group members do likewise.
Levels of Cooperation	Cooperation may be extended to the class (by ensuring that everyone in the class has learned the assigned material) and the school (by ensuring that all students in the school are progressing academically) levels.
Interaction Pattern	Students promote each other's success. Students discuss material with each other, explain how to complete the assignment, listen to each other's explanations, encourage each other to work hard, and provide academic help and assistance. This interaction pattern exists between as well as within groups.
Evaluation of Outcomes	A criteria-referenced assessment and evaluation system is used. The focus is usually on the learning and academic progress of the individual student but may also include the group as a whole, the class, and the school.

research (Appendix A) and (b) detailing the nature of constructive cooperative learning, the teacher's role in implementing it, and the basic elements that make it work (Chapters 2–6).

> So wherever I am, there's always Pooh, there's always Pooh and me. "What would I do," I said to Pooh, "if it wasn't for you?" and Pooh said, "True! It isn't much fun for one, but two can stick together," says Pooh, says he. "That's how it is," says Pooh. — *A. A. Milne*

COMPETITIVE EFFORTS

We do it on the tennis courts and putting greens, in the boardroom and the playing field, at the chalkboard and on the dance floor. It is eulogized at business club luncheons and exalted at Junior Achievement pep rallies. It is ballyhooed by economists and politicians as the cure for our financial ills, and it is glorified in locker room sermons as preparation for life in the real world. Applause for competition dates back at least as far as the ancient Greeks. The language of business, politics, and even education is filled with win-lose terms. You *win* a promotion or raise, *beat* the opposition, *outsmart* a teacher, become a *superstar*, and put competitors *in their place*. Competing with and defeating an opponent is one of the most widely recognized aspects of interpersonal interaction in our society.

Competition is working against each other to achieve a goal that only one or a few students can attain. Within competitive situations, individuals seek outcomes that are beneficial to themselves *and* detrimental to others. **Competitive learning** is the focusing of student effort on performing faster and more accurately than classmates (see Table 1.4). Students perceive that they can obtain their goals if and only if the other students in the class fail to obtain their goals (Deutsch, 1962; Johnson & Johnson, 1989).

TABLE 1.4   Aspects of Competition

Goal	Class members are instructed to perform faster and more accurately than classmates.
Levels of Competition	Competition may be focused on the group (by seeeking to be the best learner in the group), class (by seeking to be the best learner in the class), the school (by seeking to perform higher than anyone else in the school), and sometimes the nation (by seeking to perform higher than anyone else in the country) levels. It cannot be extended to intergroup competition without it becoming ingroup cooperation.
Interaction Pattern	Students obstruct each other's success. Students work alone, hide their work from each other, refuse to help or assist others, and may interfere with and seek to lower each other's efforts to learn.
Evaluation of Outcomes	A norm-referenced evaluation system is used. The focus of assessment and evaluation is on ranking students' academic performances from best to worst.

Students recognize their negatively linked fate (*The more you gain, the less for me; the more I gain, the less for you*), strive to be better than classmates (*I can defeat you*), work to deprive others (*My winning means you lose*), view rewards such as grades as limited (*Only a few of us will get As*), celebrate classmates' failures (*Your failure makes it easier for me to win*), and believe that the more able and deserving individuals become "haves" and the less able and deserving individuals become the "have nots" (*Winners always win, losers always lose*). Most students perceive school as a predominantly competitive enterprise (Johnson & Johnson, 1983a).

Considerable controversy has surrounded the use of competition in classrooms and schools. Like cooperative learning, competitive learning has both advocates and critics. This controversy may be resolved by (a) examining the research (Appendix A) and (b) detailing the nature of constructive competitive learning, the teacher's role in implementing it, and the basic elements that make it work (Chapter 7).

INDIVIDUALISTIC EFFORTS

Humans do not always interact with others. At times, people desire solitude. A long hike to a mountain lake, a walk along a deserted seashore, recording thoughts in a journal, reflecting on one's goals, planning one's day, memorizing lines in a play, and even writing a book are activities often done alone. Sometimes individuals act independently from each other without any interdependence existing among them. **Individualistic efforts** are working alone to accomplish goals unrelated to and independent from the goals of the others (Deutsch, 1962; Johnson & Johnson, 1989). Whether an individual accomplishes his or her goal has no influence on whether other individuals achieve their goals. Within individualistic situations, individuals seek outcomes that are beneficial to themselves. **Individualistic learning** is working by oneself to ensure one's own learning meets a preset criterion independently from the efforts of other students (see Table 1.5).

TABLE 1.5   Aspects of Individualistic Efforts

Goal	Class members are instructed to perform up to a present criterion independently from classmates.
Levels of Individualistic Work	Individualistic efforts focus on the person reaching a preset criterion of performance.
Interaction Pattern	Students do not interact with each other. Each works alone, independently from all others.
Evaluation of Outcomes	A criterion-referenced evaluation system is used. The focus is on determining whether a student's academic performances reaches a preset criterion.

Each student has his or her own set of materials, works at his or her own speed, tries not to disturb classmates, and seeks help and assistance only from the teacher. Students are expected and encouraged to focus on their own goals (*How well can I do*), have a strict self-interest (*What's in it for me*), see their success as dependent on only their own abilities (*If I am able, I will receive a high grade*), celebrate only their own success (*I did it!*), and ignore as irrelevant the success or failure of others (*Whether my classmates achieve or not does not affect me*).

The use of individualistic learning in classrooms has inspired some controversy, and the practice has its advocates and its critics. This controversy may be resolved by (a) examining the research (Chapter 2) and (b) detailing the nature of constructive competition, the teacher's role in implementing it, and the basic elements that make it work (Chapter 8).

Table 1.6 lists the major characteristics to these three modes of social interdependence.

TABLE 1.6   Characteristics of Social Interdependence

CHARACTERISTIC	COOPERATIVE	COMPETITIVE	INDIVIDUALISTIC
Fate	Mutual	Opposite	Independent
Benefit	Mutual	Differential	Self
Time Perspective	Long Term	Short Term	Short Term
Identity	Shared	Relative	Separate
Causation	Mutual	Relative	Self
Rewards	Unlimited	Limited	Unlimited
Motivation	Intrinsic	Extrinsic	Extrinsic
Attribution	Effort	Ability	Ability
Celebrate	Own Success, Others' Success	Own Success, Others' Failure	Own Success

Exercise 1.3   What Is It?

Review the following twelve statements. Form a pair and agree on whether each statement reflects a cooperative, competitive, or individualistic situation. Place each statement in the appropriate column in Table 1.7.

Statements

1. Strive for everyone's success.
2. Strive to be better than others.
3. Strive for one's own success only.
4. What benefits self does not affect others.
5. Joint success is celebrated.
6. What benefits self benefits others.
7. Only one's own success is celebrated.
8. Motivated to help and assist others.
9. What benefits self deprives or hurts others.
10. Motivated only to maximize one's own productivity.
11. Own success and other's failure is celebrated.
12. Motivated to ensure that no one else does better than oneself.

TABLE 1.7

COOPERATIVE	COMPETITIVE	INDIVIDUALISTIC

Exercise 1.4   Do You Agree or Disagree?

The following is a series of quotes from prominent historical figures about cooperative, competitive, and individualistic efforts. For each quote, indicate the level of your agreement.

Disagree 1—2—3—4—5 Agree

_____ 1. United we stand, divided we fall. (Watchword of the American Revolution)
_____ 2. Winning is not everything, it is the only thing. (Vince Lombardi)
_____ 3. Stand on your own two feet. (Horatio Alger)
_____ 4. A camel is a horse designed by a committee. (Anonymous)
_____ 5. It is not whether you win or lose, it is how you play the game. (Anonymous)
_____ 6. A single sequoia tree is toppled by the first wind. (Biologist)
_____ 7. Two heads are better than one. (Heywood)
_____ 8. Every time you win, you are reborn; every time you lose, you die a little. (George Allen, coach of the Washington Redskins)

_____ 9. God helps those who help themselves. (Benjamin Franklin)

_____ 10. Groups are for the weak who cannot stand on their own. (Anonymous)

_____ 11. Winning is uncool. (Anonymous student)

_____ 12. Wolves eat isolated sheep. (The Koran)

Cooperative	Competitive	Individualistic
_____ 1.	_____ 2.	_____ 3.
_____ 4.*	_____ 5.*	_____ 6.*
_____ 7.	_____ 8.	_____ 9.
_____ 10.*	_____ 11.*	_____ 12.*
_____ **Total**	_____ **Total**	_____ **Total**

*Reverse the scoring on starred items. If you score above 12, you have a positive attitude toward that type of interdependence.

THE CHOICE: APPROPRIATELY USING INTERDEPENDENCE

In a tool kit there may be a hammer, a saw, and a screwdriver. Each has its place and serves a different purpose. You do not use a hammer to cut a piece of wood in two and you do not use a saw to twist in a screw. The same is true for cooperative, competitive, or individualistic learning. Each has its place and serves a different purpose. Cooperative, competitive, and individualistic efforts are not in competition with each other. Survival of the fittest does not apply when it comes to structuring learning situations appropriately. When the three goal structures are used appropriately and in an integrated way, their sum is far more powerful than each one separately. When the goal structures are used inappropriately (such as the inappropriate and overuse of competitive or individualistic learning), problems result for both students and teachers. For every lesson you teach you will have to decide whether to have students cooperate, compete, or work individualistically. Knowing how and when to use each type of goal structure is one of the most important aspects of teaching (see Table 1.8).

TABLE 1.8   Elements of Appropriate Social Interdependence

ELEMENTS	COOPERATIVE	COMPETITIVE	INDIVIDUALISTIC
Interdependence	Positive	Negative	None
Importance of Goal	High	Low	Low
Interaction	Promotive	Oppositional	None
Accountability	Individual, Group	Individual	Individual
Social Skills	All	Comparison	None
Task	Any, Including Complex, Divisible, New	Simple, Unitary, Nondivisible, Overlearned	Simple, Unitary, Nondivisible, New
Procedures, Rules	Clear, Ambiguous	Clear	Clear

In the ideal classroom all three goal structures are used. This does not mean that they should be used equally. The basic foundation of instruction, the underlying context on which all instruction rests, is cooperation. Unless they are used within a context of cooperation, competitive and individualistic learning lose much of their effectiveness. A cooperative goal structure should dominate the classroom, being used 60 to 70 percent of the time. The individualistic goal structure may be used 20 percent of the time, and a competitive goal structure may be used 10 to 20 percent of the time. All competitive and individualistic efforts take place within a broader cooperative framework. Cooperation is the forest, competitive and individualistic efforts are but trees.

WHAT IS IN THIS BOOK?

The purposes of this book are to help you (a) make the choice of which goal structure to use with each lesson you teach and (b) implement each goal structure competently and successfully. Appendix A focuses on the research comparing the effectiveness of the three goal structures. Chapters 2 through 7 focus on your use of cooperative learning. Chapter 8 focuses on your use of competitive learning. Chapter 9 focuses on your use of individualistic learning. Chapter 10 discusses the integrated use of all three. Chapter 11 summarizes what you have learned and points toward the next steps in gaining expertise in using the three ways of structuring student–student interaction effectively.

SUMMARY

Social interdependence is to humans what water is to fish. It is constantly present, influencing everything we do. Yet because we are immersed in it, it can escape our notice. Two types of social interdependence exist: cooperative and competitive. The absence of interdependence results in individualistic efforts. Teachers have a choice of structuring every learning task competitively, individualistically, or cooperatively. Which structure is chosen determines how students interact with each other, which in turn determines the outcomes achieved. For the past fifty years competitive and individualistic efforts have dominated classrooms. Cooperative learning has been relatively ignored and underutilized by teachers even though it is by far the most important and powerful way to structure learning situations. Chapter 2, which reviews the basic research that has been conducted on the three goal structures, makes this point clearly. This does not mean, however, that competitive and individualistic learning should be abandoned. Each goal structure has its place and when they are used appropriately, they form an integrated whole. In the rest of the book, therefore, the appropriate use of each goal structure is discussed in depth.

2

Cooperative Learning

There is a power to working in groups. A group of staff and trustees at the Bronx Educational Services shaped the first nationally recognized adult literacy school. A group of citizens in Harlem founded and operated the first Little League there in more than forty years. Motorola used small manufacturing groups to produce the world's lightest, smallest, and highest-quality cellular phones (with only a few hundred parts versus more than a thousand for the competition). Ford became the most profitable car company in the United States in 1990 on the strength of the use of small groups to build its Taurus model.

Groups have existed for as long as there have been humans (and even before). Groups have been the subject of countless books. Every human society has used groups to accomplish its goals and celebrated when the groups were successful. It was groups that built the pyramids, constructed the Temple of Artemis at Ephesus, created the Colossus of Rhodes, and the hanging gardens of Babylon. It is obvious that groups outperform individuals, especially when performance requires multiple skills, judgments, and experiences. Many educators, however, overlook opportunities to use groups to enhance student learning and increase their own success.

The opportunity to capitalize on the power of groups in schools begins with understanding the answers to the following questions:

1. What is cooperative learning? This question was answered in Chapter 1.
2. Why use cooperative learning? This question is answered in Appendix A.
3. How do you structure formal cooperative learning lessons?
4. How do you use informal cooperative learning?

5. How do you use cooperative base groups?

6. What are the basic elements of cooperative learning that make it work?

7. How do you use the three types of cooperative learning in an integrated way?

Exercise 2.1 Missed Opportunities

Directions: Consider the five sources of resistance to using cooperative learning given above. Rate yourself from "1" to "5" on each source.

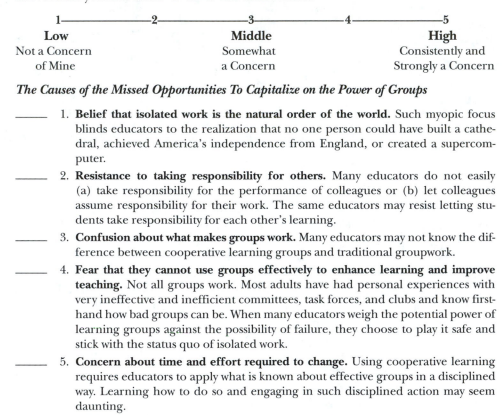

1————————2————————3————————4————————5
Low   **Middle**   **High**
Not a Concern   Somewhat   Consistently and
of Mine   a Concern   Strongly a Concern

The Causes of the Missed Opportunities To Capitalize on the Power of Groups

_____ 1. **Belief that isolated work is the natural order of the world.** Such myopic focus blinds educators to the realization that no one person could have built a cathedral, achieved America's independence from England, or created a supercomputer.

_____ 2. **Resistance to taking responsibility for others.** Many educators do not easily (a) take responsibility for the performance of colleagues or (b) let colleagues assume responsibility for their work. The same educators may resist letting students take responsibility for each other's learning.

_____ 3. **Confusion about what makes groups work.** Many educators may not know the difference between cooperative learning groups and traditional groupwork.

_____ 4. **Fear that they cannot use groups effectively to enhance learning and improve teaching.** Not all groups work. Most adults have had personal experiences with very ineffective and inefficient committees, task forces, and clubs and know firsthand how bad groups can be. When many educators weigh the potential power of learning groups against the possibility of failure, they choose to play it safe and stick with the status quo of isolated work.

_____ 5. **Concern about time and effort required to change.** Using cooperative learning requires educators to apply what is known about effective groups in a disciplined way. Learning how to do so and engaging in such disciplined action may seem daunting.

TYPES OF COOPERATIVE LEARNING GROUPS

These problems are endemic to all institutions of education, regardless of level. Children sit for 12 years in classrooms where the implicit goal is to listen to the teacher and memorize the information in order to regurgitate it on a test. Little or no attention is paid to the learning process, even though much research exists documenting that real understanding is a case of active restructuring on the part of the learner. Restructuring occurs through engagement in problem posing as well as problem solving, inference making and investigation, resolving of contradictions, and reflecting. These processes all mandate far more active learners, as well as a different model of education than the one subscribed to at present by most institutions. Rather than being powerless and dependent on the institution, learners need to be empowered to think and learn for themselves. Thus, learning needs to be conceived of as something a learner does, not something that is done to a learner.

Catherine Fosnot (1989)

Cooperative learning groups are divided into three types. **Formal cooperative learning** groups last from one class period to several weeks. You may structure any academic assignment or course requirement for formal cooperative learning. Formal cooperative learning groups ensure that students are actively involved in the intellectual work of organizing material, explaining it, summarizing it, and integrating it into existing conceptual structures. They are the heart of cooperative learning. **Informal cooperative learning** groups are ad hoc groups that last from a few minutes to one class period. You use them during direct teaching (lectures, demonstrations, films, videos) to focus students' attention on the material they are to learn, set a mood conducive to learning, help set expectations as to what the lesson will cover, ensure that students cognitively process the material you are teaching, and provide closure to an instructional session. **Cooperative base groups** are long-term (lasting for at least a year), heterogeneous groups with stable membership whose primary purpose is for members to give each other the support, help, encouragement, and assistance each needs to progress academically. Base groups provide students with long-term, committed relationships.

In addition to the three types of cooperative learning, **cooperative learning scripts** are standard cooperative procedures for (a) conducting generic, repetitive lessons (such as writing reports or giving presentations) and (b) managing classroom routines (such as checking homework and reviewing a test). Once planned and conducted several times, scripted repetitive cooperative lessons and classroom routines become automatic activities in the classroom.

When you use formal, informal, and cooperative base groups repeatedly, you will gain a routine level of expertise in doing so. **Expertise** is reflected in your proficiency, adroitness, competence, and skill in doing something. Expertise in structuring cooperative efforts is reflected in your being able to do the following:

1. Take any lesson in any subject area with any age student and structure it cooperatively.
2. Use cooperative learning (at a routine-use level) 60 to 80 percent of the time.
3. Describe precisely what you are doing and why in order to (a) communicate to others the nature and advantages of cooperative learning and (b) teach colleagues how to implement cooperative learning.
4. Apply the principles of cooperation to other settings, such as colleagial relationships and faculty meetings.

You usually gain such expertise through a progressive-refinement procedure of (a) teaching a cooperative lesson, (b) assessing how well it went, (c) reflecting on how cooperation could have been better structured, and then (d) teaching an improved cooperative lesson, (e) assessing how well it went, and so forth. You thus gain experience in an incremental step-by-step manner. The **routine-use level** of teacher expertise is the ability to structure cooperative learning situations automatically without conscious thought or planning. You can then use cooperative learning with fidelity for the rest of your teaching career.

Exercise 2.2   Types of Cooperative Learning

Form a pair. Using the spaces below, write out the definition of each type of cooperative learning in your own words.

FORMAL	INFORMAL	BASE GROUPS

EXTRAORDINARY ACHIEVEMENT

Sandy Koufax was one of the greatest pitchers in the history of baseball. Although he was naturally talented, he was also unusually well trained and disciplined. He was perhaps the only major-league pitcher whose fastball could be heard to hum. Opposing batters, instead of talking and joking around in the dugout, would sit quietly and listen for Koufax's fastball to hum. When it was their turn to bat, they were already intimidated. There was, however, a simple way for Koufax's genius to have been negated—by making the first author of this book his catcher. To be great, a pitcher needs an outstanding catcher (his great partner was Johnny Roseboro). David is such an unskilled catcher that Koufax would have had to throw the ball much slower in order for David to catch it. This would have deprived Koufax of his greatest weapon. Placing Roger and Edythe at key defensive positions in the infield or outfield, furthermore, would have seriously affected Koufax's success. Sandy Koufax was not a great pitcher on his own. Only as part of a team could Koufax achieve greatness. In baseball and in the classroom it takes a cooperative effort. Extraordinary achievement comes from a cooperative group, not from the individualistic or competitive efforts of an isolated individual.

TEACHER'S ROLE: BEING "A GUIDE ON THE SIDE"

At age 55, after his defeat by Woodrow Wilson for President of the United States, Teddy Roosevelt took a journey to South America. The Brazilian government suggested he lead an expedition to explore a vast, unmapped river deep in the jungle. Known as the River of Doubt, it was believed to be a tributary to the Amazon. Roosevelt accepted instantly. "We will go down the unknown river," he declared, and the Brazilian government organized an expedition for the trip. "I had to go," he said later, "it was my last chance to be a boy." Roosevelt, with his son Kermit and a party of eighteen, headed into the jungle. "On February 27, 1914, shortly after midday, we started down the River of Doubt into the unknown," Roosevelt wrote. The journey was an ordeal. Hostile natives of the region harassed them. Five canoes were shattered and had to be rebuilt. Food ran short and valuable equipment was lost. One man drowned when his canoe capsized. Another went berserk, killed a member of the expedition, and then disappeared into the wilderness. Roosevelt, ill with fever, badly injured his leg when he tried to keep two capsized canoes from being smashed against rocks. Unable to walk, he had to be carried. Lying in a tent with an infected leg and a temperature of 105, he requested to be left behind. Ignoring such pleas, Kermit brought his father to safety with the help of the other members of the expedition. Teddy Roosevelt barely survived, but he and his companions accomplished their mission. The party mapped the 1,000-mile River of Doubt and collected priceless specimens for the Museum of Natural History. The river was renamed in his honor, Rio Theodore.

An expedition such as Roosevelt's consists of four phases:

1. You make a series of prejourney decisions about the number of people needed, the materials and equipment required, and the route to be taken.
2. You brief all participants on the goals and objectives of the journey, emphasize that members' survival depends on the joint efforts of all, and describe the behaviors you expect of members of the expedition.
3. You make the journey, carefully mapping the area traveled and collecting the targeted specimens.
4. You report your findings to interested parties, reflect on what went right and wrong with fellow members, and write your memoirs.

A cooperative lesson is conducted in the same way. You, the teacher, make a number of preinstructional decisions, explain to students the instructional task and the cooperative nature of the lesson, conduct the lesson, and evaluate and process the results. More specifically, you follow these steps:

1. *Make preinstructional decisions.* In every lesson you (a) formulate objectives, (b) decide on the size of groups, (c) choose a method for assigning students to groups, (d) decide

which roles to assign group members, (e) arrange the room, and (f) arrange the materials students need to complete the assignment.

2. *Explain the task and cooperative structure.* In every lesson you (a) explain the academic assignment to students, (b) explain the criteria for success, (c) structure positive interdependence, (d) explain the individual accountability, and (e) explain the behaviors you expect to see during the lesson.

3. *Monitor and intervene.* While you (a) conduct the lesson, you (b) monitor each learning group and (c) intervene when needed to improve taskwork and teamwork, and (d) bring closure to the lesson.

4. *Evaluate and process.* You (a) assess and evaluate the quality and quantity of student achievement, (b) ensure students carefully process the effectiveness of their learning groups, (c) have students make a plan for improvement, and (d) have students celebrate the hard work of group members.

In each class session teachers must make the choice of being "a sage on the stage" or "a guide on the side." In doing so they might remember that *the challenge in teaching is not covering the material for the students, it's uncovering the material with the students.*

PREINSTRUCTIONAL DECISIONS

Specifying the Instructional Objectives

The Roman philosopher Seneca once said, "When you do not know to which port you are sailing, no wind is favorable." The same may be said for teaching. To plan for a lesson you must know what the lesson is aimed at accomplishing. You need to specify **academic objectives** (based on a conceptual or task analysis) and **social skills objectives** that detail what interpersonal and small group skills you wish to emphasize during the lesson. You choose social skills by

1. Monitoring the learning groups and diagnosing the specific skills needed to solve the problems students are having in working with each other.

2. Asking students to identify social skills that would improve their teamwork.

3. Keeping a list of social skills you teach to every class. The next one on the list becomes the skill emphasized in today's lesson.

4. Analyzing what social skills are required to complete the assignment.

The most sophisticated way to determine the social skills students need to complete a lesson is through creating a flowchart. A **flowchart** is a simple yet powerful visual tool to display all the steps in a process. Creating a flowchart involves six steps, as illustrated on page 19.

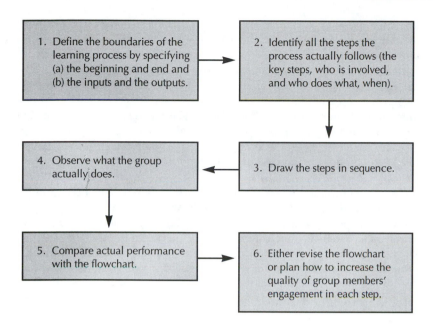

1. Define the boundaries of the learning process by specifying (a) the beginning and end and (b) the inputs and the outputs.

2. Identify all the steps the process actually follows (the key steps, who is involved, and who does what, when).

4. Observe what the group actually does.

3. Draw the steps in sequence.

5. Compare actual performance with the flowchart.

6. Either revise the flowchart or plan how to increase the quality of group members' engagement in each step.

Deciding on the Size of the Group

There is a folk saying about snowflakes. Each snowflake is so fragile and small. But when they stick together, it is amazing what they can do. The same is true for people. When we work together, there is no limit to human ingenuity and potential. For students to work together, they must be assigned to groups. To assign students to groups, you must decide (a) how large a group should be, (b) how students should be assigned to a group, (c) how long the groups will exist, and (d) what combination of groups will be used in the lesson.

Although cooperative learning groups typically range in size from two to four, *the basic rule of thumb is the smaller the better.* There is, however, no ideal size for a cooperative learning group. A common mistake is to have students work in groups of four, five, and six members before the students have the skills to do so competently. In selecting the size of a cooperative learning group, remember this advice:

Group Size Depends on "Team"
T = **T**ime Limits
E = Students' **E**xperience in Working in Groups
A = Students' **A**ge
M = **M**aterials and Equipment Available

1. *With the addition of each group member, the resources to help the group succeed increase.* As the size of the learning group increases, so does (a) the range of abilities, expertise, skills, (b) the number of minds available for acquiring and processing information, and (c) the diversity of viewpoints.

2. *The shorter the period of time available, the smaller the learning group should be.* If there is only a brief period of time available for the lesson, then smaller groups such as pairs will be more effective because they take less time to get organized, they operate faster, and there is more "air time" per member.

3. *The smaller the group, the more difficult it is for students to hide and not contribute their share of the work.* Small groups increase the visibility of students' efforts and thereby make them more accountable.

4. *The larger the group, the more skillful group members must be.* In a pair, students have to manage two interactions. In a group of three, there are six interactions to manage. In a group of four, there are twelve interactions to manage. As the size of the group increases, the interpersonal and small group skills required to manage the interactions among group members become far more complex and sophisticated.

5. *The larger the group, the less the interaction among members.* What results is less group cohesion, fewer friendships, and less personal support.

6. *The materials available or the specific nature of the task may dictate a group size.* When you have ten computers and thirty students, you may wish to assign students to groups of three. When the task is practice tennis, a group size of two seems natural.

7. *The smaller the group, the easier it is to identify any difficulties students have in working together.* Problems in leadership, unresolved conflicts among group members, issues over power and control, tendencies such as sitting back and waiting for others to do the work, and other problems students have in working together are more visible and apparent when groups are small. Groups need to be small enough to ensure all students are actively involved and participating equally.

THE GROUP SIZE WHEEL

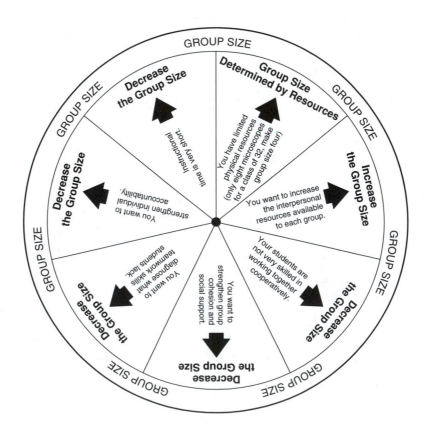

Assigning Students to Groups

Sic parvis magna (Great things have small beginnings).
Sir Francis Drake's Motto

There is no ideal group membership. What determines a group's productivity is not who its members are, but rather how well the members work together. There may be times when you use cooperative learning groups that are homogeneous in ability to teach specific skills or to achieve certain instructional objectives. Generally, however, there are advantages to heterogeneous groups in which students come from diverse backgrounds and have different abilities, experiences, and interests:

1. Students are exposed to a variety of ideas, multiple perspectives, and different problem-solving methods.
2. Students generate more cognitive disequilibrium, which stimulates learning, creativity, and cognitive and social development.
3. Students engage in more elaborative thinking, give and receive more explanations, and engage in more frequent perspective-taking in discussing material, all of which increase the depth of understanding, the quality of reasoning, and the accuracy of long-term retention.

To make groups heterogeneous, you assign students to groups using a random or stratified random procedure (see the methods listed in the table below). Teacher-selected groups can be either homogeneous or heterogeneous. When students select their own groups they usually form homogeneous ones. Each of these methods is explained next.

LITERATURE CHARACTERS	GEOGRAPHICAL AREAS
Give students cards with the names of characters in the literature they recently have read. Ask them to group with characters from the same story, play, or poem. Examples are Romeo and Juliet; Captain Hook, Peter Pan, and Wendy; and Hansel, Gretel, Witch, and Stepmother.	List a number of countries or states and have students group themselves according to most preferred to visit. Variations include grouping according to least preferred to visit, similar in terms of climate, similar in geological features, having the same exports, and so forth.
MATH METHOD	STATES AND CAPITALS
The math method of assigning students to groups has endless variations. The basic structure is to give each student a math problem and ask the student to (a) solve it, (b) find the classmates whose problems have the same answer, and (c) form a group. The math problem may vary from simple addition in the first grade to complex equations in high school classes. Thus, to form a group of three, you may distribute the following three equations throughout the class: $(3 + 3 = \_)$, $(4 + 2 = \_)$, $(5 + 1 = \_)$.	To assign students to groups of two or four, divide the number of students in the class by two (30 divided by 2 = 15). Pick a geographic area of the United States and write out on cards the names of fifteen states. Then on another set of cards write out the names of their capital cities. Shuffle the cards and pass them out to students. Then have the students find the classmate who has the matching state or capital. To form groups of four, have two adjacent states and their capitals combine.

Random Assignment   *The easiest and most effective way to assign students to groups is randomly.* You divide the number of students in your class by the size of the group desired. If you wish to have groups of three and you have thirty students in your class, you divide thirty by three. You have students number off by the result (e.g., ten). Students with the same number find each other (all ones get together, all twos get together, and so forth). A favorite variation of one of the authors is to have students count off in a different language (e.g., English, Spanish, French, Hungarian) each time they are assigned to groups.

Stratified Random Assignment   *A related procedure is stratified random assignment.* This is the same as random assignment except that you choose one (or two) characteristics of students (such as reading level, learning style, task orientation, or personal interest) and make sure that one or more students in each group have that characteristic. To assign students to learning groups randomly, stratifying for achievement level, use the following procedure:

1. Rank students from highest to lowest in terms of a pretest on the unit, a recent past test, past grades, or your best guess as a teacher.

2. Select the first group by choosing the highest student, the lowest student, and the two middle achievers. Assign them to the group unless they are all of one sex, they do not reflect the ethnic composition of the class, they are worst enemies, or they are best friends. If any of these is true, move up or down one student from the middle to re-adjust. (You may modify the procedure to assign students to groups of two or three members.)

3. Select the remaining groups by repeating this procedure with the reduced list. If there are students left over, make one or two groups of three members.

There is a danger in assigning students to groups on the basis of certain characteristics. If you form groups so that there is a white male, a white female, a black male, and a black female in every group, for example, you are giving the class a clear message that gender and ethnicity are important factors to you as a teacher. Making these categories salient may cue students' stereotypes and prejudices. *The general rule is this: If you assign students to groups based on categories, make them unique categories needed to complete the group task* (such as summarizer, creative thinker, time keeper, and library expert). As a teacher, you tell students, "In your groups there is a creative thinker, a person who is good at keeping track of time, someone who knows how to use the library, and someone who is good at summarizing all the ideas suggested in the group. To complete this assignment, you will need the resources of each member." By emphasizing the personal abilities and talents of students rather than their social categories, you focus students on the person, not the social group.

Preferences   Have students write their favorite sport to participate in on a slip of paper. Then have them find groupmates who like to participate in the same sport. Variations include favorite food, celebrity, skill, car, president, animal, vegetable, fairy-tale character, and so forth.

Teacher-Selected Groups   You, the teacher, can decide who is going to work with whom. You can ensure that nonachievement-oriented students are a minority in each group or that students who trigger disruptive behavior in each other are not together. *One of our favorite methods is creating support groups for each isolated student.* You ask students to list three classmates with whom they would like to work. From their lists, you tally for each student the number of times classmates chose the student. You can then identify the classroom isolates (students who are not chosen by any of their classmates). These are the at-risk students who need your help. You take the most socially isolated student and assign two of the most skillful, popular, support-ive, and caring students in the class to work with him or her. Then you take the sec-ond most isolated student and do the same. In this way you optimize the likelihood that the isolated students will become involved in the learning activities and build positive relationships with classmates. You want to ensure that in your classes, no stu-dent is left out, rejected, or believes that he or she does not belong.

Self-Selected Groups   The least recommended procedure is to have students select their own groups. Student-selected groups often are homogeneous with high-achieving students working with other high-achieving students, white students work-ing with other white students, minority students working with other minority students, and males working with other males. Often there is more off-task behavior in student-selected than in teacher-selected groups. A useful modification of the select-your-own-group method is to have students list whom they would like to work with and then place them in a learning group with one person they choose and one, two, or more students that the teacher selects.

For additional methods for assigning students to groups as well as a variety of team-building and warm-up activities see R. Johnson and D. W. Johnson (1985).

Length of Group Life   A common concern is, "How long should cooperative learning groups stay together?" The type of cooperative learning group you use determines one answer to this question. Base groups last for at least one and ideally for several years. Informal cooperative learning groups last for only a few minutes or at most one class period. For formal cooperative learning groups there is no formula or simple answer to this question. Groups usually stay together to complete a task, unit, or chapter. Dur-ing a course every student should work with every other classmate. Groups should stay together long enough to be successful. Breaking up groups that are having trouble functioning effectively is often counterproductive; students do not have the opportu-nity to learn the skills they need to resolve problems in collaborating with each other.

Using Combinations of Cooperative Learning Groups   In many lessons you will want to use a combination of formal and informal cooperative learning groups as well as base groups. You will use more than one size group in any one lesson. You will need ways to assign students to new groups quickly. You will need procedures for making transitions among groups, moving students from pairs to fours to pairs to threes and so forth. It sometimes helps to have timed drills on how fast students can move from a formal cooperative learning group to an informal pair and then back to their formal group.

Assigning Roles to Ensure Interdependence

In planning the lesson, you think through what are the actions that need to occur to maximize student learning. **Roles** prescribe what other group members expect from a student (and therefore what the student is obligated to do) and what that person has a right to expect from other group members who have complementary roles. There is a progression for using roles to structure cooperative efforts:

1. Do not assign roles to let students get used to working together.
2. Assign only very simple roles to students such as forming roles or the roles of reader, recorder, and encourager of participation. Rotate the roles so that each group member plays each one several times.
3. Add to the rotation a new role that is slightly more sophisticated, such as a checker for understanding. You assign the functioning roles at this point.
5. Over time add formulating and fermenting roles that do not occur naturally in the group, such as elaborator. Students typically do not relate what they are learning to what they already know until you specifically train them to do so.

Exercise 2.3   Identifying the Various Types of Roles

Form a pair. For each type of skill, there are two examples of the roles that may be assigned to ensure students work together effectively. In column one, write the letters of the two roles that teach the skill.

	SKILLS	ROLES
	Forming Skills	a. Encouraging everyone to participate
		b. Using quiet voices
	Functioning Skills	c. Relating new learning to previous learning
		d. Criticizing ideas, not people
	Formulating Skills	e. Staying with one's group
		f. Changing one's mind only if logically persuaded
	Fermenting Skills	g. Explaining, step by step, one's reasoning
		h. Giving one's ideas and conclusions

One of the challenges in using cooperative learning is to describe group roles in an age-appropriate way. How you describe a role to primary students obviously needs to be different from the way you describe the role to high school students. Examples of the ways roles are renamed to make them age appropriate may be found in Table 2.1.

TABLE 2.1   Examples of Roles Appropriate for Each Age Level

CATEGORY	ROLE	PRIMARY	INTERMEDIATE	SECONDARY
Forming	Turn-taking monitor	First you, then me	Take turns	Contribute in sequence
Functioning	Recorder	Writer	Recorder	Scribe
	Encourager of participation	Say nice things	Give positive comments	Compliment
	Clarifier, paraphraser	Now you say it	Say it in your own words	Paraphrase
	Consensus seeker	Everyone agrees	Reach agreement	Reach consensus
Formulating	Summarizer	Put together	Combine	Summarize
	Generator	Give another answer	Give additional answers	Generate alternative answers
Fermenting	Asker for justification	Ask why	Ask for reasons	Ask for justification
	Rationale giver	Say why	Give facts and reasons	Explain

Roles can be sequenced so that more and more complex and difficult roles are assigned to students each week, month, and year. Initially, students may need to be assigned roles that help them form the group. Second, roles may be assigned that help the group function well in achieving learning goals and maintaining good working relationships among members. Third, roles may be assigned that help students formulate what they are learning and create conceptual frameworks. Finally, roles may be assigned that help students ferment each other's thinking. It is at this point that cognitive and social roles merge. The social skills represented by the roles should be taught like a spiral curriculum with a more complex version of the skill taught every year.

Solving and Preventing Problems in Working Together   At times some students will refuse to participate in a cooperative group or will not understand how to help the group succeed. You can solve and prevent such problems when you give each group member a specific role to play in the group. Assigning appropriate roles may be used to fulfill the following goals:

1. Reduce problems such as one or more members' making no contribution to the group or one member dominating the group.
2. Ensure that vital group skills are enacted in the group and that group members learn targeted skills.
3. Create interdependence among group members. You structure **role interdependence** by assigning each member complementary and interconnected roles.

Arranging the Room

The design and arrangement of classroom space and furniture communicates what is appropriate behavior and what learning activities will take place. Desks in a row communicate a different message and expectation than desks grouped in small circles. Spatial design also defines the circulation patterns in the classroom. **Circulation** is the flow of movement into, out of, and within the classroom. It is movement through space. You determine what students see, when they see it, and with whom students interact by the way you design your classroom (as shown in the exercise below).

Exercise 2.4   Importance Of Classroom Design

Form a pair. Rank the following outcomes of classroom design from most important ("1") to least important ("9").

_____   *Students' academic achievement.* The way in which interior space is designed influences the amount of time students spend on task and other variables affecting achievement.

_____   *Students' visual and auditory focus.* The way in which interior space is designed creates overall visual order, focuses visual attention, and controls acoustics.

_____   *Students' participation in learning groups and activities.* Classroom design influences the patterns of student (and teacher) participation in instructional activities, the emergence of leadership in learning groups, and the patterns of communication among students and between students and teachers.

_____   *Opportunities for social contact and friendships among students.*

_____   *Learning climate.* The design of interior space affects students' and teachers' feelings (such as comfort, enjoyment, well-being, anger, and depression) and general morale. Good spatial definition helps students feel secure by delineating structured learning areas.

_____   *Classroom management.* Spatial definition prevents discipline problems by defining how and where students work, how to interact with others, and how to move through the classroom.

_____   *Students ease of access to each other, teachers, learning materials.*

_____   *Students ability to make quick transiitons from one grouping to another.*

_____   *Teachers movement from group to group to monitor student interaction carefully during the lesson.*

No single classroom arrangement will meet the requirements of all lessons. Reference points and well-defined boundaries of work spaces are needed to move students from rows to triads to pairs to fours to rows. Color, form, and lighting (a) focus students' visual attention on points of emphasis in the classroom (the learning group, you, instructional materials) and (b) define the territorial boundaries of workspaces. You can define boundaries in various ways:

1. *Using labels and signs* that designate areas.

2. *Using colors* to attract visual attention and define group and individual spaces as well as different storage areas and resource centers.

3. *Taping lines* on the floor or wall to define the different work areas.

4. *Using mobiles and forms* (such as arrows) taped on the wall or hanging from the ceiling to direct attention. You can designate work areas by hanging mobiles from the ceiling.

5. *Using lighting* to define specific work areas. Directed light (illuminating part of the room while leaving other areas dim) intensifies and directs students' attention. Brightly lit areas can draw people toward the areas and suggest activity. More dimly lit areas surrounding the lighted ones become area boundaries. As the activity in the classroom changes, the lighting could also change.

6. *Moving furniture* to define work and resource areas. Even tall plants, when placed in pots with wheels, can be moved to provide spatial boundaries.

7. *Displaying group work* to designate work spaces. If a cooperative group is to remain together for a period of several days or weeks, members may wish to build a poster or collage that designates their work area.

You can use many of these same procedures to control acoustically levels of noise in the classroom.

Planning the Instructional Materials

The types of tasks students are required to complete determine what materials are needed for the lesson. You, the teacher, decide how materials are to be arranged and distributed among group members to maximize their participation and achievement. Usually, you will wish to distribute materials to communicate that the assignment is to be a joint (not an individual) effort. You create

1. *Materials interdependence* by giving each group only one copy of the materials. The students will then have to work together in order to be successful. This is especially effective the first few times the group meets. After students are accustomed to working cooperatively, teachers can give a copy of the materials to each student.

2. *Information interdependence* by arranging materials like a jigsaw puzzle so that each student has part of the materials needed to complete the assignment. Each group member can receive different books or resource materials to be synthesized. Such procedures require that every member participate in order for the group to be successful.

3. *Interdependence from outside enemies* by structuring materials into an intergroup tournament format and having groups compete to see who has learned the most. Such a procedure was introduced by DeVries and Edwards (1973). In the teams-games-tournament format, students are divided into heterogeneous cooperative learning teams to prepare members for a tournament in which they compete with the other teams. During the intergroup competition the students individually compete against members of about the same ability level from other teams. The team whose members do the best in the competition is pronounced the winner by the teacher.

STRUCTURING THE TASK AND COOPERATIVE STRUCTURE

Explaining the Academic Task

At this point you have planned your lesson by making the preinstructional decisions and preparations. The next step is to face your class and inform students of (a) what to do to complete the assignment and (b) how to do it. The steps are explained on the flowchart.

Explaining the Task: Flowchart

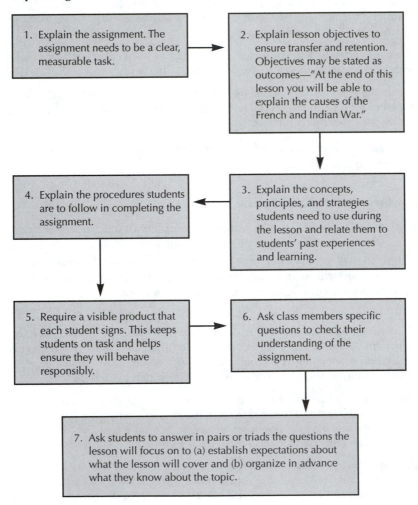

1. Explain the assignment. The assignment needs to be a clear, measurable task.

2. Explain lesson objectives to ensure transfer and retention. Objectives may be stated as outcomes—"At the end of this lesson you will be able to explain the causes of the French and Indian War."

3. Explain the concepts, principles, and strategies students need to use during the lesson and relate them to students' past experiences and learning.

4. Explain the procedures students are to follow in completing the assignment.

5. Require a visible product that each student signs. This keeps students on task and helps ensure they will behave responsibly.

6. Ask class members specific questions to check their understanding of the assignment.

7. Ask students to answer in pairs or triads the questions the lesson will focus on to (a) establish expectations about what the lesson will cover and (b) organize in advance what they know about the topic.

Explaining Criteria for Success

While explaining to students the academic task they are to complete, you need to communicate the level of performance you expect. Cooperative learning requires criterion-based evaluation. **Criterion-referenced** or **categorical judgments** are made

GRADE	PERCENT CORRECT
A	95–100
B	85–94
C	75–84
D	65–74
F	Less than 64

by adopting a fixed set of standards and judging the achievement of each student against these standards. A common version of criterion-referenced grading involves assigning letter grades on the basis of the percentage of test items answered correctly. Or you might say, "The group is not finished until every member has demonstrated mastery." Sometimes improvement (doing better this week than one did last week) may be set as the criterion of excellence. To promote intergroup cooperation, you may also set criteria for the whole class to reach. "If we as a class can score over 520 words correct on our vocabulary test, each student will receive two bonus points."

Structuring Positive Interdependence

Positive goal interdependence exists when a mutual or joint goal is established so that individuals perceive they can attain their goals if and only if their groupmates attain their goals (see Johnson & Johnson, 1992a, 1992b). Members know that they cannot succeed unless all other members of their group succeed. Positive interdependence is the heart of cooperative learning. Without positive interdependence, cooperation does not exist. Students must believe that they are in a "sink or swim together" learning situation. Positive interdependence will be discussed in detail in Chapter 4.

First, you structure positive goal interdependence. Every cooperative lesson begins with positive goal interdependence. To ensure that students think "We, not me" you say to students, "You have three responsibilities. You are responsible for learning the assigned material. You are responsible for making sure that all other members of your group learn the assigned material. And you are responsible for making sure that all other class members successfully learn the assigned material."

Second, you supplement positive goal interdependence with other types of positive interdependence (such as reward, role, resource, or identity). Positive reward interdependence, for example, may be structured through providing group rewards— *"If all members of your group score above 90 percent on the test, each of you will receive five bonus points."* Usually, the more ways positive interdependence is structured in a lesson, the better.

Positive interdependence creates peer encouragement and support for learning. Such positive peer pressure influences underachieving students to become academically involved. Members of cooperative learning groups should give two interrelated messages, "Do your work—we're counting on you!" and "How can I help you to do better?"

Structuring Individual Accountability

In cooperative groups, everyone has to do his or her fair share of the work. *An underlying purpose of cooperative learning is to make each group member a stronger in-*

dividual in his or her own right. This is accomplished by holding all members accountable to learn the assigned material and help other group members learn. You do this by

1. Assessing the performance of each individual member.

2. Giving the results back to the individual and the group to compare to preset criteria. The feedback enables members to (a) recognize and celebrate efforts to learn and contributions to groupmates' learning, (b) provide immediate remediation and any needed assistance or encouragement, and (c) reassign responsibilities to avoid any redundant efforts by members.

Individual accountability results in group members knowing they cannot hitchhike on the work of others, loaf, or get a free ride. *Ways of ensuring individual accountability* include keeping group size small, giving an individual test to each student, giving random individual oral examinations, observing and recording the frequency with which each member contributes to the group's work, having students teach what they know to someone else, and having students use what they have learned on different problems.

Structuring Intergroup Cooperation

You can extend the positive outcomes resulting from cooperative learning throughout a whole class by structuring intergroup cooperation. You establish class goals as well as group and individual goals. When a group finishes its work, you encourage members to find other groups (a) who are not finished and help them understand how to complete the assignment successfully or (b) who are finished and compare answers and strategies.

Specifying Desired Behaviors

When you use cooperative learning you must teach students the small group and interpersonal skills they need to work effectively with each other. In cooperative learning groups, students must learn both academic subject matter (taskwork) and the interpersonal and small group skills required to work as part of a group (teamwork). Cooperative learning is inherently more complex than competitive or individualistic learning because students have to simultaneously engage in taskwork and teamwork. If students do not learn the teamwork skills, then they cannot complete the taskwork. The greater the members' teamwork skills, the higher will be the quality and quantity of their learning. You define the needed teamwork skills operationally by specifying the behaviors that are appropriate and desirable within learning groups. How to do so is discussed at length in Chapter 5.

Three rules of thumb in specifying desired behaviors are as follows: *Be specific.* Operationally define each social skill through the use of a T-Chart (see Chapter 5). *Start small.* Do not overload your students with more social skills than they can learn at one time. One or two behaviors to emphasize for a few lessons is enough. Students need to know what behavior is appropriate and desirable within a cooperative learning group, but they should not be subjected to information overload. *Emphasize overlearning.* Having students practice skills once or twice is not enough. Keep emphasizing a skill until the students have integrated it into their behavioral repertoires and do it automatically and habitually.

THE COOPERATIVE LESSON

During the lesson students work together to complete the assignment. Their actions can be loosely or highly prescribed by explicit scripts (Johnson & Johnson, 1994). At the highest level of implementation you (the teacher) learn an **expert system** consisting of the five basic elements and the teacher's role and use it to create lessons uniquely tailored for your students, curriculum, needs, and teaching circumstances. Expertise in using cooperative learning is based on a conceptual, metacognitive understanding of its nature.

Besides implementing an expert system, other ways to implement cooperative lessons exist. One such method is **group investigation** (Sharan & Hertz-Lazarowitz, 1980), in which students form cooperative groups according to common interests in a topic. All group members help plan how to research their topic. Then they divide the work. Each group member carries out his or her part of the investigation. The group synthesizes its work and presents these findings to the class.

You may use highly structured scripts, structures, and curriculum packages that are implemented in a prescribed lockstep manner. Dansereau (1985) and his colleagues have developed a number of **cooperative learning scripts** that structure student interaction as they work together. Kagan (1991) has identified a number of **cooperative learning structures**—ways of organizing the interaction of students by prescribing student behavior step by step to complete the assignment. **Cooperative curriculum packages** include **Teams-Games-Tournament (TGT),** a combination of ingroup cooperation, intergroup competition, and instructional games (DeVries & Edwards, 1974). Students then meet in cooperative learning teams of four or five members (a mixture of high, medium, and low achievers) to complete a set of worksheets on the lesson. Students then play academic games as representatives of their teams. Who competes with whom is modified each week to ensure that students compete with classmates who achieve at a similar level. The highest scoring teams are publicly recognized in a weekly class newsletter. Grades are given on the basis of individual performance. **Student Team Learning (STAD)** (Slavin, 1980) is a modification of TGT that has students take a weekly quiz instead of playing an academic game. **Team-Assisted Individualization (TAI)** is a highly individualized math curriculum for grades 3 to 6 in which students work individualistically to complete math assignments using self-instructional (programmed learning) curriculum materials (Slavin, 1983). **Cooperative Integrated Reading And Composition (CIRC)** consists of a set of curriculum materials to supplement basal readers and ensure that cooperative learning is applied to reading, writing, spelling, and language mechanics (Stevens, Madden, Slavin, & Farnish, 1987).

During the lesson, students work together to complete the assignment. Using cooperative learning effectively is an art based on engineering lessons so that they include the five basic elements. There are, however, standard procedures that can be used over and over again to provide a pattern and flow to classroom life. A class session, for example, can include the following cooperative procedures:

1. Checking homework
2. Engaging in discussions
3. Taking notes
4. Reading assigned material (Read and Explain Pairs, Reading Comprehension Triads, Jigsaw)
5. Drilling and reviewing
6. Writing compositions
7. Resolving intellectual conflicts
8. Conducting projects

Exercise 2.5   Checking Homework

Task

Students are to bring their completed homework to class and understand how to do it correctly.

Cooperative

Students meet in their cooperative base groups, which are heterogeneous in terms of math and reading ability to ensure that all group members understand how to complete all parts of the assignment correctly.

Procedure

1. At the beginning of class, students meet in cooperative base groups.

2. One member of each group, **the runner,** goes to the teacher's desk, picks up the group's folder, and hands out any materials in the folder to the appropriate members.

3. The group reviews the assignment step by step to determine how much of the assignment each member completed and how well each member understands how to complete the material covered. Two roles are utilized: the **explainer** (explains step by step how the homework is correctly completed) and the **accuracy checker** (verifies that the explanation is accurate, encourages other group members, and provides coaching if needed). The role of explainer is rotated so that each member takes turns explaining step by step how a portion of the homework is correctly completed. The other members are accuracy checkers. The base groups concentrate on clarifying the parts of the assignment that one or more members do not understand.

4. At the end of the review the runner records how much of the assignment each member completed, places members' homework in the group's folder, and returns the folder to the teacher's desk.

Expected Criteria for Success

All group members understand how to complete each part of the assignment correctly.

Individual Accountability

Through regular examinations and by randomly selecting group members daily, students learn how to solve randomly selected problems from the homework.

Alternative of Directed Homework Review

Students are assigned to pairs. Teacher randomly picks questions from the homework assignment. One student explains the correct answer step by step. The other student listens, checks for accuracy, and prompts the explainer if he or she does not know the answer. Roles are switched for each question.

TURN TO YOUR NEIGHBOR SUMMARIES

A common practice in most classrooms is to hold a "whole-class discussion." You choose one student or a student volunteers to answer a question or provide a summary of what the lesson has covered so far. The student doing the explaining has an opportunity to clarify and extend what he or she knows by being actively involved in the learning process. The rest of the class is passive. As the teacher, you may ensure that all students are actively learning (and no one is passive) by requiring all students to explain their answers or to summarize simultaneously through the formulate, share, listen, and create procedure.

1. The task for students is to explain their answers and reasoning to a classmate and practice the skill of explaining. The cooperative goal is to create a joint answer that both members agree to and can explain.

2. *Students formulate an answer to a question* that requires them to summarize what the lesson has covered so far.

3. Students share their answers and reasoning with a classmate.

4. *Students listen carefully to their partner's explanation.* They should take notes, nod their heads, smile, and encourage their partner to explain the answer and reasoning in detail.

5. *The pair creates a new answer that is superior to their initial formulations* through the processes of association, building on each other's thoughts, and synthesizing.

6. The teacher monitors the pairs and assists students in following the procedure. To ensure individual accountability, you may wish to ask randomly selected students to explain the joint answer they created with their respective partners.

FORMULATE, SHARE, LISTEN, CREATE

Exercise 2.6   Read and Explain Pairs

Students may read material more effectively in cooperative pairs than individually.

1. Assign students to pairs (one high reader and one low reader in each pair). Tell students what specific pages you wish them to read. The *expected criterion for success* is that both members are able to explain the meaning of the assigned material correctly.
2. The *task* is to learn the material being read by establishing the meaning of each paragraph and integrating the meaning of the paragraphs. The cooperative goal is for both members to agree on the meaning of each paragraph, formulate a joint summary, and be able to explain its meaning to the teacher.
3. The *procedure* to be used by the student pairs is as follows:
   a. Read all the headings to get an overview.
   b. Both students silently read the first paragraph. Student A is initially the summarizer and Student B is the accuracy checker. Students rotate the roles after each paragraph.
   c. The summarizer summarizes in his or her own words the content of the paragraph to his or her partner.
   d. The accuracy checker listens carefully, corrects any misstatements, and adds anything left out. Then he or she tells how the material relates to something the student already knows.
   e. The students move on to the next paragraph, switch roles, and repeat the procedure. They continue until they have read all the assignment. They summarize and agree on the overall meaning of the assigned material.
4. During the lesson, the teacher systematically (a) monitors each reading pair and assists students in following the procedure, (b) ensures **individual accountability** by randomly asking students to summarize what they have read so far, and (c) reminds students that they can use **intergroup cooperation** (whenever it is helpful, they may check procedures, answers, and strategies with another group or compare answers with those of another group if they finish early).

Exercise 2.7   Reading Comprehension Triads

Tasks

1. Read the (poem, chapter, story, or handout) and answer the questions.
2. Practice the skill of checking.

Cooperative

1. The teacher will accept one set of answers from the group; everyone has to agree, everyone has to be able to explain each answer.
2. If all members score 90 percent or better on the test, each member will receive five bonus points.
3. To facilitate the group's work, each member will be assigned a role, such as reader, recorder, or checker.

Expected Criteria for Success

Everyone must be able to answer each question correctly.

Individual Accountability

1. One member from your group will be randomly chosen to explain the group's answers.
2. A test will be given on the assigned reading that each member takes individually.
3. Each group member will be required to explain the group's answers to a member of another group.

Expected Behaviors

Active participating, checking, encouraging, and elaborating by all members.

Intergroup Cooperation

Whenever it is helpful, check procedures, answers, and strategies with another group. When you are finished, compare your answers with those of another group and discuss.

Exercise 2.8   Jigsaw Procedure

Whenever there is material you wish to present to a class or you wish students to read, the jigsaw method is an alternative to lecture and individual reading. You assign students to cooperative groups, give all groups the same topic, and divide the material into parts like a jigsaw puzzle so that each student has part of the materials needed to complete the assignment. You give each member one unique section of the topic to learn and then teach the other members of the group. Members study the topic and teach their parts to the rest of the group. The group synthesizes the presentations of the members into the whole picture. In studying the life of Sojourner Truth (a black abolitionist and women's rights activist), for example, you give one student material on Truth's childhood, another material on her middle life, and another material on the final years of her life. Group members, therefore, cannot learn about her total life unless all members teach their parts. In a jigsaw each student then has to participate actively in order for his or her group to be successful. The *task* for students is to learn all the assigned material. The *cooperative goal* is for each member to ensure that everyone in the group learns all the assigned material. The **jigsaw** procedure is as follows:

1. *Cooperative groups.* Assign students to cooperative groups (you usually use groups of three, but you may jigsaw materials for groups of any size). Distribute a set of materials to each group so that each group gets one part of the materials. The set needs to be divisible into the number of members of the group. Number each part (Part 1, Part 2, Part 3).

2. *Preparation pairs.* Ask students to form a preparation pair with a member of another group who has the same part they do (you will wind up with a pair of Part 1s, a pair of Part 2s, a pair of Part 3s, and so on). Students have two tasks:

   a. Learning and becoming an expert on their part of the lesson materials.

   b. Planning how to teach their part of the material to the other members of their groups.

   Students are to read their part of the material together, using the pair reading procedure whereby (a) both students silently read each paragraph (or *chunk*), (b) one student summarizes its meaning and the other student checks the summary for accuracy, and (c) the students reverse roles after each paragraph. In doing so, pair members should list the major points they wish to teach, list practical advice related to major points, prepare a visual aid to help them teach the content, and prepare procedures to make the other members of their group active, not passive, learners. The *cooperative goal* is to create one teaching plan for the two members that both members are able to teach. Each member needs his or her individual copy of the plan.

3. *Practice pairs.* Ask students to form a practice pair with a member of another group who has the same part they do but who was in a different preparation pair. The *tasks* are for the members to practice teaching their part of the assigned material, listen carefully to their partner's practice, and incorporate the best ideas from the other's presentation into his or her own. The *cooperative goal* is to ensure that both members are practiced and ready to teach.

4. *Cooperative groups.* Students return to their cooperative groups. Their tasks are as follows:

   a. To teach their area of expertise to the other group members.

   b. To learn the material being taught by the other members.

   The *cooperative goal* is to ensure that members master all parts of the assigned material.

5. *Monitoring.* While the pairs and the cooperative groups work, you systematically move from group to group and assist students in following the procedures.

6. *Evaluation.* Assess students' degree of mastery of the material by giving a test that students take individually. You may wish to give members of groups whose members all score 90 percent or above five bonus points.

DRILL-REVIEW PAIRS

At times during a lesson you may wish to have students review what they have previously learned and drill on certain procedures to ensure that they have overlearned. When you do so, cooperative learning is indispensable.

Task
Correctly solve the problems or engage in the procedures.

Cooperative
The mutual goal is to ensure that both pair members understand the strategies and procedures required to solve the problems correctly. The teacher assigns two roles: *explainer* (one who explains step by step how to solve the problem) and *accuracy*

checker (one who verifies that the explanation is accurate, encourages students, and provides coaching if needed). Students rotate the two roles after each problem.

Individual Accountability

The teacher randomly chooses one member to explain how to solve a randomly selected problem.

Procedure

The teacher (a) assigns students to pairs and (b) assigns each pair to a foursome. The teacher then implements the following procedure:

1. Person A reads the problem and explains step by step the procedures and strategies required to solve it. Person B checks the accuracy of the solution and provides encouragement and coaching.

2. Person B solves the second problem, describing step by step the procedures and strategies required to solve it. Person A checks the accuracy of the solution and provides encouragement and coaching.

3. When the pair completes the problems, members check their answers with another pair. If they do not agree, they resolve the problem until there is consensus about the answer. If they do agree, they thank each other and continue to work in their pairs.

4. The procedure continues until all problems are completed.

Exercise 2.9   Cooperative Writing and Editing Pairs

When your lesson includes students writing an essay, report, poem, story, or review of what they have read, you should use cooperative writing and editing pairs.

Tasks

Write a composition and edit other students' compositions.

Criteria for Success

A well-written composition by each student. Depending on the instructional objectives, the compositions may be evaluated for grammar, punctuation, organization, content, or other criteria set by the teacher.

Cooperative Goal

All group members must verify that each member's composition is perfect according to the criteria set by the teacher. Students receive an individual score on the quality of their compositions. You can also give a group score based on the total number of errors made by the pair (the number of errors in one partner's composition plus the number of errors in the other partner's composition).

Individual Accountability

Each student writes his or her own composition.

Procedure

1. The teacher assigns students to pairs with at least one good reader in each pair.
2. Student A describes to Student B what he or she is planning to write. Student B listens carefully, probes with a set of questions, and outlines Student A's composition. The written outline is given to Student A.
3. This procedure is reversed with Student B describing what he or she is going to write and Student A listening and completing an outline of Student B's composition, which is then given to Student B.
4. The students research individualistically the material they need to write their compositions, keeping an eye out for material useful to their partners.
5. The two students work together to write the first paragraph of each composition. This ensures that both have a clear start on their compositions.
6. The students write their compositions individualistically.
7. When completed, the students proofread each other's compositions, making corrections in capitalization, punctuation, spelling, language usage, topic sentence usage, and other aspects of writing specified by the teacher. Students also give each other suggestions for revision.
8. The students revise their compositions, making all of the suggested revisions.
9. The two students then reread each other's compositions and sign their names (indicating that they guarantee that no errors exist in the composition).

While the students work, the teacher monitors the pairs, intervening where appropriate to help students master the needed writing and cooperative skills. When students complete their compositions, they discuss how effectively they worked together (listing the specific actions they engaged in to help each other), plan what behaviors they are going to emphasize in the next writing pair, and thank each other for the help and assistance received.

COOPERATIVE NOTE-TAKING PAIRS

The notes students take during a lesson are important for understanding what a student learns, both during the lesson and during reviews of the lesson. Most students, however, take notes very incompletely because of low working memory capacities, the information processing load required, and lack of skills in note taking. Students can benefit from learning how to take better notes and how to review notes more effectively.

1. Assign students to note-taking pairs. The *task* is to focus on increasing the quantity and quality of the notes taken during a lesson. The *cooperative goal* is for both stu-

dents to generate a comprehensive set of accurate notes that will enable them to learn and review the material covered in the lesson.

2. Every ten minutes or so, stop the lesson and have students share their notes. Student A summarizes his or her notes to Student B. Student B summarizes his or her notes to Student A. Each pair member must take something from his or her partner's notes to improve his or her own notes.

Exercise 2.10   *Academic Controversies*

Creating intellectual conflict (**controversy**) to improve academic learning is one of the most powerful and important instructional tools (Johnson & Johnson, 1995c). Academic controversies require a cooperative context and are actually an advanced form of cooperative learning. The basic format for structuring academic controversies is as follows:

1. Choose a topic that has content manageable by the students and on which at least two well-documented positions (pro and con) can be prepared. Organize the instructional materials into pro and con packets. Students need to know what their position is and where to find relevant information so they can build the rationale underlying the pro or con position on the issue.

2. Assign students to groups of four. Divide each group into two pairs. Assign pro and con positions to the pairs. A good reader or researcher should be in each pair.

3. Assign each pair the *tasks* of (a) learning its position and the supporting arguments and information, (b) researching all information relevant to its position (and giving the opposing pair any information found supporting the opposing position), (c) preparing a series of persuasive arguments to support its position, and (d) preparing a persuasive presentation to be given to the opposing pair. Give students the following instructions:

   Plan with your partner how to advocate your position effectively. Read the materials supporting your position. Find more information in the library reference books to support your position. Plan a persuasive presentation. Make sure you and your partner master the information supporting your assigned position and present it in a persuasive and complete way so that the other group members will comprehend and learn the information.

4. Highlight the *cooperative goals* of reaching a consensus on the issue, mastering all the information relevant to both sides of the issue (measured by a test taken individually), and writing a quality group report on which all members will be evaluated. Note that each group member will receive five bonus points if all members score 90 percent or better on the test covering both sides of the issue.

5. Have each pair present its position to the other. Presentations should involve more than one media and persuasively advocate the best case for the position. Do not allow

arguing during this time. Students should listen carefully to the opposing position and take notes. You tell students,

As a pair, present your position forcefully and persuasively. Listen carefully and learn the opposing position. Take notes, and clarify anything you do not understand.

6. Have students openly discuss the issue by freely exchanging their information and ideas. For higher-level reasoning and critical thinking to occur, it is necessary to probe and push each other's conclusions. Students ask for data to support each other's statements, clarify rationales, and show why their position is a rational one. Students evaluate critically the opposing position and its rationale, defend their own positions, and compare the strengths and weaknesses of the two positions. Students refute the claims being made by the opposing pair, and rebut the attacks on their own position. Students are to follow the specific rules for constructive controversy. Students should also take careful notes on and thoroughly learn the opposing position. Sometimes a *"time-out"* period needs to be provided so that pairs can caucus and prepare new arguments. Teachers encourage more spirited arguing, take sides when a pair is in trouble, play devil's advocate, ask one group to observe another group engaging in a spirited argument, and generally stir up the discussions.

Argue forcefully and persuasively for your position, presenting as many facts as you can to support your point of view. Listen critically to the opposing pair's position, asking them for the facts that support their viewpoint, and then present counter-arguments. Remember this is a complex issue, and you need to know both sides to write a good report.

7. Have the pairs reverse perspectives and positions by presenting the opposing position as sincerely and forcefully as they can. It helps to have the pairs change chairs. They can use their own notes, but may not see the materials developed by the opposing pair. Students' instructions are as follows:

Working as a pair, present the opposing pair's position as if you were they. Be as sincere and forceful as you can. Add any new facts you know. Elaborate their position by relating it to other information you previously learned.

8. Have the group members drop their advocacy and reach a decision by consensus. Then they should do the following:
   a. Write a group report that includes their joint position and the supporting evidence and rationale. Often the resulting position is a third perspective or synthesis that is more rational than the two assigned. All group members sign the report indicating that they agree with it, can explain its content, and consider it ready to be evaluated.
   b. Take a test on both positions individually. If all group members score above the preset criteria of excellence (90 percent), each receives five bonus points.

You can find a more detailed description of conducting academic controversies in Johnson and Johnson (1995c). Peggy Tiffany, a fourth-grade teacher in Wilmington, Vermont, regularly conducts an academic controversy on whether the wolf should be a protected species. She gives students the cooperative assignment of writing a report on the wolf in which they summarize what they have learned about the wolf and recommend the procedures they think are best for regulating wolf populations and preserving wolves within the continental United States. She randomly assigns students to groups of four, ensuring that both male and female and high-, medium-, and low-achieving students are all in the same group. She divides the group into two pairs and assigns one pair the position of an environmental organization that believes wolves should be a protected species and assigns the other pair the position of farmers and ranchers who believe that wolves should not be a protected species.

Ms. Tiffany gives each side a packet of articles, stories, and information that supports their position. During the first class period, each pair develops their position and plans how to present the best case possible to the other pair. Near the end of the period, pairs are encouraged to compare notes with pairs from other groups who represent the same position. During the second class period, each pair makes its presentation. Each member of the pair has to participate in the presentation. Members of the opposing pair take notes and listen carefully. During the third class period the group discusses the issue (following a set of rules to help them criticize ideas without criticizing people), differentiates the two positions, and assesses the degree of evidence and logic supporting each position. During the first half of the fourth hour, the pairs reverse perspectives and present each other's positions. Students drop their advocacy positions, clarify their understanding of each other's information and rationale, and begin work on their group report. Students spend the first half of the fifth period finalizing their report. The teacher evaluates the report on the quality of the writing, the evaluation of opinion and evidence, and the oral presentation of the report to the class. The students then take an individual test on the wolf and, if every member of the group achieves up to criterion, they all receive the bonus points. Finally, during the sixth class period each group makes a ten-minute presentation to the entire class summarizing its report. All four members of the group need to participate orally in the presentation.

Within this lesson you structure positive interdependence by (a) having each group arrive at a consensus, submit one written report, and make one presentation; (b) jigsawing the materials to the pairs within the group; and (c) giving bonus points if all group members score well on the test. You structure individual accountability by having (a) each member of the pair orally participate in each step of the controversy procedure, (b) each member of the group orally participate in the group presentation, and (c) each member take an individual test on the material. The social skills emphasized are those involved in systematically advocating an intellectual position and evaluating and criticizing the position advocated by others, as well as the skills involved in synthesis and consensual decision making. Students derive numerous academic and social benefits from participating in such structured controversies (Johnson & Johnson, 1995c).

Exercise 2.11   Joint Project

Task

Complete a project.

Cooperative

Each group completes one project. Members sign the project to indicate that they have contributed their share of the work, agree with the content, and can present or explain it. When a variety of materials are used (such as scissors, paper, glue, or markers), assign each team member a responsibility for one of the materials. If appropriate, assign each group member a specific role.

Criteria for Success

A completed project that each group member can explain or present.

Individual Accountability

1. Each group member may be given different color pens, markers, or pencils.
2. Each group member presents the group project to a member of another group.
3. Each student takes a test individually on the content covered by the project.

Expected Social Skills

Presenting ideas, eliciting ideas, and organizing work.

Intergroup Cooperation

Whenever it is helpful, check procedures, information, and progress with other groups.

Examples

1. Using compass readings, draw a treasure map for another group to follow.
2. Make a list of the reasons for not growing up (consider, for example, the reasons given in *Peter Pan* by J. M. Barrie).

MONITORING AND INTERVENING

> *The only thing that endures over time is the law of the farm: I must prepare the ground, put in the seed, cultivate it, water it, then gradually nurture growth and development to full maturity . . . there is no quick fix.*
>
> Stephen Covey

Once the students begin working in cooperative learning groups, the teacher's role is to monitor students' interaction and intervene to help students learn and interact more skillfully.

Monitoring Students' Behavior

Your job begins in earnest when the cooperative learning groups start working. Resist that urge to get a cup of coffee or to grade papers. You observe the interaction among group members to assess students' (a) academic progress and (b) appropriate use of interpersonal and small-group skills.

Observations can be formal (with an observation schedule on which frequencies are tallied) or anecdotal (informal descriptions of students' statements and actions). Based on your observations, you can then intervene to improve students' academic learning and interpersonal and small-group skills. Remember, *students respect what we inspect*. To *monitor* means to check continuously. Monitoring has four stages:

1. *Preparing for observing* the learning groups by deciding who will be the observers, choosing what observation forms to use, and training the observers.

2. *Observing* to assess the quality of cooperative efforts in the learning groups.

3. *Intervening when it is necessary* to improve a group's taskwork or teamwork.

4. *Having students assess the quality of their own individual participation* in the learning groups to encourage self-monitoring, having groups assess the level of their effectiveness, and having both individuals and groups set growth goals.

In monitoring cooperative learning groups, for teachers can follow these guidelines:

1. Plan a route through the classroom and the length of time spent observing each group so that all groups are observed during a lesson.

2. Use a formal observation sheet to count the number of times you observe appropriate behaviors being used by students. The more concrete the data, the more useful it is to you (the teacher) and to students.

3. Initially, do not try to count too many different behaviors. You may wish simply to keep track of who talks. Your observations should focus on positive behaviors.

4. Supplement and extend the frequency data with notes on specific student actions. Especially useful are descriptions of skillful interchanges that can be shared with students later and with parents in conferences or telephone conversations.

5. Train and utilize student observers. Student observers can obtain more complete data on each group's functioning and may learn important lessons about appropriate and inappropriate behavior. We can remember one first-grade teacher who had a student who talked all the time (even to himself while working alone). He tended to dominate any group he was in. When she introduced student observers to the class, she made him an observer. One important rule for observers was not to interfere in the task but to gather data without talking. He was gathering data on who talks and he did a good job, noticing that one student had done quite a bit of talking in the group whereas another had talked very little. The next day when he was a group member and there was another observer, he was seen starting to talk, clamping his hand over his mouth, and glancing at the observer. He knew what was being observed and he didn't want to be the only one

with marks. The teacher said he may have listened for the first time in the year. So the observer often benefits in learning about group skills.

6. Allocate sufficient time at the end of each group session for discussion of the data gathered by the observers.

Providing Task Assistance

Cooperative learning groups provide teachers with a window into students' minds. Through working cooperatively students make hidden thinking processes overt and subject to observation and commentary. From carefully listening to students explain to each other what they are learning, teachers can determine what students do and do not understand. Consequently, you may will wish to intervene to clarify instructions, review important procedures and strategies for completing the assignment, answer questions, and teach both task skills as necessary. In discussing the concepts and information to be learned, you should make specific statements, such as "Yes, that is one way to find the main idea of a paragraph," not "Yes, that is right." The more specific statement reinforces the desired learning and promotes positive transfer by helping the students associate a term with their learning. Metacognitive thought may be encouraged by asking students (a) "What are you doing?" (b) "Why are you doing it?" and (c) "How will it help you?"

Intervening to Teach Social Skills

Cooperative learning groups provide teachers with a picture of students' social skills. The social skills required for productive group work are discussed in detail in Chapter 5. They, along with activities that may be used in teaching them, are covered in even more depth in D. W. Johnson and F. Johnson (1997) and Johnson (1991, 1997). While monitoring the learning groups, you may intervene to suggest more effective procedures for working together or reinforce particularly effective and skillful behaviors. Choosing when to intervene is part of the art of teaching. In intervening, ask group members to follow the following procedure.

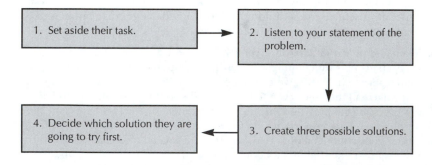

In one third-grade class, the teacher noticed when distributing papers that one student was sitting back from the other three group members. A moment later the teacher glanced over and only three students were sitting where four were a moment before. As she watched, the three students came marching over to her and complained that Johnny was under the table and wouldn't come out. "Make him come out!" they insisted (the teacher's role: police officer, judge, and executioner). The teacher told them that Johnny was a member of their group and asked what they had tried to solve their problem. "Tried?" the puzzled reply. "Yes, have you asked him to come out?" the teacher inquired. The group marched back and the teacher continued distributing papers to groups. A moment later the teacher glanced over to their table and saw no heads above the table (which is one way to solve the problem). After a few more minutes, four heads came struggling out from under the table and the group (including Johnny) went back to work with great energy. We don't know what happened under that table, but whatever it was, it was effective. What makes this story even more interesting is that the group received a 100 percent score on the paper and later, when the teacher was standing by Johnny's desk, she noticed he had the paper clutched in his hand. The group had given Johnny the paper and he was taking it home. He confided to the teacher that this was the first time he could ever remember earning a 100 on anything in school. (If that was your record, you might slip under a few tables yourself.)

EVALUATING LEARNING AND PROCESSING INTERACTION

Providing Closure to the Lesson

You provide closure to lessons by having students summarize the major points in the lesson, recall ideas, and identify final questions for the teacher (see Johnson, Johnson, & Holubec, 1992). At the end of the lesson students should be able to summarize what they have learned and to understand how these skills will use it in future lessons.

Assessing the Quality and Quantity of Learning

The quality and quantity of student learning should be regularly assessed and occasionally evaluated using a criterion-referenced system. This is covered in depth in Chapter 7. It is covered in even more depth in *Meaningful and Manageable Assessment through Cooperative Learning* (Johnson & Johnson, 1996). Cooperative learning, furthermore, provides an arena in which **performance-based assessment** (requiring students to demonstrate what they can do with what they know by performing a procedure or skill), **authentic assessment** (requiring students to demonstrate the desired procedure or skill in a real life context), and **total quality learning** (continuous improvement of the process of students helping teammates learn) can take place. A wide variety of assessment formats may be used and students may be directly involved in assessing each other's level of learning and then providing immediate remediation to ensure all group members' learning is maximized.

As an illustration, have students form into pairs and rank each of the following columns from most important ("1") to least important.

WHAT IS ASSESSED	PROCEDURES	WAYS CL HELPS
_____ Academic learning	_____ Goal setting	_____ Additional sources of labor
_____ Reasoning strategies	_____ Testing	_____ More modalities in assessment
_____ Skills, competencies	_____ Compositions	_____ More diverse outcomes
_____ Attitudes	_____ Presentations	_____ More sources of information
_____ Work habits	_____ Projects	_____ Reduction of bias
	_____ Portfolios	_____ Development of rubrics
	_____ Logs, journals	_____ Implement improvement plan

Processing How Well the Group Functioned

When students have completed the assignment, or at the end of each class session, students describe what member actions were helpful (and unhelpful) in completing the group's work and make decisions about what behaviors to continue or change. This is discussed in detail in Chapter 6. Group processing occurs at two levels: in each learning group and in the class as a whole. In **small group processing,** each group member discusses how effectively the group worked together and what could be improved. In **whole-class processing** teachers give the class feedback and have students share incidents that occurred in their groups. Processing is made up of four parts:

1. **Feedback:** You ensure that each student, each group, and the class as a whole receives (and gives) feedback on the effectiveness of taskwork and teamwork. Feedback given to students should be descriptive and specific, not evaluative and general (see Johnson, 1997).

2. **Reflection:** You ensure that students analyze and reflect on the feedback they receive. You avoid questions that can be answered yes or no. Instead of saying, "Did everyone help each other learn?" you should ask, "How frequently did each member (a) explain how to solve a problem and (b) correct or clarify other member's explanations?

3. **Improvement goals:** You help individuals and groups set goals for improving the quality of their work.

4. **Celebration:** You encourage the celebration of members' hard work and the group's success.

SUMMARY AND CONCLUSIONS

At this point you know what cooperative learning is and how it is different from competitive and individualistic learning. You know that three types of cooperative learning groups exist: formal cooperative learning groups, informal cooperative learning groups, and cooperative base groups. You know that the essence of cooperative learning is positive interdependence where students recognize that "we are in this together, sink or swim." Other essential components include individual accountability (every student is accountable for both learning the assigned material and helping other group members learn), face-to-face interaction among students (students promote each other's successes), the appropriate use of interpersonal and group skills, and the ability to process how effectively the learning group has functioned. These five essential components of cooperation form the conceptual basis for constructing cooperative procedures. You know that the research supports the proposition that cooperation results in greater effort to achieve, more positive interpersonal relationships, and greater psychological health and self-esteem than do competitive or individualistic efforts. You know the teacher's role in implementing formal cooperative learning. Any assignment in any subject area may be structured cooperatively. In using formal cooperative learning, the teacher decides on the objectives of the lesson, makes a number of preinstructional decisions about the size of the group and the materials required to conduct the lesson, explains to students the task and the cooperative goal structure, monitors the groups as they work, intervenes when it is necessary, and then evaluates.

Teachers who have mastered the use of cooperative learning have told us many times, "Don't say it is easy!" We know it's not. It can take years to become an expert. There is a lot of pressure to teach like everyone else, to have students learn alone, and not to let students look at each other's papers. Students will not be accustomed to working together and are likely to have a competitive orientation. You may wish to start small by using cooperative learning for one topic or in one class until you feel comfortable, and then expand into other topics or classes. *Implementing formal cooperative learning in your classroom is not easy, but it is worth the effort.*

In addition to formal cooperative learning, teachers use informal cooperative learning and cooperative base groups. These techniques will be discussed in the next two chapters.

3

Informal Cooperative Learning

It is 12,896 B.C. A small group of hunters surround a band of reindeer as they ford an icy river. The hunters are armed with harpoons tipped with spear heads carved from reindeer antler. As the reindeer wallow in the water the hunters run in and slaughter them. It is the coordinated action of the group of Cro-Magnon hunters that makes them more successful than their Neanderthal cousins, who hunt as individuals.

Our origins are somehow linked with the fate of the Neanderthals. We have never been proud of our extinct predecessors, partly because of their looks. Nevertheless, the Neanderthals represent a high point in the human story. Their lineage goes back to the earliest members of the genus *Homo*. They were the original pioneers. Over thousands of years, Neanderthals moved out of Africa by way of the Near East into India, China, Malaysia, and into southern Europe. In recent times, 150,000 or so years ago, they pioneered glacial landscapes. The Neanderthals were the first to cope with climates hospitable only to woolly mammoths and reindeer.

There is no anatomical evidence that the Neanderthals were inferior to us (the Cro-Magnons) cerebrally and no doubt whatever that they were our physical superiors. Their strongest individuals could probably lift weights of half a ton or so. Physically, we are quite puny in comparison. But we gradually replaced the Neanderthals during an overlapping period of a few thousand years. It may have mainly been a matter of attrition and population pressure. As the glaciers from Scandinavia advanced, northern populations of Neanderthals moved south while our ancestors were moving north out of Africa. We met in Europe. They vanished about 30,000 years ago.

Numerous explanations exist for the disappearance of the Neanderthals. Perhaps they evolved into us. Perhaps we merged. Perhaps there was an intergroup competition for food, with the Neanderthals unable to meet our challenge and dying off in marginal areas. Perhaps the Neanderthals were too set in their ways and were unable to evolve and refine better ways to cooperate whereas we were continually organizing better cooperative efforts to cope with changing climatic conditions. There seems to be little doubt that we were more able to form and maintain cooperative efforts within small groups.

During the time we (the Cro-Magnons) overlapped with the Neanderthals, our ancestors developed highly sophisticated cooperative effects characterized by social organization, group-hunting procedures, creative experimentation with a variety of materials, sharing of knowledge, divisions of labor, trade, and transportation systems. We sent out scouts to monitor the movements of herds of animals we preyed on. The Neanderthals probably did not. We cached supplies and first aid materials to aid hunting parties far away from our home bases. The Neanderthals did not. Neanderthals apparently engaged their prey chiefly in direct combat. We learned more efficient ways of hunting, such as driving animals over cliffs, that changed fundamentally our relationship with the rest of the animal kingdom (i.e, instead of behaving like lions and other carnivores by going after young, old, and sick animals to weed out the less fit, large-scale game drives wiped out entire herds and perhaps entire species). We developed more sophisticated tools and weapons to kill from a distance such as the spear thrower and the bow and arrow. The Neanderthals probably did not. The Neanderthals used local materials to develop tools. We were more selective, often obtaining special fine-grained and colorful flints from quarries as far as 250 miles away. This took a level of intergroup cooperation and social organization that Neanderthals did not develop. We improved the toolmaking process through experimentation and sharing knowledge. The Neanderthals did not. The Neanderthals used stone almost exclusively for tools. We used bone and ivory to make needles and other tools. We "tailored" our clothes and made ropes and nets. Our ability to obtain more food than we needed resulted in trading and the formation of far-ranging social networks. Status hierarchies, the accumulation of wealth, artistic efforts, laws, and story telling to preserve traditions followed as more complex forms of cooperation were developed. Whether we replaced or evolved from the Neanderthals, our ingenuity was especially evident in organizing cooperative efforts to increase our standard of living and the quality of our lives. We excelled at organizing effective small-group efforts.

Humans are small-group beings. We always have been and we always will be. As John Donne said, "No man is an island, entire of itself." Throughout the history of our species we have lived in small groups. For 200,000 years, humans lived in small hunting and gathering groups. For 10,000 years, humans lived in small farming communities. It is only recently, during the past 100 years or so, that large cities have become the rule rather than the exception.

THE COOPERATIVE CLASSROOM

Classrooms perhaps should primarily be small-group places, and there is more to using cooperative learning groups than formal cooperative learning. Teachers also use informal cooperative learning and cooperative base groups. Informal cooperative learning is used with direct teaching. Base groups involve long-term cooperative efforts. The three types of cooperative learning are then integrated into coherent lessons.

Direct Teaching, Lecturing

> *Our survey of teaching methods suggests that . . . if we want students to become more effective in meaningful learning and thinking, they need to spend more time in active, meaningful learning and thinking—not just sitting and passively receiving information.*
>
> McKeachie (1986)

Direct teaching includes lecturing, showing films and videos, giving demonstrations, and having guest speakers. Lecturing is currently the most common teacher behavior in secondary and elementary schools (as well as in colleges and universities). Even in training programs within business and industry, lecturing dominates. A **lecture** is an extended presentation in which the teacher presents factual information in an organized and logically sequenced way. It typically results in long periods of uninterrupted teacher-centered, expository discourse that relegates students to the role of passive "spectators" in the classroom. A lecture has three parts: the introduction, the body, and the conclusion. Proponents of lecturing advise teachers to "Tell them what you are going to tell them; then tell them; then tell them what you told them." First you describe the learning objectives in a way that alerts students to what is to be covered in the lecture. You then present the material to be learned in small steps organized logically and sequenced in ways that are easy to follow. You end with an integrative review of the main points. Normally, lecturing includes using reference notes, occasionally using visuals to enhance the information being presented, and responding to students' questions as the lecture progresses or at its end. Occasionally, students are provided with handouts to help them follow the lecture. The lecturer presents the material to be learned in more or less final form, gives answers, presents principles, and elaborates the entire content of what is to be learned.

APPROPRIATE USE OF LECTURING

Some of the reasons why lecturing is so popular are that it can be adapted to different audiences and time frames and it keeps the teacher at the center of all communication and attention in the classroom. Lecturing and other forms of direct teaching are appropriate under certain conditions (see Table 3.1). From the research directly evaluating lecturing (see reviews by Bligh, 1972; Costin, 1972; Eble, 1983; McKeachie, 1967; Verner & Dickinson, 1967) it may be concluded that lecturing is appropriate when the purpose is to

1. **Disseminate information.** Lecturing is appropriate when faculty wish to communicate a large amount of material to many students in a short period of time, when faculty wish to supplement curriculum materials that need updating or elaborating, when the material has to be organized and presented in a particular way, or when faculty want to provide an introduction to an area.

TABLE 3.1   **Direct Teaching and Lecturing**

APPROPRIATE USE	PROBLEMS	ENEMIES
Disseminate information	Decreases student attention	Preoccupation with past or future
Present information not available elsewhere	Requires intelligent, motivated auditory learner	Emotional moods, such as anger, frustration
Save students time in locating information	Promotes lower-level learning of factual information	Student lack of interest in material presented
Arouse students' interest in a topic	All students need same information, presented orally, impersonally, at same pace, no dialogue	Failure to understand material being presented
Teach students who are auditory learners	Students tend not to like it	Feelings of alienation from class and school
	Assumes students learn auditorially, have high working memory, possess required prior knowledge, are good note takers, have information processing strategies and skills	Entertaining, clear presentations that misrepresent complexity of material

2. **Present material that is not available elsewhere.** Lecturing is appropriate when information is not available in a readily accessible source, the information is original, or the information might be too complex and difficult for students to learn on their own.

3. **Expose students to content in a brief time that might take them much longer to locate on their own.** Lecturing is appropriate when faculty need to teach information that must be integrated from many sources and students do not have the time, resources, or skills to do so.

4. **Arouse students' interest in the subject.** When a lecture is presented by a highly authoritative person or in a skillful way with lots of humor and examples, students may be intrigued and want to find out more about the subject. Skillful delivery of a lecture includes maintaining eye contact, avoiding distracting behaviors, modulating voice pitch and volume, and using appropriate gestures. Achievement is higher when presentations are clear (Good & Brouws, 1977; Smith & Land, 1981), delivered with enthusiasm (Armento, 1977), and delivered with appropriate gestures and movements (Rosenshine, 1968).

5. **Teach students who are primarily auditory learners.**

Problems with Lecturing

While direct teaching may be appropriately used, there are also problems with direct teaching that teachers must keep in mind. Much of the research on lecturing has compared lecturing with group discussion. Although the conditions under which lecturing is more successful than group discussion have *not* been identified, a number of problems with lecturing have been found.

The first problem with lectures is that students' attention to what the teacher is saying decreases as the lecture proceeds. Research in the 1960s by D. H. Lloyd, at the University of Reading in Berkshire, England, found that student attending during lectures followed a pattern: five minutes of settling in, five minutes of readily assimilating material, confusion and boredom with assimilation falling off rapidly and remaining low for the bulk of the lecture, and some revival of attention at the end of the lecture (Penner, 1984). The concentration during lectures of medical students, who presumably are highly motivated, rose sharply and peaked ten to fifteen minutes after the lecture began, and fell steadily thereafter (Stuart & Rutherford, 1978). J. McLeish, in a research study in the 1960s, analyzed the percentage of content contained in student notes at different time intervals throughout the lecture (reported in Penner, 1984). He found that students wrote notes on 41 percent of the content presented during the first fifteen minutes, they wrote notes on 25 percent of the content presented in a thirty-minute time period, and they wrote notes on only 20 percent of what had been presented during forty-five minutes.

The second problem with lecturing is that it takes an educated, intelligent person oriented toward auditory learning to benefit from listening to lectures. Verner and Cooley (1967) found that, in general, very little of a lecture can be recalled except by listeners with above-average education and intelligence. Even under optimal conditions, when intelligent, motivated people listen to a brilliant scholar talk about an interesting topic, a lecture can present serious problems. Verner and Dickinson (1967, p. 90) give this example:

> *Ten percent of the audience displayed signs of inattention within fifteen minutes. After eighteen minutes one-third of the audience and ten percent of the platform guests were fidgeting. At thirty-five minutes everyone was inattentive; at forty-five minutes, trance was more noticeable than fidgeting; and at forty-seven minutes some were asleep and at least one was reading. A causal check twenty-four hours later revealed that the audience recalled only insignificant details, and these were generally wrong.*

The third problem with lecturing is that it tends to promote only lower-level learning of factual information. Bligh (1972), after an extensive series of studies, concluded that while lecturing was as (but not more) effective as reading or other methods in transmitting information, lecturing was clearly less effective in promoting thinking or in changing attitudes. A survey of 58 studies conducted between 1928 and 1967 comparing various characteristics of lectures versus discussions found that lectures and discussions did not differ significantly on lower-level learning (such as learning facts and principles), but discussion appeared superior in developing higher-level problem-solving capabilities and positive attitudes toward the course (Costin, 1972). McKeachie and Kulik (1975) separated studies on lecturing according to whether they focused on factual learning, higher-level reasoning, attitudes, or motivation. They found lecture to be superior to discussion for promoting factual learning, but discussion was found to be superior to lecture for promoting higher-level reasoning, positive attitudes, and motivation to learn. Lecturing at best tends to focus on the lower-level of cognition and learning. When the material is complex, detailed, or abstract; when students need to analyze, synthesize, or integrate the knowledge being studied; or when long-term retention is desired, lecturing is not such a good idea. Formal cooperative learning groups should be used to accomplish goals such as these.

The fourth problem with lecturing is that it is based on the assumptions that all students need the same information, presented orally, presented at the same pace, without dialogue with the presenter, and in an impersonal way. Although students have different levels of knowledge about the subject being presented, the same information is presented to all. The material covered in a lecture may often be communicated just as well in a text assignment or a handout. Lectures can waste student time by telling them things that they could read for themselves. Although students learn and comprehend at different paces, a lecture proceeds at the lecturer's pace. Although students who listen carefully and cognitively process the information presented will have questions that need to be answered, lectures typically are forms of one-way communication and the large number of classmates inhibit question asking. If students cannot ask questions, misconceptions, incorrect understanding, and gaps in understanding cannot be identified and corrected. Stones (1970), for example, surveyed more than 1,000 college students and found that 60 percent stated that the presence of a large number of classmates would deter them from asking questions, even if the teacher encouraged them to do so. Lecturing by its very nature impersonalizes learning. Research indicates that personalized learning experiences have more impact on achievement and motivation.

The fifth problem with lecturing is that students tend not to like it. Costin's (1972) review of the literature indicates that students like the course and subject area better when they learn in discussion groups than when they learn by listening to lectures. This is important in introductory courses where disciplines often attempt to attract majors.

Finally, lecturing is based on a series of assumptions about the cognitive capabilities and strategies of students. When you lecture you assume that all students learn auditorially, have high working memory capacity, have all the required prior knowledge, have good note-taking strategies and skills, and are not susceptible to information processing overload.

Enemies of the Lecture

Besides the identified problems with lecturing and direct teaching, there are obstacles to making direct teaching and lecturing effective. We call these obstacles the enemies of the lecture:

1. *Preoccupation with what happened during the previous hour or with what happened on the way to class.* For lectures to succeed, faculty must take students' attention away from events in the hallway or campus and focus student attention on the subject area and topic being dealt with in class.

2. *Emotional moods that block learning and cognitive processing of information.* Students who are angry or frustrated about something are *not* open to new learning. For lectures to work, faculty must set a constructive learning mood. Humor helps.

3. *Disinterest by students who go to sleep or who turn on a tape recorder while they write letters or read comic books.* For lectures to work, faculty must focus student attention on the material being presented and ensure that they cognitively process the information and integrate it into what they already know.

4. *Failure to understand the material being presented in the lecture.* Students can learn material incorrectly and incompletely because of lack of understanding. To make lectures work

there has to be some means of checking the accuracy and completeness of students' understanding of the material being presented.

5. *Feelings of isolation and alienation and beliefs that no one cares about them as persons or about their academic progress.* To make lectures work, students have to believe that there are other people in the class who will provide help and assistance because they care about the students as people and about the quality of their learning.

6. *Entertaining lectures that misrepresent the complexity of the material being presented.* Although entertaining and impressing students is nice, it often does not help students understand and think critically about complex material. To make lectures work students must think critically and use higher-level reasoning in cognitively processing course content. One of our colleagues is a magnificent lecturer. His explanation of the simplex algorithm for solving linear programming problems is so clear and straightforward that the students go away with the view that it is very simple. Later when they try to solve a problem on their own, they find that they don't have a clue as to how to begin. Our colleague used to blame himself for not explaining well enough. Sometimes he blamed the students. Now he puts small cooperative groups to work on a simple linear programming problem, circulates and checks the progress of each student, provides help where he feels it is appropriate, and only gives his brilliant lectures when the students understand the problem and are ready to hear his proposed solution. Both he and the students are much happier with their increased understanding.

After considering these problems and barriers, it may be concluded that alternative teaching strategies have to be interwoven with lecturing if the lecture method is to be effective. Even though lecturing and direct teaching have traditionally been conducted within competitive and individualistic structures, they can be made cooperative. Perhaps the major procedure to interweave with lecturing is informal cooperative learning groups.

INFORMAL COOPERATIVE LEARNING GROUPS

Sometimes teachers need to lecture, show a movie or videotape, give a demonstration, or have a guest speaker. In such cases, informal cooperative learning may be used to ensure that students are active (not passive) cognitively. **Informal cooperative learning** consists of having students work together to achieve a joint learning goal in temporary, ad hoc groups that last from a few minutes to one class period. Their *purposes* are to focus student attention on the material to be learned, set a mood conducive to learning, help organize in advance the material to be covered in a class session, ensure that students cognitively process the material being taught, and provide closure to an instructional session. Informal cooperative learning groups also ensure that misconceptions, incorrect understanding, and gaps in understanding are identified and corrected, and learning experiences are personalized. They may be used at any time, but are especially useful during lecturing or direct teaching.

During lecturing and direct teaching the instructional challenge for the teacher is to ensure that students do the intellectual work of organizing material, explaining it, summarizing it, and integrating it into existing conceptual networks. This may be achieved by having students do the advance organizing, cognitively process what they are learning, and provide closure to the lesson. Breaking up lectures with short cooperative processing times will give you slightly less lecture time, but it will help counter what is proclaimed as the main problem of lectures: The information passes from the notes of the professor to the notes of the student without passing through the mind of either one.

LECTURING WITH INFORMAL COOPERATIVE LEARNING GROUPS

The following procedure will help you plan a lecture that keeps students more actively engaged intellectually. It entails having **focused discussions** before and after the lecture (i.e., bookends) and interspersing **pair discussions** throughout the lecture. Two important aspects of using informal cooperative learning groups are to (a) make the task and the instructions explicit and precise and (b) require the groups to produce a specific product (such as a written answer). The procedure is as follows.

1. *Introductory Focused Discussion:* Assign students to pairs. The person nearest each student will do. You may wish to require different seating arrangements each class period so that students will meet and interact with a number of other students in the class. Then give the pairs the cooperative assignment of completing the initial (advance organizer) task. Give them only four or five minutes to do so. The discussion task is aimed at *promoting advance organizing* of what the students know about the topic to be presented and *establishing expectations* about what the lecture will cover.

2. *Lecture Segment 1:* Deliver the first segment of the lecture. This segment should last from ten to fifteen minutes. This is about the length of time a motivated adult can concentrate on a lecture. For unmotivated adolescents, the time may be shorter.

3. *Pair Discussion 1:* Give the students a discussion task focused on the material you have just presented that may be completed within three or four minutes. Its purpose is to ensure that students are actively thinking about the material being presented. The discussion task may be to (a) give an answer to a question posed by the teacher, (b) give a reaction to the theory, concepts, or information being presented, or (c) relate material to past learning so that it is integrated into existing conceptual frameworks (i.e., elaborate the material being presented). Discussion pairs respond to the task in the following way:

   a. Each student *formulates* his or her answer.

   b. Students *share* their answer with their partner.

   c. Students *listen* carefully to their partner's answer.

   d. Pairs *create* a new answer that is superior to each member's initial formulation through the process of association, building on each other's thoughts, and synthesizing.

   Randomly choose two or three students to give thirty-second summaries of their discussions. *It is important that students are randomly called on to share their answers after each discussion task.* Such **individual accountability** ensures that the pairs take the tasks seriously and check each other to ensure that both are prepared to answer.

4. *Lecture Segment 2:* Deliver the second segment of the lecture.

5. *Pair Discussion 2:* Give a discussion task focused on the second part of the lecture.

6. Repeat this sequence of lecture segment and pair discussion until the lecture is completed.

Informal Cooperative Learning

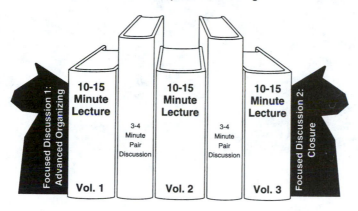

FIGURE 3.1 Informal Cooperative Learning

7. *Closure Focused Discussion:* Give an ending discussion task to summarize what students have learned from the lecture. Students should have four or five minutes to summarize and discuss the material covered in the lecture. The discussion should result in students integrating what they have just learned into existing conceptual frameworks. The task may also point students toward what the homework will cover or what will be presented in the next class session. This provides closure to the lecture.

Process the procedure with students regularly to help them increase their skill and speed in completing short discussion tasks (see Figure 3.1). Processing questions may include (a) "How well prepared were you to complete the discussion tasks?" and (b) "How could you come even better prepared tomorrow?"

The informal cooperative learning group is not only effective for getting students actively involved in understanding what they are learning, it also provides time for you to gather your wits, reorganize your notes, take a deep breath, and move around the class listening to what students are saying. Listening to student discussions can give you direction and insight into how well the concepts you are teaching are being grasped by your students (who, unfortunately, may not have graduate degrees in the topic you are presenting).

Besides the use of formal and informal cooperative learning groups, there is a need for a permanent cooperative base group that provides relatively long-term relationships among students. It is to this use of cooperative learning that we now turn.

CONCLUSIONS

In informal cooperative learning, students interact for only a few minutes. In formal cooperative learning, students may interact for one or several class periods. In the next chapter, cooperative groups that last for a semester, a year, or several years will be discussed.

4

Cooperative Base Groups

COOPERATIVE BASE GROUPS

Author William Manchester wrote several years ago in *Life* magazine about revisiting Sugar Loaf Hill in Okinawa, where 34 years before he had fought as a marine. He describes how he had been wounded, sent to a hospital, and, in violation of orders, escaped from the hospital to rejoin his unit at the front. Doing so meant almost certain death. "Why did I do it?" he wondered. The answer lies in long-term relationships in which group members depend on and support each other.

Children and youth must attend school if they are to achieve valuable knowledge, form constructive peer relationships, and develop personally and socially in healthy ways. Students must also believe that they belong. They must socially bond and attach to teachers and classmates. Caring and committed relationships cannot be created from memos and announcements over the loudspeaker that "in this school you are required to like each other." Caring and committed relationships develop over time as individuals work together to achieve worthwhile goals. At least one cooperative group, therefore, must last for some time.

Cooperative base groups are long-term, heterogeneous cooperative learning groups with stable membership whose primary responsibilities are to provide support, encouragement, and assistance in completing assignments and to hold each other accountable for striving to learn. Typically, cooperative base groups (a) are heterogeneous in membership (especially in terms of achievement motivation and task orientation), (b) meet regularly (for example, daily or biweekly), and (c) last for the duration of the class (a semester or year) and preferably until the students graduate. When students know that the cooperative base group will stay together until each member graduates, they become committed to finding ways to motivate and encourage their groupmates. Problems in working with each other cannot be ignored or waited out.

Two types of base groups exist: class base groups and school base groups. The agendas of both types of base groups can include the following:

1. **Academic support tasks,** such as checking to see what assignments each member has and what help he or she needs to complete them. Base group members give each other encouragement, assistance, and support for mastering the course content and completing all assignments. The group discusses assignments, answers any questions about assignments, provides information about what a member missed, and plans, reviews, and edits papers. Members can prepare each other to take tests and go over the questions missed afterward. Members can share their areas of expertise (such as art or computers). Above all, members monitor each other's academic progress and make sure all members are achieving.

2. **Personal support tasks,** such as listening sympathetically when a member has problems with parents or friends, having general discussions about life, giving each other advice about relationships, and helping each other solve nonacademic problems. Base groups provide interpersonal relationships that personalize the course. Teachers may increase the likelihood of personal support by conducting trust-building exercises with the base groups, such as sharing their favorite movie, a childhood experience, a memory from high school, and so forth.

3. **Routine tasks** such as taking attendance or collecting homework. The base group provides a structure for managing course procedures such as attendance, homework, and assessments.

CLASS BASE GROUPS

The larger the class and the more complex the subject matter, the more important it is to have base groups. The members of base groups should exchange phone numbers and information about schedules as they may wish to meet outside of class. All members are expected to contribute actively to the group's work, strive to maintain effective working relationships with other members, complete all assignments and assist groupmates in completing their assignments, and indicate agreement with the work of the base group by signing the weekly contract. At the beginning of each session class members meet in their base groups to perform the following activities (see also Table 4.1).

TABLE 4.1   Base Group Agendas

OPENING TASKS	CLOSING TASKS
Greeting and welcoming	Reviewing and clarifying assignments
Checking homework	Discussing what was learned
Reviewing the progress of ongoing assignments	Discussing applications of learned material
Completing relationship and group building task	Celebrating members' hard work

1. Greet each other and check to see that none of their group is under undue stress. Members ask, "How are you today?" and "Are we all prepared for class?"

2. Check to see if members have completed their homework or need help in doing so. Members ask, "Did you do your homework?" and "Is there anything you did not understand?" If extensive help is needed, an appointment is made. Periodically, the base group may be given a checklist of academic skills and assesses which ones each member needs to practice.

3. Review what members have completed since the previous class session. Members should be able to give a brief, terse, succinct summary of what they have read, thought about, and done. They may come to class with resources they have found and want to share or copies of work they have completed and wish to distribute to their base group members.

4. Get to know each other better and provide positive feedback by discussing such questions as, "What is the best thing that has happened to you this week?" "What is your favorite television show?" "Who is your favorite music group?"

Class base groups are available to support individual group members. If a group member arrives late or must leave early on an occasion, the group can provide information about what that student missed. Additionally, group members may assist one another in writing required papers. Assignments may be discussed in the base groups, papers may be planned, reviewed, and edited in the base groups, and any questions regarding the course assignments and class sessions may be first addressed in the base groups. If the group is not able to resolve the issue, it should be brought to the attention of the teacher or the teaching assistant.

Some attention should be paid to building a base group identity and group cohesion. The first week the base groups meet, for example, base groups can pick a name, design a flag, or choose a motto. If a teacher with the proper expertise is available, the groups will benefit from participating in a *challenge course* involving ropes and obstacles. By completing this type of physical challenge together, groups build cohesion quickly.

The class session closes with students meeting in base groups. Closing tasks may be as follows:

1. Ensure all members understand their assignments? Find out what help each member needs to complete them?

2. Summarize at least three things members learned in today's class session?

3. Summarize how members will use or apply what they have learned?

4. Celebrate the hard work and learning of group members.

SCHOOL BASE GROUPS

School base groups should stay together for at least a year and ideally for four years. At the beginning of the academic year, students are assigned to school base groups (or the base groups from the previous year should be reconvened). Class schedules should be arranged so members attend as many of the same classes as possible. During the year, base groups typically meet either (a) at the beginning and end of each day or (b) at the beginning and end of each week. **Daily base groups** meet first thing in the morning and last thing in the afternoon. School opens with a base group meeting in which members welcome each other to school, check to see if everyone has completed and understands the homework, and get to know each other better. At the end of the day members meet in their base groups to see that everyone understands their homework assignments, has the help and assistance they need to do their work (during the evening students can confer on the telephone or even study together at one member's house), share what members learned during the day, and discuss how they will apply what they learned in future assignments.

When base groups meet at the beginning and end of each week, members discuss the academic progress of each member, provide help and assistance to each other, and hold each member accountable for completing assignments and progressing satisfactorily through the academic program. The meeting on Monday morning refocuses the students on school, provides any emotional support required after the weekend, reestablishes personal contact among base group members, and helps students set their academic goals for the week (what is still to be done on assignments that are due and so forth). Members should carefully review each other's assignments and ensure that members have the help and assistance needed. In addition, they should hold each other accountable for committing serious effort to succeed in school. The meeting on Friday afternoon helps students review the week, set academic goals for the weekend (what homework has to be done before Monday), and share weekend plans and hopes.

THE ADVISEE OR HOME ROOM BASE GROUP

In many schools it will seem difficult to implement base groups. Two opportunities are advisor–advisee groups or homerooms. Teachers may take their advisees and divide students into base groups; then they can plan an important agenda for students to follow during a daily or a weekly meeting. Or the homeroom time can be spent in having students meet in base groups.

In the school where the authors of this textbook teach, all students are assigned an advisor. The teacher then meets once a week with all of his or her advisees. The meeting lasts for thirty minutes. The base groups are given four tasks:

1. A quick *self-disclosure task,* for which group members respond to questions such as "What is the most exciting thing you did over the vacation break? What is the worst thing that happened to you last weekend? What is your biggest fear? What is your favorite ice cream?"

2. An *administrative task,* such as deciding what classes to register for next semester.

3. An *academic task,* such as "You have midterms coming up. As a group, write out three pieces of advice for taking tests. I will type up the suggestions from each group and hand them out next week."

4. A *closing task,* such as wishing each other good luck for the day or week.

COOPERATIVE LEARNING AND SOCIAL SUPPORT

Like anyone else, students can feel isolated, lonely, and depressed. Their achievements can be seen as meaningless when parents get divorced, their peers reject them, or they are victims of crime. Anyone, no matter how intelligent or creative, can have such feelings. Recently in a Minnesota school district, a popular star athlete committed suicide. Even though he was widely liked, the note he left indicated feelings of loneliness, depression, and isolation. He is not unusual. A recent national survey reported that growing feelings of worthlessness and isolation led 30 percent of the brightest teenagers in the United States to consider suicide, and 4 percent have tried it.

We are witnessing an epidemic of depression and anxiety among our adolescents and young adults (Seligman, 1988), and it seems to be spreading downward as more and more elementary school students are becoming depressed. The stark emptiness of the self and the vacuousness of "me" are revealed when students are faced with a personal crisis. We often deny that personal well-being cannot exist without commitment to and responsibility for joint well-being. An important advantage of placing students in cooperative learning groups and having them work together with a wide variety of peers to complete assignments is the sense of belonging, acceptance, and caring that results. In times of crisis, such community may mean the difference between isolated misery and deep personal talks with caring friends.

School life can be lonely. Many students start school without a clear support group. Students can attend class without ever talking to other students. Although many students are able to develop relationships with classmates and fellow students to provide themselves with support systems, other students are unable to do so. Schools have to structure carefully student experiences to build a learning community. A *learning community* is characterized by two types of social support. The *first* is an academic support group that provides any needed assistance and helps students succeed academically. The *second* is a personal support group made up of people who care about and are personally committed to the student. Working in formal and informal cooperative groups provides an opportunity to begin long-term relationships, but for some students it is not enough. Base groups may be needed. Two years ago, for example, a student in a class on the social psychology of education stated, "This is my last quarter of course work for my doctorate. I have taken 120 quarter hours of courses. This is the first class in which I really got to know other students on a personal level. I got to know the members of my base group. Why didn't this happen in all my classes?"

It is important that some of the relationships built within cooperative learning groups are permanent. School has to be more than a series of temporary encounters that last for only a semester or year. Students should be assigned to permanent base groups to create permanent caring and committed relationships with classmates who will provide the support, help, encouragement, and assistance students need to make academic progress and develop cognitively and socially in healthy ways.

NEED FOR LONG-TERM PERMANENT RELATIONSHIPS

> *To state quite simply what we learn in time of pestilence: . . . There are more things to admire in men than to despise.*
>
> Albert Camus (1947)

Social Support

A **social support system** consists of significant others who collaboratively share a person's tasks and goals and provide resources (such as emotional concern, instrumental aid, information, and feedback) that enhance the individual's well-being and help the individual mobilize his or her resources to deal with challenging and stressful situations (Johnson & Johnson, 1989). A social support system consists of support to achieve and be productive and personal support. Social support is most often reciprocated.

Levels of social support are low in many schools because (a) learning situations are dominated by competitive and individualistic efforts (which promotes isolation and self-centeredness and (b) the school is organized on a mass-production, bureaucratic structure, which strives for depersonalized relationships in order to eliminate bias and favoritism. Classmates and teachers are assumed to be replaceable parts in the education machine and, therefore, it is assumed that any classmate will do and any teacher will do. Relationships that do develop in schools may be, at best, temporary shipboard romances as students know each other for a semester or year and then move on to different classes and new short-term relationships. Even relationships with teachers may last for only one semester or one year. For effective social support systems to develop, some relationships in schools need to be permanent. This requires more than being in proximity to each other. Cooperative long-term relationships are a prerequisite to creating a meaningful social support system for each student (Johnson & Johnson, 1989).

The longer a cooperative group exists, the more influence members will have over each other, the more caring their relationships will tend to be, the greater the social support they will provide for each other, and the more committed they will be to each other's success. Permanent cooperative base groups provide the arena in which caring and committed relationships can be created that will provide the social support to improve attendance, personalize the school experience, increase achievement, and improve the quality of life within the classroom.

Meaning, Purpose, and Psychological Health

The feelings and commitment that drove William Manchester to risk his life to help protect his comrades do not automatically appear when students walk into the school building. *Meaning* is created from involvement in interdependent efforts in which one strives to contribute to the well-being of others and the common good as well as achieve personal benefits. The significance of one's actions depends on the degree to which the actions balance concern for self with concern for others and the community as a whole.

The major barrier to meaning and significance is egocentrism and the focus on one's own well-being at the expense of or indifference to the well-being of others. Among many current high school and college students, their own pleasures and pains, successes and failures, occupy center stage in their lives (Conger, 1988; Seligman, 1988). Each person tends to focus on gratifying his or her own ends without concern for others. Physical, psychological, and material self-indulgence has become a primary concern (Conger, 1988; National Association of Secondary School Principals, 1984). Over the past twenty years, self-interest has become more important than commitment to community, country, or God. Young adults have turned away from careers of public service to careers of self-service. Many young adults have a *delusion of individualism,* believing that (a) they are separate and apart from all other individuals and, therefore, (b) others' frustration, unhappiness, hunger, despair, and misery have no significant bearing on their own well-being. With the increase in the past two decades in adolescents' and youth's concern for personal well-being, there has been a corresponding diminished concern for the welfare of others (particularly the less advantaged) and of society itself (Astin, Green, & Korn, 1987; Astin, Green, Korn, & Schalit, 1986). Self-orientation interferes with consideration of others' needs in that it actively prevents concern for others as equally deserving persons.

Meaning does not spring from competitive or individualistic efforts in which students strive for outcomes that benefit no one but themselves. Purpose does not grow from an egocentric focus on one's own material gain. Without involvement in interdependent efforts and the resulting concern for others, it is not possible to realize oneself except in the most superficial sense (Conger, 1981; Slater, 1971). Excessive concern for self leads to a banality of life, self-destructiveness, rootlessness, loneliness, and alienation (Conger, 1988). Individuals are empowered, are given hope and purpose, and experience meaning when they contribute to the well-being of others within an interdependent effort. Almost all people, when asked what makes their life meaningful, respond "friends, parents, siblings, spouses, lovers, children, and feeling loved and wanted by others" (Klinger, 1977).

Accountability and Motivation

Cooperative base groups create the long-term caring and committed relationships in which students are motivated and held accountable to work hard and do their best. Not every student is blessed with a high IQ or complex talents. But every student can work hard to maximize his or her achievements, conceptual understanding of the material being studied, level of reasoning, and creativity. Numerous students, however, spend very little time studying, even those students who get good grades. Students often avoid hard subjects like math, science, and foreign languages and simply coast along, doing far less than they are capable of doing. To increase the effort students commit to learning and achievement, they must be involved in caring and committed relationships within which they are (a) held accountable for exerting considerable effort to learn and (b) given the help, assistance, encouragement, and recognition they need to sustain their efforts to achieve. Many a student who couldn't care less what a teacher thinks will say, "I did my homework because I couldn't face my group and tell them I didn't do it. I couldn't let my group down."

Changing Students' Attitudes about Academic Work

Many students do not value schoolwork, do not aspire to do well in school, do not plan to take the more difficult courses, and plan to just get by. One of the responsibilities of the faculty is to change the attitudes of these students so that they value school, education, and the hard work necessary to learn. In doing so, several general principles, supported by research (see Johnson & F. Johnson, 1991), can guide your efforts:

1. Attitudes are changed in groups, not individual by individual. Focus your efforts on having students within small groups persuade each other to value education.
2. Attitudes are changed as a result of small group discussions that lead to public commitment to work harder in school and take education more seriously. Attitudes are rarely modified by information or preaching.
3. Messages from individuals who care about and are committed to the student are taken more seriously than messages from indifferent others. Build committed and caring relationships between academically oriented and nonacademically oriented students.
4. Personally tailor appeals to value education to the student. General messages are not nearly as effective as personal messages. The individuals best able to construct an effective personal appeal are peers who know the student well.
5. Plan for the long-term, not sudden, conversions. Internalization of academic values will take years of persuasion by caring and committed peers.
6. Support from caring and committed peers is essential to modifying old attitudes and behaviors and maintaining new attitudes and behaviors. Remember, "You can't do it alone. You need help from your friends."

Students may be best encouraged to value education, work hard in school, take the valuable but difficult courses (such as math, science, and foreign languages), and aspire to go to graduate school by placing them in permanent base groups that provide members with help and encouragement and hold members accountable for working hard in school. The base group provides a setting in which academic values may be encouraged and the necessary caring and committed relationships may be developed.

Base Groups and Dropping Out of School

Base groups provide a means of both preventing and combating dropping out of school. Any student who believes that "in this school, no one knows me, no one cares about me, no one would miss me when I'm gone," is at risk of dropping out. Base groups provide a set of personal and supportive relationships that may prevent many students from dropping out of school. Dropping out often results when a student feels alienated from the school and the other students. *Base groups also provide a means of fighting a student's inclination to drop out.* A faculty member may approach a base group and say, "*Roger thinks he is dropping out of school. Go find and talk to him. We're not going to lose Roger without a fight.*"

The Necessities of Life

There are certain basics in life that all students need to develop in healthy ways. One set of necessities involves good nutrition, adequate sleep, and appropriate clothing and shelter. Another set involves caring and committed relationships. All students need to know that there are people in the world who are committed to them and will provide them with help and assistance when it is needed. Schools need to ensure that every student is involved in caring and committed relationships with peers. One way to do so is through cooperative base groups.

CONCLUSIONS

Love is loyalty. Love is teamwork. Love respects the dignity of the individual. Heartpower is the strength of your corporation.

Vince Lombardi

In revisiting Sugar Loaf Hill in Okinawa, William Manchester gained an important insight.

"I understand at last, why I left the hospital that long-ago Sunday and, in violation of orders, returned to the front and almost certain death. It was an act of love. Those men on the line were my family, my home. They were closer to me than I can say, closer than any friends had been or ever would be. They were comrades; three of them had saved my life. They had never let me down, and I couldn't do it to them. I had to be with them, rather than let them die and me live with the knowledge that I might have saved them. Men, I now knew, do not fight for flag or country, for the Marine Corps or glory or any other abstraction. They fight for their friends."

Long-term committed efforts to achieve come from the heart, not the head. It takes courage and hope to continue the quest. Striving for increased expertise is an arduous and long-term enterprise. Students can become exhausted, frustrated, and disenchanted. They can be tempted to exert minimal effort and just get by. They can be tempted to give up. In the process of working to achieve shared goals students come to care about one another on more than just a professional level. Extraordinary accomplishments result from personal involvement with the task and each other.

Base groups are long-term heterogeneous cooperative learning groups with stable membership whose primary responsibilities are to provide support, encouragement, and assistance in completing assignments and hold each other accountable for striving to learn. Base groups may be used in two ways. The first is to have a base group in each course. The second is to organize all students within the school into base groups and have the groups function as an essential component of school life. School base groups stay together for at least a year and preferably for four years or until all members have graduated. Base groups focus the power of long-term relationships on supporting academic progress, motivating academic effort, creating positive attitudes toward learning, increasing retention and graduation rates, and providing the caring and commitment necessary for a full and complete school experience.

To use cooperative learning effectively, teachers must understand the basic elements that make cooperation work. These basic elements are described in the next chapter. In addition, formal cooperative learning, informal cooperative learning, and cooperative base groups form a gestalt that allows teachers to create a learning community within classrooms and schools. The integrated use of the three types of cooperative learning will be discussed in Chapter 6.

5

Basic Elements of Cooperative Learning

The Killer Bees is a boys' high school basketball team from Bridgehampton, New York, a small, middle-class town on Long Island (described in Katzenbach & Smith, 1993). Bridgehampton High School's total enrollment has declined since 1985 from sixty-seven to forty-one, with fewer than twenty males attending the high school. There have never been more than seven players on the team. Yet, since 1980 the Killer Bees have amassed a record of 164 wins and 32 losses, qualified for the state championship playoffs six times, won the state championship twice, and finished in the final four two other times. None of their players was ever really a star and the team was never tall. Not one of the Killer Bees went on to play professional basketball. Although every Killer Bee graduated and most went on to college, few had the talent to play basketball in college.

How did the Killer Bees become so successful with so few players and so little talent? The Killer Bees consistently won against bigger supposedly more talented opponents for at least three reasons. The first is that the Killer Bees' game was *team basketball.* They won, not by superior talent, but through superior teamwork. The second reason is that team members adopted an incredible work ethic. They practiced 365 days a year on skill development and teamwork. The third reason was the versatility and flexibility in how they played their opponents. The source of the Killer Bee's focus on teamwork, hard work, and versatility was a richness and depth of purpose that eludes most teams. Their mission was more than winning basketball games. They were committed to bringing honor and recognition to their community and protecting and enhancing their legacy. They were also committed to each other. The commitment of team members was reciprocated by the community, whose members came to every game and relentlessly cheered the team on.

FIGURE 5.1   Cooperative Efforts

It is the potential for such performances that make cooperative groups the key to successful education. Teamwork can do for learning what it did for the Killer Bees' basketball performance. The truly committed cooperative learning group is probably the most productive instructional tool educators have (Figure 5.1). Creating and maintaining truly committed cooperative learning groups, however, is far from easy. In most classrooms they are rare, perhaps because many educators

1. Are confused about what is (and is not) a cooperative learning group as well as about the basics that make cooperative learning groups work.
2. Lack the discipline to implement the basics of cooperative efforts in a rigorous way.

This chapter differentiates cooperative learning groups from other types of groups, notes the characteristics of pseudo and traditional classroom groups, and discusses the basic elements of cooperation. Finally, the chapter notes that educators need to develop the discipline to structure the basics of cooperation in every learning group.

MAKING POTENTIAL GROUP PERFORMANCE A REALITY

Not all groups are cooperative groups. Placing people in the same room and calling them a cooperative group does not make them one. Having a number of people work together does not make them a cooperative group. Study groups, project groups, lab groups, committees, task forces, departments, and councils are groups, but they are not necessarily cooperative. Groups do not become cooperative groups simply because that is what someone labels them.

The authors have studied cooperative learning groups for thirty years. We have interviewed thousands of students and teachers in a wide variety of school districts in a number of different countries over three different decades to discover how groups are used in the classroom and where and how cooperative groups work best. On the basis of our findings and the findings of other researchers such as Katzenbach and Smith (1993), we have developed a learning group performance curve to clarify the difference between traditional classroom groups and cooperative learning groups (Figure 5.2).

The learning group performance curve illustrates that how well any small group performs depends on how it is structured. On the performance curve, four types of learning groups are described. It begins with the individual members of the group and illustrates the relative performance of these students to pseudo groups, traditional classroom groups, cooperative learning groups, and high-performance cooperative learning groups.

A *pseudo-learning group* is a group whose members have been assigned to work together but they have no interest in doing so. They meet, but do not want to work together or help each other succeed. Members often block or interfere with each other's learning, communicate and coordinate poorly, mislead and confuse each other, loaf, and seek a free ride. The interaction among group members detracts from individual learning without delivering any benefit. The result is that the sum of the whole is less than the potential of the individual members. The group does not mature because members have no interest in or commitment to each other or the group's future.

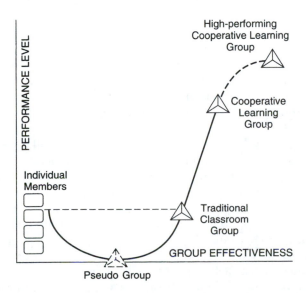

FIGURE 5.2   The Learning Group Performance Curve

A *traditional classroom learning group* is a group whose members have accepted that they are to work together but see little benefit from doing so. Interdependence is low. The assignments are structured so that very little if any joint work is required. Members do not take responsibility for anyone's learning other than their own. Members interact primarily to share information and clarify how the assignments are to be done. Then they each do the work on their own, and their achievements are individually recognized and rewarded. Students are accountable as separate individuals, not as members of a team. Students do not receive training in social skills, and a group leader is appointed who is in charge of directing members' participation. The quality of the group's efforts is not processed.

A *cooperative learning group* is more than a sum of its parts. It is a group whose members are committed to the common purpose of maximizing each other's learning. It has a number of defining characteristics. *First,* the group's goal of maximizing the learning of all members provides a compelling purpose that motivates members to roll up their sleeves and accomplish something beyond their individual achieve-

ments. Each member takes responsibility for the performance of himself or herself, all teammates, and the group as a whole. Members believe that "they sink or swim together," and "if one of us fails, we all fail." *Second,* in a cooperative group the focus is on both group and individual accountability. Group members hold themselves and each other accountable for doing high-quality work, and they also hold themselves and each other accountable for achieving the overall group goals. *Third,* group members do real work together. They not only meet to share information and perspectives, they produce discrete work products through members' joint efforts and contributions. They also give whatever assistance and encouragement is needed to promote each other's success. Through promoting each other's success, group members provide both academic and personal support based on a commitment to and caring about each other. *Fourth,* members are taught social skills and are expected to use them to coordinate their efforts and achieve their goals. Both taskwork and teamwork skills are emphasized. All members accept the responsibility for providing leadership. *Finally,* groups analyze how effectively they are achieving their goals and how well members are working together. They emphasize continuous improvement of the quality of their learning and teamwork processes.

A *high-performance cooperative learning group* is a group that meets all the criteria for being a cooperative learning group and outperforms all reasonable expectations, given its membership. What differentiates the high-performance group from the cooperative learning group is the level of commitment members have to each other and the group's success. Jennifer Futernick, who is part of a high-performing, rapid response team at McKinsey & Company, calls the emotion binding her teammates together a form of love (Katzenbach & Smith, 1993). Ken Hoepner of the Burlington Northern Intermodal Team (also described by Katzenbach and Smith, 1993) stated: "Not only did we trust each other, not only did we respect each other, but we gave a damn about the rest of the people on this team. If we saw somebody vulnerable, we were there to help." Members' mutual concern for each other's personal growth enables high-performance cooperative groups to perform far above expectations and also to have lots of fun. The bad news about high-performance cooperative groups is that they are rare. Most groups never achieve this level of development. Table 5.1 compares traditional and cooperative learning groups.

TABLE 5.1   Comparison of Learning Groups

TRADITIONAL LEARNING GROUPS	COOPERATIVE LEARNING GROUPS
Low interdependence. Members take responsibility only for self. Focus is on individual performance only.	High positive interdependence. Members are responsible for own and each other's learning. Focus is on joint performance.
Individual accountability only.	Both group and individual accountability. Members hold self and others accountable for high-quality work.
Assignments are discussed with little commitment to each other's learning.	Members promote each other's success. They do real work together and help and support each other's efforts to learn.
Teamwork skills are ignored. Leader is appointed to direct members' participation.	Teamwork skills are emphasized. Members are taught and expected to use social skills. All members share leadership responsibilities.
No group processing of the quality of its work. Individual accomplishments are rewarded.	Group processes quality of work and how effectively members are working together. Continuous improvement is emphasized.

Exercise 5.1   Types of Groups

Demonstrate your understanding of the different types of groups listed below by matching the definitions with the appropriate group. Check your answers with your partner and explain why you believe your answers to be correct.

TYPE OF GROUP	DEFINITION
_____ Psuedo group	a. A group which students work together to accomplish shared goals. Students percieve they can reach their learning goals if and only if the other group members also reach their goals.
_____ Traditional learning group	b. A group whose members have been assigned to work together but they have no interest in doing so. The structure promotes competition at close quarters.
_____ Cooperative learning group	d. A group that meets all the criteria for being a cooperative group and outperforms all reasonable expectations, given its membership.
_____ High-performance cooperative learning group	c. A group whose members agree to work together but see little benefit from doing so. The structure promotes individualistic work with talking.

FORCES HINDERING GROUP PERFORMANCE

Performance and small groups go hand in hand. Although cooperative groups outperform individuals working alone, there is nothing magical about groups. There are conditions under which groups function effectively and conditions under which groups function ineffectively. *Potential barriers to group effectiveness* are as follows (Johnson & F. Johnson, 1997):

1. *Lack of group maturity.* Group members need time and experience working together to develop into an effective group. Temporary, ad hoc groups usually do not develop enough maturity to function with full effectiveness.

2. *Uncritically giving one's dominant response.* A central barrier to higher-level reasoning and deeper-level understanding is the uncritical giving of members' dominant response to academic problems and assignments. Instead, members should generate a number of potential answers and choose the best one.

3. *Social loafing—hiding in the crowd.* When a group is working on an additive task (group product is determined by summing together individual group members' efforts), and individual members can reduce their effort without other members realizing that they are doing so, many people tend to work less hard. Such social loafing has been demonstrated on a variety of additive tasks such as rope pulling, shouting, and clapping.

4. *Free riding—getting something for nothing.* On disjunctive tasks (if one member does it, all members receive the benefit), there is the possibility of a free ride. When group members realize that their efforts are dispensable (group success or failure depends very little on whether or not they exert effort), and when their efforts are costly, group members are less likely to exert themselves on the group's behalf.

5. *Motivation losses due to perceived inequity—not being a sucker.* When other group members are free riding, there is a tendency for the members who are working to reduce their efforts to avoid being a "sucker."

6. *Groupthink.* Groups can be overconfident in their ability and resist any challenge or threat to their sense of invulnerability by avoiding any disagreements and seeking concurrence among members.

7. *Lack of sufficient heterogeneity.* The more homogeneous the group members, the less each member adds to the group's resources. Groups must develop the right mix of taskwork and teamwork skills necessary to do their work. Heterogeneity ensures a wide variety of resources are available for the group's work.

8. *Lack of teamwork skills.* Groups with members who lack the small group and interpersonal skills required to work effectively with others often underperform their most academically able members.

9. *Inappropriate Group Size,* The larger the group, the fewer members that can participate, the less essential each member views his or her personal contribution, the more teamwork skills required, and the more complex the group structure.

Not every group is effective. Most everyone has been part of a group that wasted time, was inefficient, and generally produced poor work. But some groups accomplish wondrous things. Educators must be able to spot the characteristics of ineffective groups and take action to eliminate them. The hindering factors are eliminated by the basics of cooperation.

APPLYING THE BASICS OF COOPERATION

Educators fool themselves if they think well-meaning directives to "work together," "cooperate," and "be a team," will be enough to create cooperative efforts among students. There is a discipline to creating cooperation. The basics of structuring cooperation are not a series of elements that characterize good groups. They are a regimen that, if followed rigorously, will produce the conditions for effective cooperation. Cooperative learning groups are rare because educators (and students) seek shortcuts to quality groupwork and assume that traditional classroom groups will do. Like persons who wish to lose weight without dieting, they seek easy alternatives to the disciplined application of the basics of effective groups.

The basics of cooperation are not new and startling to most educators. They already have a good idea of what the basics are. The performance potential of learning groups, however, is frequently lost due to educators not applying what they know about cooperative efforts in a disciplined way. The basic components of effective cooperative efforts are positive interdependence, face-to-face promotive interaction, individual and group accountability, appropriate use of social skills, and group processing.

POSITIVE INTERDEPENDENCE: WE INSTEAD OF ME

> *All for one and one for all.*
> Alexandre Dumas

Within a football game, the quarterback who throws the pass and the receiver who catches the pass are positively interdependent. The success of one depends on the success of the other. It takes two to complete a pass. One player cannot succeed without the other. Both have to perform competently if their mutual success is to be assured. If one fails, they both fail.

The discipline of using cooperative groups begins with structuring positive interdependence (see Johnson & Johnson, 1992a, 1992b). Group members have to know that they "sink or swim together." It is positive interdependence that requires group members to roll up their sleeves and work together to accomplish something beyond individual success. It is positive interdependence that creates the realization that members have two responsibilities: to learn the assigned material and to ensure that all members of their group learn the assigned material. When positive interdependence is clearly understood, it highlights the fact that (a) each group member's efforts are required and indispensable for group success (i.e., there can be no free riders) and (b) each group member has a unique contribution to make to the joint effort because of his or her resources or role and task responsibilities (i.e., there can be no social loafing).

Structuring positive interdependence involves three steps. *The first is assigning the group a clear, measurable task.* Members have to know what they are supposed to do. *The second step is to structure positive goal interdependence* so members believe that they can attain their goals if and only if their groupmates attain their goals. In other words, members know that they cannot succeed unless all other members of their group succeed. Positive goal interdependence ensures that the group is united around a common goal, a concrete reason for being, such as "learn the assigned material and make sure that all members of your group learn the assigned material." Positive goal interdependence may be structured by informing group members they are responsible for the following:

1. All members scoring above a specified criterion when tested individually.
2. All members improving their performance over their previous scores.
3. The overall group score (determined by adding the individual scores of members together) being above a specified criterion.
4. One product (or set of answers) being successfully completed by the group.

Individuals will contribute more energy and effort to meaningful goals than to trivial ones. Being responsible for others' success as well as for one's own gives cooperative efforts a meaning that is not found in competitive and individualistic situations. The efforts of each group member, therefore, contribute not only to one's own success but also to the success of groupmates. When there is meaning to what they do, ordinary people exert extraordinary effort. It is positive goal interdependence that gives meaning to the efforts of group members.

The third step is to supplement positive goal interdependence with other types of positive interdependence. Reward/celebration interdependence is structured when (a) each group member receives the same tangible reward for successfully completing a joint task (if all members of the group score 90 percent correct or better on the test, each will receive five bonus points) or (b) group members jointly celebrate their success. Regular celebrations of group efforts and success enhance the quality of cooperation. If students are to look forward to working in cooperative groups, and enjoy doing so, they must feel that (a) their efforts are appreciated and (b) they are respected as an individual. A long-term commitment to achieve is largely based on feeling recognized and respected for what one is doing. Thus, students' efforts to learn and promote each other's learning need to be (a) observed, (b) recognized, and (c) celebrated. The celebration of individual efforts and group success involves structuring reward interdependence. Ways of structuring positive reward interdependence include the following:

1. Celebrating their joint success when all members reach criterion.
2. Adding bonus points to all members' academic scores when everyone in the group achieves up to the criterion or when the overall group score reaches the criterion.
3. Receiving nonacademic rewards (such as extra free time, extra recess time, stickers, stars, or food) when all group members reach criterion.
4. Receiving a single group grade for the combined efforts of group members. This should be cautiously done until all students (and parents) are very familiar with cooperative learning.

Exercise 5.2   Types of Positive Interdependence

Positive goal interdependence. Students perceive that they can achieve their learning goals if and only if all the members of their group also attain their goals. Members of a learning group have a mutual set of goals that they are all striving to accomplish.

Positive celebration/reward interdependence. Group celebrates success. A joint reward is given for successful group work and members' efforts to achieve.

Positive resource interdependence. Each member has only a portion of the information, resources, or materials necessary for the task to be completed and the member's resources have to be combined in order for the group to achieve its goal.

Positive role interdependence. Each member is assigned complementary and interconnected roles that specify responsibilities that the group needs in order to complete a joint task.

Positive identity interdependence. The group establishes a mutual identity through a name, flag, motto, or song.

Environmental interdependence. Group members are bound together by the physical environment in some way. An example is putting people in a specific area in which to work.

Positive fantasy interdependence. A task is given that requires members to imagine that they are in a life or death situation and must collaborate in order to survive.

Positive task interdependence. A division of labor is created so that the actions of one group member have to be completed if the next team member is to complete his or her responsibility.

Positive outside enemy interdependence. Groups are placed in competition with each other. Group members then feel interdependent as they strive to beat the other groups and win the competition.

Role interdependence is structured when each member is assigned complementary and interconnected roles (such as reader, recorder, checker of understanding, encourager of participation, and elaborator of knowledge) that specify responsibilities that the group needs in order to complete the joint task. Roles prescribe what other group members expect from a person (and therefore the person is obligated to do) and what that person has a right to expect from other group members who have complementary roles. In cooperative groups responsibilities are often divided into (a) roles that help the group achieve its goals and (b) roles that help members maintain effective working relationships with each other. Such roles are vital to high-quality learning. The role of checker, for example, focuses on periodically asking each groupmate to explain what is being learned. Rosenshine and Stevens (1986) reviewed a large body of well-controlled research on teaching effectiveness and found "checking for comprehension" to be one specific teaching behavior that was significantly associated with higher levels of student learning and achievement. Although the teacher cannot continually check the understanding of every student (especially if there are thirty or more students in the class), the teacher can engineer such checking by having students work in cooperative groups and assigning one member the role of checker.

Resource interdependence is structured when each member has only a portion of the information, materials, or resources necessary for the task to be completed and members' resources have to be combined in order for the group to achieve its goal. Ways of structuring resource interdependence include the following:

1. Limiting the resources given to the group. Only one pencil, for example, may be given to a group of three students.
2. Jigsawing materials so that each member has part of a set of materials. A group could be given the assignment of writing a biography of Abe Lincoln and information on Lincoln's childhood given to one member, information on Lincoln's early political career given to another, information on Lincoln as president given to a third, and information on Lincoln's assassination given to the fourth member.
3. Having each member make a separate contribution to a joint product. Each member, for example, could be asked to contribute a sentence to a paragraph, an article to a newsletter, or a chapter to a book.

Identity interdependence is structured when the group establishes a mutual identity through a name or a group symbol such as a motto, flag, or song. Outside enemy interdependence (striving to perform higher than other groups) and fantasy interdependence (striving to solve hypothetical problems such as how to deal with being shipwrecked on the moon). Task interdependence is structured by creating a division of labor so that the actions of one group member have to be completed if the next group member is to complete his or her responsibilities. Environmental interdependence exists when group members are bound together by the physical environment in some way (such as a specific area to meet in).

The heart of cooperative efforts is positive interdependence. Without positive interdependence, cooperation does not exist. Positive interdependence may focus on joint outcomes or on the mutual effort required to achieve the group's goals. Positive goal and reward interdependence (with the related identity, outside enemy, fantasy, and environmental interdependence) result in members realizing that all group members do the following (Johnson & Johnson, 1989):

1. Share a common fate where they all gain or lose on the basis of the overall performance of group members. One result is a sense of personal responsibility (a) for the final outcome and (b) to do their share of the work.
2. Strive for mutual benefit so that all members of the group will gain. There is a recognition that what helps other group members benefits oneself and what promotes one's own productivity benefits the other group members.

3. Have a long-term time perspective so that long-term joint productivity is perceived to be of greater value than short-term personal advantage.
4. Have a shared identity based on group membership. Besides being a separate individual, one is a member of a team. The shared identity binds members together emotionally and creates an expectation for a joint celebration based on mutual respect and appreciation for the success of group members. The experience creates a positive cathexis so that group members like each other. Feelings of success are shared and pride is taken in other members' accomplishments as well as one's own.

Positive resource, role, and task interdependence result in individuals realizing that the performance of group members is mutually caused. No member is on his or her own. Each person views himself or herself as instrumental in the productivity of other group members and views other group members as being instrumental in his or her productivity. Members realize that their efforts are required in order for the group to succeed (i.e., there can be no "free riders") and that their potential contribution to the group as being unique (because of their role, resources, or task responsibilities). Each member shares responsibility for other members' productivity (mutual responsibility) and is obligated to other members for their support and assistance (mutual obligation). As a result of the mutual causation, cooperative efforts are characterized by positive inducibility in that group members are open to being influenced by each other and substitutability in that the actions of group members substitute for each other so that if one member of the group has taken the action there is no need for other members to do so. Group members have a mutual investment in each other.

The authors have conducted a series of studies investigating the nature of positive interdependence and the relative power of the different types of positive interdependence (Frank, 1984; Hwong, Caswell, Johnson, & Johnson, 1993; Johnson, Johnson, Stanne, & Garibaldi, 1990; Johnson, Johnson, Ortiz, & Stanne, 1991; Lew, Mesch, Johnson, & Johnson, 1986a, 1986b; Mesch, Johnson, & Johnson, 1988; Mesch, Lew, Johnson, & Johnson, 1986). Six questions concerning positive interdependence have been addressed by our research. The *first* question is whether group membership in and of itself is sufficient to produce higher achievement and productivity or whether group membership and positive interdependence are required. The results of Hwong, Caswell, Johnson, and Johnson (1993) indicate that positive interdependence is necessary. Knowing that one's performance affects the success of groupmates seems to create "responsibility forces" that increase one's efforts to achieve.

The *second* question is whether interpersonal interaction is sufficient to increase productivity or whether positive interdependence is required. Debra Mesch and Marvin Lew conducted a series of studies in which they investigated whether the relationship between cooperation and achievement was due to the opportunity to interact with peers or positive goal interdependence. Their results are quite consistent. The individuals achieved higher results under positive goal interdependence than when they worked individualistically but had the opportunity to interact with classmates (Lew, Mesch, Johnson, & Johnson, 1986a, 1986b; Mesch, Johnson, & Johson, 1988; Mesch, Lew, Johnson, & Johnson, 1986).

The *third* question is whether goal or reward interdependence is most important in promoting productivity and achievement. The results of the Mesch and Lew studies indicate that although positive goal interdependence is sufficient to produce higher achievement and productivity than an individualistic effort, the combination of goal and reward interdependence is even more effective. The impact of the two types of outcome interdependence seem to be additive.

The *fourth* question is whether different types of reward interdependence have differential effects on productivity. Michael Frank's (1984) study indicates not. Both working to achieve a reward and working to avoid the loss of a reward produced higher achievement than did individualistic efforts.

The *fifth* question is whether goal or resource interdependence is most important for enhancing productivity and achievement. Johnson and Johnson (in press) found that goal interdependence promoted higher achievement than did resource interdependence. The study by Johnson, Johnson, Stanne, and Garibaldi indicated that although goal interdependence in and of itself increased achievement, the combination of goal and resource interdependence increased achievement even further. Compared with individualistic efforts, the use of resource interdependence alone seemed to decrease achievement and lower productivity.

Finally, there is a question as to whether positive interdependence simply motivates individuals to try harder or facilitates the development of new insights and discoveries through promotive interaction. The latter position is supported by the fact that some studies have found that members of cooperative groups use higher level reasoning strategies more frequently than do individuals working individualistically or competitively.

In summary, our research indicates that positive interdependence provides the context within which promotive interaction takes place, group membership and interpersonal interaction among students do not produce higher achievement unless positive interdependence is clearly structured, the combination of goal and reward interdependence increases achievement over goal interdependence alone, and resource interdependence does not increase achievement unless goal interdependence is present also.

INDIVIDUAL ACCOUNTABILITY/PERSONAL RESPONSIBILITY

> *What children can do together today, they can do alone tomorrow.*
>
> Vygotsky

Among the early settlers of Massachusetts there was a saying, "*If you do not work, you do not eat.*" Everyone had to do his or her fair share of the work. *The discipline of using cooperative groups includes structuring group and individual accountability.* **Group accountability** exists when the overall performance of the group is assessed and the results are given back to all group members to compare against a standard of performance. **Individual accountability** exists when the performance of each individual member is assessed, the results are given back to the individual and the group to compare against a standard of performance, and the member is held responsible by groupmates for contributing his or her fair share to the group's success. On the basis of the feedback received, (a) efforts to learn and contribute to groupmates' learning can be recognized and celebrated, (b) immediate remediation can take place by providing any needed assistance or encouragement, and (c) groups can reassign responsibilities to avoid any redundant efforts by members.

The purpose of cooperative groups is to make each member a stronger individual in his or her own right. Individual accountability is the key to ensuring that all group members are in fact strengthened by learning cooperatively. After participating in a cooperative lesson, group members should be better prepared to complete similar tasks by themselves. There is a pattern to classroom learning. *First,* students learn knowledge, skills, strategies, or procedures in a cooperative group. *Second,* students apply the knowledge or perform the skill, strategy, or procedure alone to demonstrate their personal mastery of the material. Students learn it together and then perform it alone.

Individual accountability results in group members knowing they cannot hitchhike on the work of others. When it is difficult to identify members' contributions, when members' contributions are redundant, and when members are not responsible for the final group outcome, members sometimes engage in social loafing or seek a free ride (Harkins & Petty, 1982; Ingham, Levinger, Graves, & Peckham, 1974; Kerr & Bruun, 1981; Latane, Williams, & Harkins, 1979; Moede, 1927; Petty, Harkins, Williams, & Latane, 1977; Williams, 1981; Williams, Harkins, & Latane, 1981). Common ways to structure individual accountability include the following:

1. Keeping the size of the group small. The smaller the size of the group, the greater the individual accountability.
2. Giving an individual test to each student.
3. Giving random oral examination. Students are randomly selected to present his or her group's work to you (in the presence of the group) or to the entire class.
4. Observing each group and recording the frequency with which each member contributes to the group's work.
5. Assigning one student in each group to the role of checker. The *checker* asks other group members to explain the reasoning and rationale underlying group answers.
6. Having students teach what they learned to someone else. When all students do this, it is called simultaneous explaining.

Positive Interdependence and Accountability

In cooperative situations, group members share responsibility for the joint outcome. Each group member takes *personal responsibility* for (a) contributing his or her efforts to accomplish the group's goals and (b) helping other group members do likewise. The greater the positive interdependence structured within a cooperative learning group, the more students will feel personally responsible for contributing their efforts to accomplish the group's goals. The shared responsibility adds the concept of *ought* to members' motivation—one *ought* to do one's share, contribute, and pull one's weight. The shared responsibility also makes each group member personally accountable to the other group members. Students will realize that if they fail to do their fair share of the work, other members will be disappointed, hurt, and upset.

FACE-TO-FACE PROMOTIVE INTERACTION

In an industrial organization it's the group effort that counts. There's really no room for stars in an industrial organization. You need talented people, but they can't do it alone. They have to have help.

John F. Donnelly, president of Donnelly Mirrors

The discipline of using cooperative groups includes ensuring that group members meet face to face to work together to complete assignments and promote each other's success. Group members need to do real work together. Promotive interaction exists when individuals encourage and facilitate each other's efforts to complete tasks in order to reach the group's goals. Through promoting each other's success, group members build both an academic and a personal support system for each member. There are three steps to encouraging promotive interaction among group members. *The first is to schedule time for the group to meet.* As simple as this step seems, many learning groups are not given sufficient meeting time to mature and develop. *The second step is to highlight the positive interdependence that requires members to work together to achieve the group's goals.* It is positive interdependence that creates the commitment to each other's success. *The third step is to encourage promotive interaction among group members.* Monitoring groups and celebrating instances of members' promotive interaction is one way to do so.

Although positive interdependence in and of itself may have some effect on outcomes, it is the face-to-face promotive interaction among individuals fostered by the positive interdependence that most powerfully influences efforts to achieve caring and committed relationships, and psychological adjustment and social competence (Johnson & Johnson, 1989). Promotive interaction is characterized by individuals providing each other with efficient and effective help and assistance, exchanging needed resources such as information and materials and processing information more efficiently and effectively, providing each other with feedback in order to improve subsequent performance, challenging each other's conclusions and reasoning in order to promote higher-quality decision making and greater insight into the problems being considered, advocating the exertion of effort to achieve mutual goals, influencing each other's efforts to achieve the group's goals, acting in trusting and trustworthy ways, being motivated to strive for mutual benefit, and establishing a moderate level of arousal characterized by low anxiety and stress. Members do real work together.

INTERPERSONAL AND SMALL GROUP SKILLS

I will pay more for the ability to deal with people than any other ability under the sun.

John D. Rockefeller

Placing socially unskilled students in a group and telling them to cooperate does not guarantee that they are able to do so effectively. We are not born instinctively knowing how to interact effectively with others. Interpersonal and small-group skills do not magically appear when they are needed. Students must be taught the social skills required for high-quality collaboration and be motivated to use them if cooperative groups are to be productive. The whole field of group dynamics is based on the premise that social skills are the key to group productivity (Johnson & F. Johnson, 1997).

A fourth arena in the disciplined use of cooperative groups is teaching group members the small-group and interpersonal skills they need to work effectively with each other. In cooperative learning groups, students are required to learn academic subject matter (taskwork) and also to learn the interpersonal and small group skills required to function as part of a group (teamwork). If students do not learn teamwork skills, then they cannot complete taskwork. If group members are inept at teamwork, their taskwork will tend to be substandard. On the other hand, the greater the members' teamwork skills, the higher will be the quality and quantity of their learning. Cooperative learning is inherently more complex than competitive or individualistic learning because students have to engage in taskwork and teamwork simultaneously. To coordinate efforts that will achieve mutual goals, students must (a) get to know and trust each other, (b) communicate accurately and unambiguously, (c) accept and support each other, and (d) resolve conflicts constructively (Johnson, 1995a, 1995b; Johnson & F. Johnson, 1997).

Exercise 5.3   *How Valuable Are Social Skills?*

Given below are six of the more important outcomes of being socially skilled. Form a pair, and then rank the outcomes from most important ("1") to least important ("6").

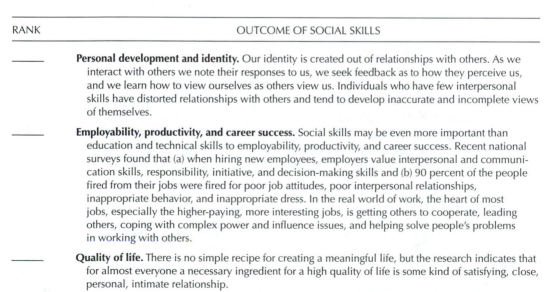

RANK	OUTCOME OF SOCIAL SKILLS
_____	**Personal development and identity.** Our identity is created out of relationships with others. As we interact with others we note their responses to us, we seek feedback as to how they perceive us, and we learn how to view ourselves as others view us. Individuals who have few interpersonal skills have distorted relationships with others and tend to develop inaccurate and incomplete views of themselves.
_____	**Employability, productivity, and career success.** Social skills may be even more important than education and technical skills to employability, productivity, and career success. Recent national surveys found that (a) when hiring new employees, employers value interpersonal and communication skills, responsibility, initiative, and decision-making skills and (b) 90 percent of the people fired from their jobs were fired for poor job attitudes, poor interpersonal relationships, inappropriate behavior, and inappropriate dress. In the real world of work, the heart of most jobs, especially the higher-paying, more interesting jobs, is getting others to cooperate, leading others, coping with complex power and influence issues, and helping solve people's problems in working with others.
_____	**Quality of life.** There is no simple recipe for creating a meaningful life, but the research indicates that for almost everyone a necessary ingredient for a high quality of life is some kind of satisfying, close, personal, intimate relationship.

(continued)

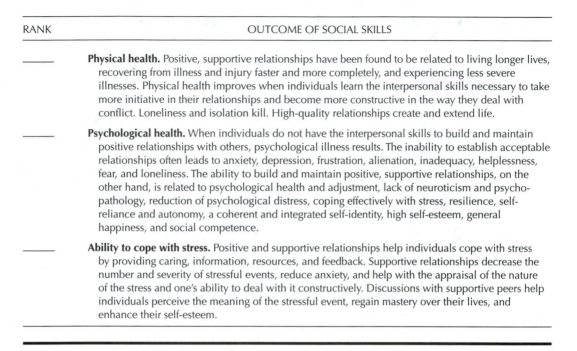

RANK	OUTCOME OF SOCIAL SKILLS
_____	**Physical health.** Positive, supportive relationships have been found to be related to living longer lives, recovering from illness and injury faster and more completely, and experiencing less severe illnesses. Physical health improves when individuals learn the interpersonal skills necessary to take more initiative in their relationships and become more constructive in the way they deal with conflict. Loneliness and isolation kill. High-quality relationships create and extend life.
_____	**Psychological health.** When individuals do not have the interpersonal skills to build and maintain positive relationships with others, psychological illness results. The inability to establish acceptable relationships often leads to anxiety, depression, frustration, alienation, inadequacy, helplessness, fear, and loneliness. The ability to build and maintain positive, supportive relationships, on the other hand, is related to psychological health and adjustment, lack of neuroticism and psychopathology, reduction of psychological distress, coping effectively with stress, resilience, self-reliance and autonomy, a coherent and integrated self-identity, high self-esteem, general happiness, and social competence.
_____	**Ability to cope with stress.** Positive and supportive relationships help individuals cope with stress by providing caring, information, resources, and feedback. Supportive relationships decrease the number and severity of stressful events, reduce anxiety, and help with the appraisal of the nature of the stress and one's ability to deal with it constructively. Discussions with supportive peers help individuals perceive the meaning of the stressful event, regain mastery over their lives, and enhance their self-esteem.

The more socially skillful students are, and the more attention teachers pay to teaching and rewarding the use of social skills, the higher the achievement that can be expected within cooperative learning groups. In their studies on the long-term implementation of cooperative learning, Marvin Lew and Debra Mesch (Lew, Mesch, Johnson, & Johnson, 1986a, 1986b; Mesch, Johnson, & Johnson, 1988; Mesch, Lew, Johnson, & Johnson, 1986) investigated the impact of a reward contingency for using social skills as well as positive interdependence and a contingency for academic achievement on performance within cooperative learning groups. In the cooperative skills conditions students were trained weekly in four social skills, and each member of a cooperative group was given two bonus points toward the quiz grade if all group members were observed by the teacher to demonstrate three out of four cooperative skills. The results indicated that the combination of positive interdependence, an academic contingency for high performance by all group members, and a social skills contingency promoted the highest achievement.

GROUP PROCESSING

Take care of each other. Share your energies with the group. No one must feel alone, cut off, for that is when you do not make it.

Willi Unsoeld, renowned mountain climber

The final phase of the discipline of using cooperative groups is structuring group processing. Effective group work is influenced by whether or not groups reflect on (process) how well they are functioning. A *process* is an identifiable sequence of events taking place over time, and *process goals* refer to the sequence of events instrumental in achieving outcome goals (Johnson & F. Johnson, 1997). **Group processing** may be defined as reflecting on a group session to (a) describe what member actions were helpful and unhelpful and (b) make decisions about what actions to continue or change. The *purpose* of group processing is to clarify and improve the effectiveness of the members in contributing to the collaborative efforts necessary to achieve the group's goals.

PROCESSING STARTERS

1. Name three things your group did well in working together. Name one thing your group could do even better.

2. Think of something that each group member did to improve group effectiveness. Tell that person what it is.

3. Tell your group members how much you appreciate their help today.

4. Rate yourself from 1 (low) to 10 (high) on (name a cooperative skill like encouraging participation or checking for understanding). Share your rating with your group and explain why you rated yourself the way you did. Plan how to increase the frequency with which group members use this skill.

There are five steps in structuring group processing in order to improve continuously the quality of the group's taskwork and teamwork (see Johnson, Johnson, & Holubec, 1993a). *The first step is to assess the quality of the interaction among group members as they work to maximize each other's learning.* The easiest way to conduct such assessments of the process of how the group gets its work done is for the teacher to observe the cooperative learning groups as they work. The teacher systematically moves from group to group and uses a formal observation sheet or checklist to gather specific data on each group. The frequency with which targeted social skills are used can be recorded.

Systematic observation allows teachers to attain a window into students' minds. Listening to students explain how to complete the assignment to groupmates provides better information about what students do and do not know and understand than do correct answers on tests or homework assignments. Listening in on students' explanations provides valuable information about how well the students understand the instructions, the major concepts and strategies being learned, and the basics of working together effectively. Wilson (1987, p. 18) conducted a three-year, teaching-improvement study as part of a college faculty development program. Both faculty and students agreed that faculty needed help on knowing if the class understood the material or not.

Teachers are not the only ones who can observe groups and record data about their functioning. A student observer can be appointed for each learning group (rotating the responsibility for each lesson), and at the end of a lesson, each group member can fill out a checklist as to the frequency with which they engaged in each targeted social skill. It is often helpful to assess the quality of the overall group product so groups can compare how well they performed with specific patterns of interaction among members.

The second step in examining the process by which the group does its work is to give each learning group feedback. Teachers need to allocate some time at the end of each class session for each cooperative group to process how effectively members worked together. Group members need to describe what actions were helpful and unhelpful in completing the group's work and make decisions about what behaviors to continue or change. The data collected can be taken from the checklists and placed in a Pareto chart to focus the discussion on current levels of effectiveness and ways to improve the quality of the group's work. Individual efforts that contribute to the group's success need to be recognized and celebrated. Such small-group processing (a) enables learning groups to focus on maintaining good working relationships among members, (b) facilitates the learning of cooperative skills, (c) ensures that members receive feedback on their participation, (d) ensures that students think on the metacognitive as well as the cognitive level, and (e) provides the means to celebrate the success of the group and reinforce the positive behaviors of group members. Some of the keys to successful small-group processing are allowing sufficient time for it to take place, providing a structure for processing (such as instructing students to "List three things your group is doing well today and one thing you could improve"), emphasizing positive feedback, making the processing specific rather than general, maintaining student involvement in processing, reminding students to use their cooperative skills while they process, and communicating clear expectations as to the purpose of processing.

Group processing provides a structure for group members to hold each other accountable for being responsible and skillful group members. In order to contribute to each other's learning, group members need to attend class, be prepared (i.e., have done the necessary homework), and contribute to the group's work. A student's absenteeism and lack of preparation often demoralizes other members. Productive group work requires members to be present and prepared, and there should be some peer accountability to be so. When groups process, they discuss any member actions that need to be improved in order for everyone's learning to be maximized.

The third step is for groups to set goals as to how to improve their effectiveness. Members suggest ways the teamwork could be improved and the group decides which suggestions to adopt. Discussing group functioning is essential. A common teaching error is to provide too brief a time for students to process the quality of their collaboration. Students do not learn from experiences that they do not reflect on. If the learning groups are to function better tomorrow than they did today, members must receive feedback, reflect on how their actions may be more effective, and plan how to be even more skillful during the next group session.

The fourth step is to process how effectively the whole class is functioning. In addition to small-group processing, teachers should periodically conduct whole-class processing sessions. At the end of the class period the teacher can then conduct a whole-class processing session by sharing with the class the results of his or her observations. If each group had a student observer, the observation results for each group may be added together to get an overall class total.

The fifth step is to conduct small-group and whole-class celebrations. It is feeling successful, appreciated, and respected that builds commitment to learning, enthusiasm about working in cooperative groups, and a sense of self-efficacy about subject-matter mastery and working cooperatively with classmates.

Stuart Yager examined the impact on achievement of (a) cooperative learning in which members discussed how well their group was functioning and how they could improve its effectiveness, (b) cooperative learning without any group processing, and (c) individualistic learning (Yager, Johnson, & Johnson, 1985). The results indicate that the high-, medium-, and low-achieving students in the cooperation-with-group-processing condition achieved higher on daily achievement, postinstructional achievement, and retention measures than did the students in the other two conditions. Students in the cooperation-without-group-processing condition, furthermore, achieved higher on all three measures than did the students in the individualistic condition. Johnson, Johnson, Stanne, and Garibaldi (1990) conducted a follow-up study comparing cooperative learning with no-processing, cooperative learning-with-teacher processing (the teacher specified which cooperative skills to use, observed the groups, and gave whole-class feedback as to how well students were using the skills), cooperative learning with teacher and student processing (the teacher specified which cooperative skills to use, observed the groups, gave whole-class feedback as to how well students were using the skills, and had learning groups discuss how well they interacted as a group), and individualistic learning. Forty-nine high ability African American high school seniors and entering college freshmen at Xavier University participated in the study. A complex computer-assisted problem-solving assignment was given to the students. All three cooperative conditions performed higher than did the individualistic condition. The combination of teacher and student processing resulted in greater problem-solving success than did the other cooperative conditions. Julie Archer-Kath (Archer-Kath, Johnson, & Johnson, in press) studied the impact of the combination of group and individual feedback with group feedback only on student performance and attitudes. Fifty-six eighth-grade midwestern students studying German were used as subjects. The investigators found that the combination of group and individual feedback resulted in higher achievement motivation, actual achievement, and more positive attitudes toward each other, the subject area, the teacher, and themselves.

POSITIVE INTERDEPENDENCE AND INTELLECTUAL CONFLICT

The greater the positive interdependence within a learning group, the greater the likelihood of intellectual disagreement and conflict among group members. When members of a cooperative learning group become involved in a lesson, their different

information, perceptions, opinions, reasoning processes, theories, and conclusions will result in intellectual disagreement and conflict. When such controversies arise, they may be dealt with constructively or destructively, depending on how they are managed and the level of interpersonal and small-group skills of the participants. When managed constructively, controversy promotes uncertainty about the correctness of one's conclusions, an active search for more information, a reconceptualization of one's knowledge and conclusions, and, consequently, greater mastery and retention of the material being discussed and a more frequent use of higher-level reasoning strategies (Johnson & Johnson, 1979, 1989, 1992a). Individuals working alone in competitive and individualistic situations do not have the opportunity for such intellectual challenge and, therefore, their achievement and quality of reasoning suffer.

REDUCING PROBLEM BEHAVIORS

When students first start working in cooperative learning groups they sometimes engage in unhelpful behaviors. Whenever inappropriate student behavior occurs, your first move should be toward strengthening the perceived interdependence.

STUDENT IS NOT PARTICIPATING OR BRINGING WORK OR MATERIALS		
Jigsaw materials	Assign student role essential for group success	Reward group if all members achieve up to criterion to increase peer pressure to participate

A STUDENT IS TALKING ABOUT EVERYTHING BUT THE ASSIGNMENT	
Give a reward that the student or group finds especially attractive	Structure task so steady contributions are required for group success

A STUDENT IS WORKING ALONE AND IGNORING THE GROUP DISCUSSION	
Limit resources in the group (if there is only one pencil, the member will be unable to work alone)	Jigsaw materials so that the students cannot complete the assignment without other members' information

A STUDENT IS REFUSING TO LET OTHER MEMBERS PARTICIPATE		
Jigsaw resources	Assign other members essential roles (such as reader, recorder, or summarizer)	Reward group on the basis of the lowest two scores by group members

SUMMARY

In certain groups, such as sports teams and combat units, factors such as contagious excitement, strong norms favoring maximal effort, and intense feelings of commitment, loyalty, and obligation often make group members demonstrate levels of motivation and effort far beyond what would be expected from an individual acting alone. During a basketball game in 1989, for example, Jay Burson, a player on the Ohio State University team, continued to play in a game after he had suffered a broken neck. There are many examples where people like Jay Burson doubled their efforts or placed themselves in great jeopardy because of their devotion and loyalty to other group members and the group.

Cooperative learning groups and student learning are inextricably connected. The truly committed cooperative learning group is probably the most productive instructional tool teachers have at their disposal, provided that teachers know what cooperative efforts are and have the discipline to structure them in a systematic way. Despite the fact that most educators are familiar with cooperative learning groups, many educators are imprecise in their thinking about cooperative efforts. For that reason, gaining a clear understanding of (a) what a cooperative learning group is and is not and (b) the basics of making cooperative efforts effective can provide insights useful for strengthening the performance of cooperative learning groups. Imprecise thinking about cooperative learning groups, however, pales in comparison to the lack of discipline most educators bring to using cooperative learning groups in instructional situations.

Not all groups are cooperative groups. Groups can range from pseudo learning groups to traditional classroom groups to cooperative learning groups to high-performance cooperative learning groups. High-performance cooperative learning groups are rare. Most cooperative groups never reach this level. Many educators who believe that they are using cooperative learning are, in fact, using traditional classroom groups. There is a crucial difference between simply putting students in groups to learn and in structuring cooperation among students. Cooperation is not having students sit side by side at the same table to talk with each other as they do their individual assignments. Cooperation is not assigning a report to a group of students in which one student does all the work although the others put their names on the product as well. Cooperation is not having students do a task individually with instructions that the ones who finish first are to help the slower students. Cooperation is much more than being physically near other students, discussing material with other students, helping other students, or sharing material among students, although each of these is important in cooperative learning.

Educators can examine any learning group and decide where on the group performance curve it now is. Pseudo learning groups and traditional classroom groups are characterized by group immaturity, members uncritically giving their dominant response in completing assignments, members engaging in social loafing and free riding, members losing motivation to learn, groupthink, homogeneity of skills and abilities, and inappropriate group size and resources. Cooperative learning groups are characterized by members perceiving clear positive interdependence, holding each other personally and individually accountable to do his or her fair share of the work, promoting each other's learning and success, appropriately using the interpersonal and small-group skills needed for successful cooperative efforts, and processing as a group how effectively members are working together. These five essential components must be present for small-group learning to be truly cooperative.

Creating cooperative learning groups is not easy. It takes daily, disciplined application of the basics of cooperative efforts. These basics are tough standards and present a difficult implementation challenge to teachers. At the same time, working hard to ensure that the basics are present in each learning group will accelerate teachers' efforts to ensure that all students are achieving up to their full potential.

Understanding how to implement the five basic elements in formal cooperative learning lessons, informal cooperative learning activities, and cooperative base groups sets the stage for using all three in an integrated way. That is the topic of the next chapter.

6

Integrated Use of All Types of Cooperative Learning

Pull together. In the mountains you must depend on each other for survival.

Willi Unsoeld, mountain climber

Structuring cooperative learning in classrooms involves integrating the use of the three types of cooperative learning groups. Each course may have a mixture of cooperative formal, informal, and base groups. This chapter begins by presenting two examples of how cooperative learning may be used. The examples are followed by a discussion of personalizing the learning environment of the class.

FIFTY-MINUTE CLASS SESSION

Teacher Welcome

The teacher formally starts the class by welcoming the students and instructing them to meet in their base groups (see Table 6.1).

TABLE 6.1 Integrated Use of All Types of Cooperative Learning for Fifty-Minute Session

STEP	ACTIVITY	TIME
1	Teacher welcome and opening base group meeting	10
2	Choice 1: Direct teaching, informal cooperative learning	35
3	Choice 2: Work in formal cooperative learning groups	35
4	Choice 3: Direct teaching, formal cooperative learning groups	35
5	Closing base group meeting	5

Opening Base Group Meeting

The introduction and warm-up for the class are provided within base groups. The initial **base group** meeting includes the following tasks:

1. Greet each other and check to see that none of their group is under undue stress. Members ask, "How are you today?" and "Are we all prepared for class?"
2. Check to see if members have completed their homework or need help in doing so. Members ask, "Did you do your homework?" "Is there anything you did not understand?"
3. Share resources they have found or copies of work they have completed and wish to distribute to their base group members.
4. Deepen their relationships by discussing such questions as "What is the best thing that has happened to you this week?" "What is your favorite television show?"

Base group activities must be completed within about five minutes. Regularly structuring this time is essential for helping students get into a good learning mood, communicating high expectations about completing homework and helping others, and providing a transition between the student's (and teacher's) previous hour and the current class session.

Choice 1: Direct Teaching with Informal Cooperative Learning

Direct teaching begins and ends with a focused discussion in an informal cooperative learning group and has paired discussions interspersed throughout the lecture (see Chapter 5). During the discussions each student completes the following tasks:

1. *Formulates* an answer individually (30 seconds).
2. *Shares* his or her answer with the student's partner (1 minute).
3. *Listens* carefully to his or her partner's answer (1 minute).
4. *Creates* an answer that is superior to each partner's individual answers (1 minute).

Students are slow and awkward at following this procedure initially, but once they become familiar with it they work intensely. Again, this is an important time for the teacher to circulate among the students, listen in, and learn what they already know about the topic. In the long run it is important to vary the type of informal cooperative learning groups, using simultaneous explanation pairs one day and cooperative note-taking pairs another.

Choice 2: Complete Assignment in Formal Cooperative Learning Groups

If a group assignment is given, it is carefully structured to be cooperative (see Chapter 3). The teacher notes the objectives of the lesson, makes a series of preinstructional decisions, communicates the task and the positive interdependence, monitors the groups as they work and intervenes when needed, evaluates students' learning, and has groups process how effectively members are working together. Formal cooperative learning groups are used when the teacher wishes to achieve an instructional objective that includes conceptual learning, problem solving, or the development of students' critical thinking skills. Formal cooperative learning groups are needed for simulations of firsthand experiences, role playing, or the sharing of expertise and resources among members.

Choice 3: Short Direct Teaching and Short Group Assignment

The third choice for the teacher is to use a combination of direct teaching with informal cooperative learning and an assignment to be completed in formal cooperative learning groups. The group assignment may be carried over into the following class period.

Closing Base Group Meeting

The class session ends in a base group meeting in which members list three or four major learnings and one or two questions about the material covered. The summaries and questions are handed in as the students leave. Commenting on what was learned and answering a few of the questions sends a message to the students that the activity is important. The summaries and questions provide the teacher with valuable information about what the students are learning. Finally, members of the base groups should celebrate their hard work and success.

NINETY-MINUTE CLASS SESSION

The basic structure of a ninety-minute period is essentially the same as for the fifty-minute period except it is easier to both lecture and have cooperative learning groups complete an assignment within one class session. Class begins with a base group meeting, the teacher gives a lecture using informal cooperative learning groups (to ensure that students are cognitively active while the teacher disseminates information), conducts a formal cooperative learning activity to promote problem-solving and higher-level learning, and closes the class with a second base group meeting (see Table 6.2).

TABLE 6.2   Integrated Use of All Types of Cooperative Learning for Ninety-Minute Session

STEP	ACTIVITY	TIME
1	Opening base group meeting	10
2	Direct teaching with informal cooperative learning	25
3	Work on assignment in formal cooperative learning	40
4	Direct teaching with informal cooperative learning	10
5	Closing base group meeting	5

Teacher Welcome

The teacher formally starts the class by welcoming the students and instructing them to meet in their base groups.

Opening Base Group Meeting

The base group meetings can be longer (up to fifteen minutes) and more complex activities can be conducted. Valuable information can be gleaned by eavesdropping on the base groups and noting which parts of the assignment caused difficulty.

Direct Teaching with Informal Cooperative Learning

Direct teaching may follow. In using a variety of informal cooperative learning group procedures, faculty need to structure carefully the five basic elements of cooperative learning within the learning situation.

Complete Assignment in Formal Cooperative Learning Groups

Formal cooperative learning groups become the heart of longer class periods. Students take increasing responsibility for each other's learning, and the teacher takes increasing responsibility for guiding this process. Faculty should structure positive interdependence in a variety of ways and give students the opportunity to promote each other's learning face to face. It is helpful to use a variety of formal cooperative learning procedures, such as jigsaw, problem solving, joint projects, and peer composition (see Chapter 3). Occasional reporting by the students to the whole class (by randomly calling on individual students to report for their group, of course) can help the teacher guide the overall flow of the class. Carefully monitor the cooperative groups and use formal observation sheets to collect concrete data on group functioning to use during whole-class and small-group processing.

Direct Summary with Informal Cooperative Learning

At the end of the class session teachers will wish to call the class together and summarize what was covered and point toward what will be covered in the next class session. In doing so, students should be asked to consider one or two issues phrased as questions. Informal cooperative learning is used. The teacher poses a question, students *formulate* their answer to the question, turn to another student and *share* their answer, *listen* to their partner's answer, and *create* a new answer that is better than either one.

Closing Base Group Meeting

The class session closes with students meeting in base groups. Include the following closing tasks:

1. Ensure all members understand the assignment? Find out what help each member needs to complete it?

2. Summarize at least three things members learned in today's class session?
3. Summarize how members will use or apply what they have learned?
4. Celebrate the hard work and learning of group members.

EXAMPLES OF INTEGRATED USE OF COOPERATIVE LEARNING

Example 1

An example of the integrated use of the cooperative learning procedures is as follows. Students arrive at class and meet in their base groups to welcome each other, complete a self-disclosure task (such as "What is each member's favorite television show?"), check each other's homework to make sure all members understand the academic material and are prepared for the class session, and tell each other to have a great day.

The teacher then begins a lesson on the limitations of being human. To help students cognitively organize in advance what they know about the advantages and disadvantages of being human, the teacher uses **informal cooperative learning.** The teacher asks students to form a triad and ponder, "What are five things you cannot do with your human limitations that a billion-dollar being might be designed to do?" Students have four minutes to respond. In the next ten minutes, the teacher explains that although the human body is a marvelous system, we (like other organisms) have very specific limitations. We cannot see bacteria in a drop of water or the rings of Saturn unaided. We cannot hear as well as a deer or fly like an eagle. Humans have never been satisfied being so limited and, therefore, we have invented microscopes, telescopes, and our own wings. The teacher then instructs students to turn to the person next to them and answer the questions, "What are three limitations of humans, what have we invented to overcome them, and what other human limitations might we be able to overcome?"

Formal cooperative learning is now used in the lesson (for the billion-dollar being lesson, see *Topics in Applied Science,* Jefferson County Schools, Golden, Colorado). The teacher has the thirty-two students count off from 1 to 8 to form groups of four randomly. Group members sit so they can face each other and face the teacher. Each member is assigned a role: researcher/runner, summarizer/time keeper, collector/recorder, and technical advisor (role interdependence). Every group gets one large two-foot-by-three-foot piece of paper, a marking pen, a rough draft sheet for designing the being, an assignment sheet explaining the task and cooperative goal structure, and four student self-evaluation checklists (resource interdependence). The *task* is to design a billion-dollar being that overcomes the human limitations thought of by the class and the group. The group members are to draw a diagram of the being on the scratch paper, and when they have something they like, they can transfer it to the larger paper. The teacher establishes **positive goal interdependence** by asking for one drawing from the group that all group members contribute to and can explain. The *criterion for success* is to complete the diagram in the thirty-minute time limit. The teacher ensures *individual accountability* by observing each group to ensure that members are fulfilling their roles and that any one member can explain any part of the being at any time. The teacher informs students that the *expected social skills* to be used by all students are encouraging each other's participation, contributing ideas, and summarizing. She or he defines the skill of encouraging participation and has each student practice it twice before the lesson begins. While students work in their groups, the teacher *monitors* by systematically observing each group and intervening to provide academic assistance and help in using the interpersonal and small-group skills required to work together effectively. At the end of the lesson the groups hand in their diagrams of the billion-dollar being to be assessed and *evaluated*. Group members then *process* how well they worked together by identifying actions each member engaged in that helped the group succeed and one thing that could be added to improve their group next time.

The teacher uses **informal cooperative learning** to provide closure to the lesson by asking students to meet in new triads and write out six conclusions about the limitations of human beings and what we have done to overcome them.

At the end of the class session the **cooperative base groups** meet to review what students believe is the most important thing they have learned during the day, what homework has been assigned, what help each member needs to complete the homework, and to tell each other to have a fun afternoon and evening.

Example 2

An example of the integrated use of the types of cooperative learning is as follows. Students arrive at school in the morning and meet in their base groups to welcome each other, complete a self-disclosure task (such as "What is each member's favorite television show?"), check each student's homework to make sure all members understand the academic material and are prepared for the day, and tell each other to have a great day. The teacher then begins a lesson on world interdependence. The teacher has a series of objects and wants students to identify all the countries involved in creating the objects. To help students cognitively organize in advance what they know about the world economy the teacher uses informal cooperative learning by asking students to turn to the person seated next to them and identify the seven continents and one good that is produced in each continent. They have four minutes to do so.

Formal cooperative learning is now used in the lesson. The objectives for the lesson are for students to learn about global economic interdependence and to improve their skill in encouraging each other's participation. The teacher has the thirty students count off from 1 to 10 to form triads randomly. They sit so they can either face each other or face the teacher. The teacher hands out the objects that include a silk shirt with plastic buttons, a cup of tea (a saucer and cup with a tea bag and a lump of sugar in it), and a walkman and earphones (with a cassette tape of a Nashville star) made by Phillips (a European company). The teacher assigns members of each triad the roles of hypothesizer (who hypothesizes about the number of products in each item and where they came from), a reference guide (who looks up each hypothesized country in the book to see what products it exports), and a recorder. After each item the roles are rotated so that each student fulfills each role once.

The teacher introduces world economic interdependence by noting the following:

1. A hand-held calculator most often consists of electronic chips from the United States, is assembled in Singapore or Indonesia, is placed in a steel housing from India, and is stamped with a label Made in Japan on arrival in Yokohama (the trees and chemicals used to make the paper and ink in the label are all made and processed elsewhere and the plastic in the keys and body are all made elsewhere).
2. Modern hotels in Saudi Arabia are built with room modules made in Brazil, construction labor from South Korea, and management from the United States.
3. The global economic interdependence is almost beyond imagining.

The teacher then assigns the academic task of identifying how many countries contributed to the production of each object. She establishes **positive goal interdependence** by stating that it is a cooperative assignment and, therefore, all members of the group must agree on an answer before it is recorded and all members must be able to explain each of the group's answers. The criteria for success were to hand in a correctly completed report form and for each member to score 90 percent or better on the test to be given the next day on world economic interdependence. The teacher establishes **positive reward interdependence** by stating that if the record sheet is accurate, each member will receive fifteen points and if all members of the group achieve 90 percent or better on the test, each member will receive five bonus points. Individual accountability is established by the roles assigned and the individual test. In addition, the teacher will observe each group to make sure all students are participating and learning. The teacher informs students that the *expected social skill* to be used by all students is encouraging each other's participation. The teacher then defines the skill and has each student practice it twice before the lesson begins.

While students work in their groups, the teacher **monitors** by systematically observing each group and intervening to provide academic assistance and help in using the interpersonal and small-group skills required to work together effectively. At the end of the lesson the groups hand in their report forms to be **evaluated** and **process** how well they worked together by identifying three things members did to help the group achieve and one thing that could be added to improve their group next time.

Next, the teacher then uses a **generic cooperative lesson structure** to teach vocabulary. Studying vocabulary words is a routine that occurs every week in this class. The teacher instructs students to move into their vocabulary pairs, take the vocabulary words identified in the world interdependence lesson, and for each word (a) write down what they think the word means, (b) look it up in the text and write down its official definition, (c) write a sentence in which the word is used, and (d) learn how to spell the word. When they have done that for each word, the pair is to make up a story in which all of the words are used. Pairs then exchange stories and carefully determine whether all the words are used appropriately and spelled correctly. If not, the two pairs discuss the word until everyone is clear about what it means and how it should be used.

The teacher uses informal cooperative learning to provide closure to the lesson by asking students to meet with a person from another group and write out four conclusions they derived from the lesson and circle the one they believed was the most important.

At the end of the school day the cooperative base groups meet to review what students believe is the most important thing they have learned during the day, what homework has been assigned, what help each member needs to complete the homework, and to tell each other to have a fun afternoon and evening.

THE EVOLUTION OF COOPERATIVE LEARNING

In implementing cooperative learning, teachers need a time line to guide their efforts. Although a few teachers take cooperative learning strategies and change their classrooms overnight, most teachers engage in a slower, more evolutionary approach. Both the collaborative skills of the students and the instructional skills of the teachers take time to develop and build. Overloading students and teachers with new demands and new situations rarely results in productive change. Teachers are well advised to take what they already know about using learning groups, add a clear cooperative goal structure, and slowly expand the use of cooperative learning until it dominates the classroom. Generally, teachers pass through the following stages as they become proficient in structuring learning situations cooperatively:

1. *Nonuse.* Teachers have not heard of cooperative learning or are under pressures that prevent consideration of new instructional strategies.
2. *Decision to use and initial preparation.* Teachers learn enough about cooperative learning to be interested in trying it. They plan their first lesson.
3. *Initial use.* Teachers are using cooperative learning less than 10 percent of the time. They are attempting to deal with the initial start-up issues:
   a. Logistical issues of moving furniture and making transitions in and out of cooperative learning, getting students to sit together and engage in such "forming" (see Chapter 5) behaviors as "using quiet voices," and getting students to turn and look at the teacher when instructions are given.
   b. Communication issues of clearly defining the positive interdependence and individual accountability so that students understand what actions are appropriate and inappropriate.
4. *Beginning use.* Teachers use cooperative learning between 10 and 20 percent of the time. They typically focus on the following issues:
   a. Teacher monitoring issues of determining how effectively students collaborate and counting frequencies of positive behaviors to share with the whole class or individual groups.
   b. Student monitoring and processing issues of training students to observe the collaborative interaction of group members and process how effectively their group is functioning. This can be done with any age student. Teachers have had kindergarten and first-grade students observing their group for "who talks," "who takes turns," and "who asks someone else to speak."
   c. Teaching students the collaborative skills they need to function effectively in cooperative learning groups. Teachers will move from *forming* to *functioning* skills. They

may wish to emphasize the *formulating and fermenting* skills after students have mastered the basics of working collaboratively. Some care has to be taken in translating the skills into phrases and actions that are appropriate for the age and the background of the students being taught.

5. **Mechanical use.** Teachers follow the general procedures for implementing cooperative learning in a step-by-step fashion by planning each lesson and reviewing recommended procedures before each lesson. Teachers at this point are usually using cooperative learning from 20 to 50 percent of the time. Some of the issues teachers deal with are the following:

  a. Using a variety of ways to structure positive interdependence and individual accountability, to monitor and process, and to evaluate.

  b. Expanding the use of cooperative learning from one subject area or class to several subject areas or classes.

  c. Thinking in terms of curriculum units (rather than single lessons) being cooperative and in terms of alternating among cooperative, competitive, and individualistic learning rather than the isolated use of cooperative learning.

  d. Teaching collaborative and academic skills simultaneously.

6. *Routine use.* Teachers automatically structure cooperative learning situations without conscious thought or planning. The concurrent focus on academic and collaborative skills happens spontaneously. Teachers are usually using cooperative learning more than 50 percent of the time and are dealing with the following issues:

  a. Integrating cooperative, competitive, and individualistic lessons.

  b. Varying how cooperative learning is structured according to tasks, students, and circumstances.

  c. Integrating cooperative learning with other teaching strategies in their repertoire.

  d. Applying collaborative skills and understanding of positive interdependence to faculty relationships and other settings.

It may take a year for teachers to develop into mechanical users of cooperative learning and it often takes up to two years for teachers to become firmly routine users (see Figure 3.1). In planning how you will progress from beginning to routine use of cooperative learning the following advice may be helpful:

1. Do not try to move too fast. Start with a single lesson. Move to conducting at least one cooperative lesson per week and then to modifying a curriculum unit to be primarily cooperative. Finally, think of integrating cooperative, competitive, and individualistic learning within a class or subject area.

2. Persevere! Do not stop growing in your use of cooperative learning even though some students are not very skillful and no one else in your school seems to care. Lay out a long-range plan and stay with it. Especially persevere with students who have a hard time collaborating with peers.

3. Seek support from one or more colleagues and engage in joint sharing of successes, problems, new ideas, and curriculum modification.

4. Make sure the teacher who has your students the following year understands what cooperative learning is and how good your students are in collaborating.

5. Plan carefully for the start of each school year so that cooperative learning is emphasized right away.

PERSONALIZING THE LEARNING ENVIRONMENT

Learning is a personal experience. The more frequently cooperative learning is used, the more personalized the learning will be. Haines and McKeachie (1967) demonstrated that students in classes stressing competition for grades showed more tension, self-doubt, and anxiety than did students working in cooperative learning groups. The learning environment may be personalized in a number of ways.

First, monitor cooperative groups closely. Circulate among the groups, systematically observe, and often stop to (a) join in and interact with group members or (b) intervene within a group. The more attentive teachers are to individual students, the more effective and personal the teaching. It is easier to make a direct comment to a student in a small group than in a whole-class setting.

Second, work to establish classroom norms that promote individuality, creativity, and sensitivity to students' needs. All students need to feel respected, free, and motivated to make the maximum contributions of what they are capable.

Third, demonstrate a willingness to learn from students. Every teacher–student interaction carries potential for learning for both the teacher and students. When faculty accept and learn from students' contributions, the learning experience becomes more personal for the students.

Fourth, present students with a realistic assessment of what they have learned and with high expectations as to what they can learn if they make the effort. Faculty offer students a tension between present and future, actuality and possibility. In a detailed and practical study of skills possessed by effective teachers of adults, Schneider, Klemp, and Kastendiek (1981) concluded that effective teachers (a) believe that average students are competent, (b) identify and affirm students' capabilities, (c) express the view that students are capable of change, and (d) accept student suggestions for changes in learning plans when the changes are consistent with the students' learning objectives. Daloz (1987) found that effective teachers were described by students as "giving me confidence in myself," "kept pushing me and telling me I could do it," and "having faith in me even when I did not." Through their expectations of students, faculty can communicate where students are and what they can become without allowing either to eclipse the other.

Fifth, send them out of class feeling happy. John Wooden, the basketball coach at UCLA for many years, wrote out a detailed lesson plan for every one of his practices. At the end of each lesson plan he wrote, "Send the players to the showers happy." Similarly, Durward Rushton (a principal in Hattisburg, Mississippi) states that each student should feel personally *secure*, have a sense of *belonging*, and experience some *success* each class session (SBS). Teachers should adopt similar attitudes toward creating a positive atmosphere for each class session. One step to doing so is eliminating put-downs. Being put down by a teacher is the most common response given to the question "What is your most memorable experience from high school?" (Kohl, personal communication, 1989). Many students are afraid to contribute in class, some for lack of confidence, others because they fear their ideas are not worthy. The simple procedure of saying something positive about every student's comment, question, or answer to a question has remarkable power for transforming a classroom.

A simple means for promoting a personalized learning environment is having students (and you) wear name tags to help students learn each other's names. Teachers often comment that for their students, the most important word in the English language is their name. Name tagging is a simple procedure that makes a profound difference in the atmosphere of the classroom. Students immediately warm up to their colleagues and seem to appreciate the opportunity to meet and greet each other. The short time that this activity consumes is more than compensated by the improvement in the learning mood of the students. On the first day have students complete a name tag. In the center the student (and teacher) places his or her name (actually the way he or she prefers to be addressed) in print large enough to be read twenty feet away. In the corners are placed other information about the student, such as, birthplace, favorite place, hobbies, favorite artist, something the student is looking forward to, and major or profession. Finally, surrounding their name students are asked to place two or three adjectives that describe them. The students are then given about ten minutes to meet and learn something about as many other students in the class as possible.

CONCLUSIONS

Formal cooperative learning, informal cooperative learning, and cooperative base groups form a gestalt that allows teachers to present coherent lessons in which all activities lead to the achievement of mutual learning goals. The integrated use of the three types of cooperative learning provides the context in which competitive and individualistic activities may be used effectively.

7

Assessment and Evaluation

CONDUCTING ASSESSMENTS

In the time of change, learners inherit the earth, while the learned find themselves beautifully equipped to deal with a world that no longer exists.

Eric Hoffer

In 1955 Edward Banfield lived for nine months in a small town in southern Italy that he called Montegrano (Johnson & Johnson, 1996). What Banfield noticed most was the town's alienated citizenry, grinding poverty, and pervasive corruption. He concluded that the primary source of Montegrano's plight was the distrust, envy, and suspicion that characterized its inhabitants' relations with each other. They viewed communal life as little more than a battleground. Town members consistently refused to help one another unless it would result in material gain. Many actually tried to prevent their neighbors from succeeding, believing that others' good fortune would inevitably undercut their own. Consequently, they remained socially isolated and impoverished, unable to cooperate to solve common problems or pool their resources and talents to build viable economic enterprises.

Montegrano's citizens were not inherently more selfish or foolish than people elsewhere. But for a number of complex historical and cultural reasons, they lacked the norms, habits, attitudes, and networks that encourage people to work together for the common good. They lacked what Alexis de Tocqueville called "the habits of the heart." Habits of the heart include taking responsibility for the common good, trusting others to do the same, being honest, having self-discipline, reciprocating good deeds, and perfecting the skills necessary for cooperation and

103

conflict management. The relationship between democracy and such habits is supported by the fact that in the United States, since the early 1960s voter turnout in national elections has fallen by a quarter and the number of citizens saying that "most people can be trusted" has dropped by more than a third.

There is far more to assessment than giving students grades (Johnson & Johnson, 1996). It is vital to assess what students know, understand, and retain over time (academic learning). It is equally important to assess (a) the quality and level of their reasoning processes and (b) their skills and competencies (such as oral and written communication skills and skills in using technology). In today's complex and ever-changing world, a broad view of education is needed rather than a narrow focus on the memorization of facts. More than ever, schools need to focus on teaching students appropriate work habits (such as completing work on time and striving for quality work and continuous improvement) and attitudes (such as a love of learning, a desire to read good literature, or a commitment to democracy).

Exercise 7.1   Your Assessment Plan

Listed below are generic assessment targets and procedures. In planning your assessment program, check the targets that you wish to assess and then check the procedures you wish to use. Match the procedures with the targets so it is clear how you will assess each target.

WHAT IS ASSESSED	PROCEDURES USED TO ASSESS
_____ Academic learning	_____ Goal-setting conferences
_____ Reasoning process/strategies	_____ Standardized tests
_____ Skills and competencies	_____ Teacher-made tests
_____ Attitudes	_____ Written compositions
_____ Work habits	_____ Oral presentations
	_____ Projects
	_____ Portfolios
	_____ Observations
	_____ Questionnaires
	_____ Interviews
	_____ Learning logs and journals
	_____ Student management teams

TABLE 7.1   Assessment Issues

PURPOSE	FOCUS	SETTING	STAKEHOLDERS	STAKES
Diagnostic	Process of learning	Artificial (classroom)	Students-parents	Low
Formative	Process of instruction	Authentic (real world)	Teachers, administrators	High
Summative	Outcomes of learning		Policy makers	
	Outcomes of instruction		Colleges, employers	

In achieving these complex and long-term responsibilities of the school, teachers need to conduct three types of assessments: *diagnostic* (diagnosing students' present level of knowledge and skills), *formative* (monitoring progress toward learning goals to help form the instructional program), and *summative* (providing data to judge the final level of students' learning). These assessments need to focus on both the process and the outcomes of learning and instruction (see Table 7.1). Assessments need to take place in more authentic settings as well as in the classroom. The number of stakeholders in education have increased as the world economic and the interdependence among nations have increased. The stakes of many of the assessments also have increased, as students' futures are more and more determined by what they have learned and how many years of formal education they have completed. As the seriousness of educators' responsibilities has increased, so has the need to use a wider variety of assessment procedures.

Exercise 7.2   Essential Definitions

Form a pair and match the correct definition with each concept listed below. Combine with another pair and check answers.

CONCEPT	DEFINITION
_____ 1. Instruction	a. Change within a student that is brought about by instruction.
_____ 2. Learning	b. Judging the merit, value, or desirability of a measured performance.
_____ 3. Rubric	c. Standards against which the quality and quantity of performances are assessed (what counts or is important).
_____ 4. Assessment	d. Structuring of situations in ways that help students change, through learning.
_____ 5. Criteria	e. Collecting information about the quality or quantity of a change in a student, group, teacher, or administrator.
_____ 6. Evaluation	f. Articulation of gradations of quality and quantity for each criterion, from poor to exemplary.

MAKING ASSESSMENTS MEANINGFUL AND MANAGEABLE

Educators face two major issues in conducting effective and responsible assessments (Johnson & Johnson, 1996):

1. Making assessments meaningful to the various stakeholders (see Table 7.2).
2. Making assessments manageable so they will actually get done.

Many educators forget that the most significant motivating forces for students are those that increase their competencies in a way that benefits those they care about. Such personal meaning is created by three factors:

1. *Structuring positive interdependence among students.* It is positive interdependence that creates positive relationships among students, a commitment to each other's learning and well-being, a desire to contribute to the common good, the motivation to strive to be one's best for the sake of others as well as for oneself, and the conviction that there is more to life than selfish self-interest.
2. *Involving students in the learning and assessment processes.* Students need to be involved in formulating their learning goals, choosing the paths for achieving the goals, assessing their progress and success, planning how to improve, and implementing their plan in the event that serious management problems arise.
3. *Ensuring that assessment data is organized in a way that it may be used.* Useful results help students to seek remediation for what they misunderstood, reviews to fill in gaps in what they know, and new learning experiences that will help students to take the next steps to advance their knowledge and skills.

These three issues are interrelated. Positive interdependence creates the context for involvement. The involvement creates the ownership of the learning and assessment processes and the motivation to use the assessment improves one's understanding and competencies. The more clearly the results point toward the next steps to be taken to increase the quality and quantity of the learning, the more likely students are to engage in the assessment process. Implementing plans to improve learning requires the help of collaborators, which returns the cycle to positive interdependence (see Table 7.3).

Serious management problems arise when students are involved in formulating their learning goals, choosing the paths for achieving the goals, assessing their progress and success, planning how to improve, and implementing their plan. One

TABLE 7.2   Meaningful Assessment

INVOLVEMENT IN PROCESS		USE OF OUTCOMES	
LESS MEANING	MORE MEANING	LESS MEANING	MORE MEANING
Isolated goals	Interdependent goals	Individual celebration	Joint celebration
Work alone	Joint effort with others	New isolated goals	New interdependent goals
Self-assess only	Assess other's work as well as one's own		
Receive feedback only	Both give and receive feedback		

TABLE 7.3   Meaningful Assessments

POSITIVE INTERDEPENDENCE	INVOLVEMENT	USEFUL RESULTS
Common purpose	Setting goals, planning paths to achieve goals, assessing progress, planning for improvement, implementing plans	Clarify of next steps to improve
Positive relationships	Ownership	Use of results
MEANING	MEANING	MEANING

teacher working by himself or herself can no longer manage the entire assessment system. The most natural sources of help for teachers are students and colleagues. Students provide the most help because they are available at all times. To be constructive participants in the assessment process, however, students need to be organized into cooperative learning groups. Students oriented toward competition or only their own individualistic efforts resist contributing to the others' continuous improvement. To organizational theorists such as Deming, competitive and individualistic structures are "forces for destruction" (Walton, 1986). To provide quality assessment, students have to be as committed to classmates' learning and academic success as they are to their own. Such commitment only comes from clear positive interdependence.

Cooperative learning groups provide the setting, context, and environment in which assessment becomes part of the instructional process and students learn almost as much from assessing the quality of their own and their classmates' work as they do from participating in the instructional activities.

1. Cooperative learning allows assessment to be integrated into the learning process. Continuous assessment requires continuous monitoring and support, which can best be done within cooperative learning groups.
2. The new assessment practices are so labor intensive that students who are sincerely committed to each other's learning and success may need to be involved.
3. Cooperative learning groups allow more modalities to be used in the learning and assessment process while focusing on more diverse outcomes.
4. Cooperative learning groups allow groupmates to be sources of information in addition to the teacher and the curriculum materials.
5. Involving groupmates in assessment reduces possible biases resulting from the teacher being the sole source of feedback and the heavy reliance on reading and writing as assessment modalities.
6. Cooperative learning groups help each student in analyzing assessment data, interpreting the results, and implementing improvement plans.

It is difficult to imagine a class in which cooperative learning groups do not help make the assessment system more manageable or how a comprehensive assessment program can be managed without cooperative learning groups.

This chapter is a summary of the book, *Meaningful and Manageable Assessment through Cooperative Learning* (Johnson & Johnson, 1996). Readers interested in more detail and a wide variety of practice procedures are referred to that book.

ASSESSMENT PROCEDURES

Assessment begins with setting learning goals. Once students have formulated and agreed to their learning goals, a variety of assessment procedures can be used. The assessment procedures include tests, compositions, presentations, projects, portfolios, observations, interviews, questionnaires, and learning logs and journals.

SETTING AND MANAGING LEARNING GOALS

Without clear learning and instructional goals, assessment cannot take place (Johnson & Johnson, 1996). The goals are created and reemphasized in three types of conferences with each student: A *goal-setting conference* is conducted to establish a contract containing the student's learning goals, *progress-assessment conferences* are conducted to review the student's progress in achieving his or her goals, and a *post-evaluation conference* is conducted in which the student's accomplishments are explained to interested parties (see Table 7.4).

Each student must commit to achieving a learning goal that specifies what he or she needs to accomplish in the immediate future and identifies his or her responsibilities for helping other students learn. These goals are established in a goal-setting conference. The goal-setting conference may be between the teacher and the student (T/S), the teacher and the cooperative learning group (T/G), the cooperative learning group and the student (G/S), or a cooperative learning group and another group (G/G). In all cases, the emphasis is on helping students set and take ownership for learning goals that meet the START criteria (specific, trackable, achievable,

TABLE 7.4   Types of Conferences

CONFERENCE	INDIVIDUAL STUDENT	COOPERATIVE LEARNING GROUP
Goal-Setting Conference	Each class period, day, week, or instructional unit each student sets personal learning goals and publicly commits himself or herself to achieve them in a learning contract.	Each class period, day, week, or instructional unit each cooperative group sets group learning goals and members publicly commit themselves to achieve them in a learning contract.
Progress-Assessment Conferences	The student's progress in achieving his or her learning goals is assessed, what the student has accomplished so far and what is yet to be done is reviewed, and the student's next steps are detailed.	The group's progress in achieving its learning goals is assessed, what the group has accomplished so far and what is yet to be done is reviewed, and the group's next steps are detailed.
Post-Evaluation Conference	The student explains his or her level of achievement (what the student learned and failed to learn during the instructional unit) to interested parties (student's cooperative learning group, teachers, and parents), which naturally leads to the next goal-setting conference.	The group explains its level of achievement (what the group has accomplished and failed to accomplish during the instructional unit) to interested parties (members, teachers, and parents), which naturally leads to the next goal-setting conference.

START GOALS
S = Specific
M = Measurable, trackable
A = Challenging but achievable
R = Relevant
T = Transfer

relevant, transferable). The goal-setting conference contains four steps:

1. Diagnosing current level of expertise (what does the student now know?).
2. Setting START goals focusing on student's (a) academic achievement, reasoning, social skills, attitudes, and work habits and (b) responsibilities for helping groupmates learn.
3. Organizing support systems and resources to help each student achieve his or her goals successfully.
4. Constructing a plan for utilizing the resources to achieve the goals and formalizing the plan into a learning contract (see Table 7.5).

TABLE 7.5   My Learning Contract

LEARNING GOALS		
My Academic Goals	My Responsibilities for Helping Others' Learn	My Group's Goals
1. _____	_____	_____
2. _____	_____	_____
3. _____	_____	_____
4. _____	_____	_____

THE PLAN FOR ACHIEVING MY LEARNING GOALS,
MEETING MY RESPONSIBILITIES, AND HELPING MY GROUP

THE TIME LINE FOR ACHIEVING MY GOALS

Beginning date: _____   Third road mark: _____

First road mark: _____   Final Date: _____

Second road mark: _____

Signatures

_____   _____

_____   _____

The truth is that most teachers do not have the time to conference with each individual student, whether it is a goal-setting conference, a progress-assessment conference, or a post-evaluation conference. This does not mean that such conferences cannot happen. Teachers can engineer and supervise such conferences through appropriate use of cooperative learning groups. Groups can regularly have progress-assessment conferences with each member while the teacher listens in or pulls aside individual students for conferences.

TESTS AND EXAMINATIONS

Both standardized and teacher-made tests may be used to assess student learning (Johnson & Johnson, 1996). Standardized tests are often high-stake events for which students need to be carefully prepared. Teacher-made tests are often a routine part of an instructional program to assess quickly and efficiently a broad sampling of students' knowledge. They may be multiple-choice, true-false, matching, short answers, interpretative, or essay tests. Although many effective assessment procedures exist, testing remains a mainstay of what teachers do. Cooperative learning groups may be used with tests through the GIG (group preparation, individual test, group test), group discussion, and teams-games-tournament procedures.

THE GIG PROCEDURE FOR GIVING TESTS

You should frequently give tests and quizzes to assess (a) how much each student knows and (b) what students still need to learn. Whenever you give a test, cooperative learning groups can serve as bookends by preparing members to take the test and providing a setting in which students review the test. Using the following procedure will result in (a) optimizing each student's preparation for the test, (b) making each student accountable to peers for his or her performance on the test, (c) assessing how much each student knows, (d) assessing what students still need to learn, (e) providing students with immediate clarification of what they did not understand or learn, (f) providing students with immediate remediation of what they did not learn, and (g) preventing arguments between you and your students over which answers are correct and why. The procedure is as follows:

1. Students prepare for and review for a test in cooperative learning groups.

2. Each student takes the test individually, making two copies of his or her answers. Students submit one set of answers to you to grade and keep one set for the group discussion.

3. Students retake the test in their cooperative learning groups.

Preparing for a Test in Cooperative Groups
Students meet in their cooperative learning groups and are given (a) study questions and (b) class time to prepare for the examination. The task is for students to discuss each study question and come to consensus about its answer. The cooperative goal is to

ensure that all group members understand how to answer the study questions correctly. If students disagree on the answer to any study questions, they must find the page number and paragraph in the resource material explaining the relevant information or procedures. When the study/review time is up, the students give each other encouragement for doing well on the upcoming test.

Taking the Test Individually

Each student takes the test individually, making two copies of his or her answers. The task (and individual goal) is to answer each test question correctly. Students submit one copy of the answers to you (the teacher). You score the answers and evaluate student performance against a preset criterion of excellence. Students keep one copy for the group discussion. After all group members have finished the test, the group meets to take the test again.

Retaking the Test in Cooperative Groups

Students meet in their cooperative learning groups and retake the test. The *task* is to answer each question correctly. The *cooperative goal* is to ensure that all group members understand the material and procedures covered by the test. Members do so by (a) reaching consensus on the answer for each question and the rationale or procedure underlying the answer and (b) ensuring that all members can explain the answer and the rationale or procedure. Members complete the following procedure:

1. Compare their answers on the first question.

2. If there is agreement, one member explains the rationale or procedure underlying the question and the group moves on to the second question.

3. If there is disagreement, members find the page number and paragraph in the resource materials explaining the relevant information or procedures. The group is responsible for ensuring that all members understand the material they missed on the test. If necessary, group members assign review homework to each other. When all members agree on the answer and believe other members comprehend the material, the group moves on to the third question.

4. The learning groups repeat this procedure until they have covered all test questions.

5. The group members celebrate how hard members have worked in learning the material and how successful they were on the test.

COMPOSITIONS AND PRESENTATIONS

Every educated person should be able to present what they know in written and oral form. These are difficult competencies and to become skilled writers and presenters, students need to write and present every day. This presents an assessment problem, as someone has to read each composition and listen to each presentation in order to provide helpful feedback. Using cooperative learning groups to assess members' performances accomplishes five goals at the same time. It allows students to (a) engage in the performance frequently, (b) receive immediate and detailed feedback on their efforts, (c) observe closely the performances of others, (d) see what is good or lacking in others' performances, and (e) provide the labor needed to allow students to engage in a performance frequently. Two of the most common performances assessed are compositions and presentations. Students are assigned to composition pairs. The students discuss and outline each other's composition in their pairs, and then each one researches his or her topic alone. In pairs the students write the first paragraph of each composition, write the composition alone, edit each other's composition, rewrite the composition alone, re-edit each other's compositions, sign-off on partner's composition verifying that it is ready to be handed in, and then process the quality of the partnership (see the composition rubric presented in Table 7.6). The procedure for presentations is very similar.

TABLE 7.6 Persuasive Argument Composition Rubric

Name: _____ Date: _____ Grade: _____

Title of Composition: _____

SCORING SCALE: LOW 1—2—3—4—5 HIGH

CRITERIA	SCORE	WEIGHT	TOTAL
Organization			
Thesis statement and introduction	_____	6	
Rationale presented to support thesis	_____		
Conclusion logically drawn from rationale	_____		
Effective transitions	_____		(30)
Content			
Topic addressed	_____	8	
Reasoning clear with valid logic	_____		
Evidence presented to support key points	_____		
Creativity evident	_____		(40)
Usage			
Topic sentence beginning every paragraph	_____	4	
Correct subject-verb agreement	_____		
Correct verb tense	_____		
Complete sentences (no run-ons, fragments)	_____		
Mix of simple and complex sentences	_____		(20)
Mechanics			
Correct use of punctuation	_____	2	
Correct use of capitalization	_____		
Few or no misspellings	_____		(10)
Scale: 93–100 = A, 85–92 = B, 77–84 = C	_____	20	(100)

TABLE 7.7   Examples of Projects

Mythological rap song: Write and present a rap song about the gods and goddesses in Greek mythology.

Select a famous writer, artist, politician, or philosopher from the Renaissance period and become that person on a panel of experts.

Teach cycles through gardening (different students are in charge of seeds, fertilizing, and so forth).

Videotape a community project.

Write plays, skits, or role plays.

Run a school post office.

Participate in an international festival by presenting multicultural activity.

Write alternative endings with dramatizations.

Turn a short story or event in history into a movie.

Present a newscast.

Pamphlet: Select and research a disease and prepare an instructional pamphlet to present to the class.

Research an international conflict in the world today (for each country a student researches, he or she can present a different aspect of the country related to the war history, resolutions, maps, and so forth).

Paint a mural of the history of the earth and humankind (each group takes a section: Greek, Roman, Middle Ages art).

Prepare a time line (personal, history, literature, art, geology).

Publish a school or class newspaper.

Dramatize a mock court.

Paint a mural based on a reading.

Create a new invention using the computer.

Design an ideal school and have class enact it.

Design a science fair project.

INDIVIDUAL AND GROUP PROJECTS

A standard part of most every course is allowing students to be creative and inventive in integrating diverse knowledge and skills. This is especially important in assessing multiple intelligences and the ability to engage in complex procedures such as scientific investigation. Projects allow students to use multiple modes of learning. The use of cooperative learning groups allows projects to be considerably more complex and elaborate than projects completed by any one student (see Table 7.7).

PORTFOLIOS

Students become far more sophisticated and educated when they can organize their work into a portfolio that represents the quality of their learning in a course or school year. There is no substitute for having students collect and organize their work samples and write a rationale connecting the work samples into a complete and holistic picture of the student's achievements, growth, and development. The resulting portfolio may feature the student's best works or the process the student is using to learn. Like all other complex and challenging tasks, students need considerable help in constructing their portfolios and in presenting them to teachers, parents, and other interested stakeholders. Portfolios, therefore, may be more manageable when they are constructed within cooperative learning groups. The group can help each member select appropriate work samples and write a coherent and clear rationale. The

TABLE 7.8   Cooperative Group Portfolio

What is a cooperative base group?	A **cooperative base group** is a long-term, heterogeneous cooperative learning group with stable membership. It may last for one course, one year, or for several years. Its purposes are to give the support, help, encouragement, and assistance each member needs to make good academic progress and develop cognitively and socially in healthy ways.
What is a group portfolio?	A **group portfolio** is an organized collection of group work samples accumulated over time and individual work samples from each member.
What are its contents?	Cover that creatively reflects group's personality
	Table of contents
	Description of the group and its members
	Introduction to portfolio and rationale for the work samples included
	Group work samples (products by the group that any one member could not have produced alone)
	Observation data of group members interacting as they worked on group projects
	Self-assessment of the group by its members
	Individual members' work samples that were revised on the basis of group feedback (compositions, presentations, and so forth)
	Self-assessment of members, including their strengths and weaknesses in facilitating group effectiveness and other members' learning
	List of future learning and social skills goals for the group and each of its members
	Comments and feedback from faculty and other groups

portfolio may also include the group's assessment of the student's learning and growth (see Table 7.8).

An extension of portfolios is to have the student, the teacher, and the student's cooperative learning group each independently decide on what represents the student's best work and why. They then have a conference to compare their assessments and resolve any differences.

CONTENTS OF PORTFOLIOS

1. *Cover sheet* that creatively reflects the nature of the student's (or group's) work
2. *Table of contents* that includes the title of each work sample and its page number
3. The *rationale* explaining what work samples are included, why each one is significant, and how they all fit together to form a holistic view of the student's (or group's) work
4. The *work samples*
5. A *self-assessment* written by the student or the group members
6. *Future goals* based on the student's (or group's) current achievements, interests, and progress
7. *Other's comments and assessments* from the teacher, cooperative learning groups, and other interested parties such as the parents

Exercise 7.3   *Preparing to Use Portfolios*

1. Who will construct the portfolios?

    _____   Individual students with teacher input and help.

    _____   Individual students with the input and help of cooperative learning groups.

    _____   Cooperative base groups (whole-group work and individual members' work to be included) with the teacher's input and help.

2. What type of portfolio do you want to use?

    _____   Best works portfolio   _____   Process/growth portfolio

3. What are the purposes and objectives of the portfolio?

    a.

    b.

    c.

4. What categories of work samples should go into the portfolio?

    a.

    b.

    c.

5. What criteria will students or groups use to select their entries?

    a.

    b.

    c.

6. Who will develop the rubrics to assess and evaluate the portfolios?

    _____   Faculty   _____   Students

OBSERVING

There is a limit to the information gained by having students turn in completed tests, compositions, projects, and portfolios. Answers on a test and homework assignments tell teachers whether students can arrive at a correct answer. They cannot, however, inform teachers as to the quality of the reasoning strategies students are using, students' commitment to classmates' success and well-being, or the extent to which students can work effectively with others. Teachers must find a way to make students' covert reasoning processes overt, demonstrate behaviorally their attitudes and work habits, and show how skillfully they can work with others. Observing students in action thus becomes one of the most important assessment procedures. Observing students has three stages:

1. *Preparing for observing.* Deciding what actions to observe, who will observe, what the sampling plan will be; constructing an observation form; and training observers to use the form.

2. *Observing.* Observations may be formal or informal, structured or unstructured.

3. *Summarizing the data for use by students and other stakeholders.* In summarizing observations, the data may be displayed in bar or run charts. Feedback is then given to the students or other interested parties, and the recipients reflect on the feedback and set improvement goals.

One of the primary uses of observation procedures is to assess the use of social skills. *First,* you teach students the targeted social skill. You show the need for the skill, define it with a T-chart, set up practice situations in which students can use the skill, ensure that students receive feedback on their use of the skill and reflect on how to improve, and ensure that students persevere in practicing the skill until it becomes automatic. *Second,* you structure cooperative learning situations so students can use the social skills and you can observe their doing so. *Third,* you intervene in the cooperative learning groups to ensure that members are using the social skills appropriately and to recognize them for doing so. *Fourth,* you have students complete checklists or questionnaires to self-diagnose their mastery of the targeted social skills. *Fifth,* you assign students to set improvement goals for increasing their social competence. *Sixth,* you assess students' knowledge of social skills. *Finally,* you report on the level of students' social skills to interested stakeholders, such as the students, parents, and potential employers.

INTERVIEWING

Closely related to observing students in action is interviewing students. Like observing, interviews can make covert behaviors appear more overt by asking students more and more detailed questions about their reasoning processes and strategies. The strengths of the interview are that it is personal and flexible. The personal nature of interviews allows you to build a more positive, supportive, and trusting relationship with each student. The flexibility of interviews allows you to interview either one student or a small group of students before, during, and after a lesson and to use the interview for both assessment and teaching purposes. Socrates is an example of a teacher who used interviewing as his major instructional strategy.

BEING A SOCRATES

1. Choose a topic being studied.

2. Develop two or three general questions on what the student knows about the topic to begin an interview.

3. After asking the opening questions, probe what the student knows while looking for inconsistencies, contradictions, or conflicts in what the student is saying.

4. Ask follow-up questions that highlight the conflicts within the student's reasoning and make the contradictions focal points for the student's attention.

5. Continue the interview until the student has resolved the conflicts by moving toward a deeper-level analysis of what he or she knows and arriving at greater and greater insights into the material being studied.

6. Conclude the interview by pointing the student toward further resources to read and study.

ATTITUDE QUESTIONNAIRES

All learning has affective components and in many ways the attitudes students develop may be more important than their level of academic learning. Getting an A in a math class, for example, does a student little good if he or she has learned to hate math and never wants to take a math class again. Obviously, loving math and wanting to take math courses throughout one's educational career is far more important than the level of achievement in any one math class. Attitudes largely determine whether students continue to study the subject area, become uninterested, or wish to avoid it in the future. In assessing student attitudes, you (a) decide which attitudes to measure, (b) construct a questionnaire, (c) select a standardized measure if it is appropriate, (d) give the measures near the beginning and end of each instructional unit, semester, or year, (e) analyze and organize the data for feedback to interested stakeholders, (f) give the feedback in a timely and orderly way, and (g) use the results to make decisions about improving the instructional program. In constructing a questionnaire, each question needs to be well worded and requiring either an open-ended (fill-in-the-blank or free) response or closed-ended (dichotomous, multiple-choice, ranking, or scale) response. The questions are then arranged in an appropriate sequence and given an attractive format. A standardized questionnaire, such as the Classroom Life instrument, may be used to measure a broader range of student attitudes. Table 7.9 illustrates one way to ascribe point values to criteria.

TABLE 7.9   Assigning Point Values to Entries

POINTS	CRITERIA
20	Completeness of entries
10	Entries recorded on time
15	Originality of entries
15	Higher-level reasoning demonstrated
15	Connections made with other subject areas
25	Personal reflection
100	Total

STUDENT ATTITUDE SURVEY

Respond to statements below with your best opinion. Do not leave any blank.

1. My general opinion about history is _____ .

2. History is my _____ subject.

3. If someone suggested I take up history as my life's work, I would reply

_____ .

4. History is my favorite school subject.   _____ True   _____ False

5. Do you intend to take another course in history?

_____ Yes   _____ No   _____ I'm not sure

6. How interested are you in learning more about history?

Very interested   1:2:3:4:5:6:7   Very uninterested

7.   **History**

Ugly   1:2:3:4:5:6:7   Beautiful

Bad   1:2:3:4:5:6:7   Good

Worthless   1:2:3:4:5:6:7   Valuable

Negative   1:2:3:4:5:6:7   Positive

LEARNING LOGS AND JOURNALS

Students often do not spend enough time reflecting on what they are learning and how it relates in a personal way to their lives. Learning logs and journals help students document and reflect on their learning experiences. *Logs* tend to emphasize short entries concerning the subject matter being studied. Logs are especially useful in conjunction with informal cooperative learning. *Journals* tend to emphasize more narrative entries concerning personal observations, feelings, and opinions in response to readings, events, and experiences. These entries often connect what is being studied in one class with other classes or with life outside of the classroom. Journals are especially useful for having students apply what they are learning to their "action theories."

TOTAL QUALITY LEARNING

Total quality learning begins with assigning students to teams and assigning them the task of continuously improving the quality of the processes of learning and assessment. **Continuous improvement** is the ongoing search for changes that will increase the quality of the processes of learning, instructing, and assessing. Each time students write a composition, for example, they should find at least one way to improve their writing skills. The changes do not have to be dramatic. Small, incremental changes are fine.

To improve continuously the processes of learning and assessment, students need to engage in eight steps. *First,* they must form teams. Quality learning is not possible without cooperative learning groups. *Second,* team members analyze the assignment and select a learning process for improvement. *Third,* members define the process to improve, usually by drawing a flowchart or cause-and-effect diagram. *Fourth,* team members engage in the process. *Fifth,* students gather data about the process, display the data, and analyze it. Tools to help them do so include observation forms, Pareto charts, run charts, scatter diagrams, and histograms. *Sixth,* on the basis of the analysis, team members make a plan to improve the process. *Seventh,* students implement the plan by engaging in the learning process in a modified and improved way. *Finally,* the team institutionalizes the changes that do in fact improve the quality of the learning process.

One way to enhance the use of total quality learning is through the use of student management teams. A **student management team** consists of three or four students plus the instructor who assume responsibility for the success of the class by focusing on how to improve either the instructor's teaching or the content of the course. The group members monitor the course through their own experience and the comments of classmates. There are four stages of using student management teams: forming the team by recruiting and choosing members, building a cooperative team by structuring the five basic elements, improving the instruction and content of the course, and reaping the long-term gains from the process by carrying on the improvements to the next course.

TEACHING TEAMS AND ASSESSMENT

The days are gone when a teacher, working in isolation from colleagues, could instruct, assess, and report results by himself or herself. The practices have become so labor intensive and complex that one teacher cannot expect to do them alone. Realistically, colleagial teaching teams are needed to coordinate and continuously improve the instruction, assessment, and reporting process. Teachers need to begin their instruction, assessment, and reporting efforts by forming a colleagial teaching team. This allows them to capitalize on the many ways teams enhance productivity. The team focuses its efforts on continuously improving both student learning and the quality of instruction. The team as a whole conducts the assessment and reporting process by developing rubrics, applying the rubrics effectively, and reporting results to interested audiences. The team then establishes a continuous improvement process by focusing on maximizing the quality of instruction for each member. While engaging in the continuous improvement process, the team also engages in continuous retraining aimed at improving the effectiveness of their use of the assessment procedures. The use of colleagial teaching teams provides the framework for developing schoolwide criteria and standards to be used in assessment.

GIVING GRADES

Teachers need to assess student learning and progress frequently, but they do not need to evaluate or give grades. Assessing involves checking on how students are doing, what they have learned, and what problems or difficulties they have experienced. Grades are symbols that represent a value judgment concerning the relative quality of a student's achievement during a specified period of instruction. Grades are necessary to give students and other interested audiences information about students' level of achievement, evaluate the success of an instructional program, provide students access to certain educational opportunities, and reward students who excel. Grading systems may involve a single grade or multiple grades. It is vital that grades are awarded fairly as they can have considerable influence on students' futures. Being fair includes using a wide variety of assignments to measure achievement. Grades may be supplemented with checklists and narratives to give a more complex and complete summative evaluation of student achievement. Having students work in cooperative groups adds further opportunity to measure aspects of students' learning and assign grades in a variety of ways.

Exercise 7.4   Giving Students Grades in Cooperative Learning

The way grades are given depends on the type of interdependence the instructor wishes to create among students. Norm-referenced grading systems place students in competition with each other. Criterion-referenced grading systems require students to either work individualistically or cooperatively. Here are a number of suggestions for giving grades in cooperative learning situations.

1. *Individual score plus bonus points based on all members reaching criterion.* Group members study together and ensure that all have mastered the assigned material. Each then takes a test individually and is awarded that score. If all group members achieve over a preset criterion of excellence, each receives a bonus. An example is presented in Table 7.10.

TABLE 7.10

CRITERIA	BONUS	MEMBERS	SCORES	BONUS	TOTAL
100	15 Points	Bill	100	10	110
90–99	10 Points	Juanita	95	10	105
80–89	5 Points	Sally	90	10	100

TABLE 7.11

CRITERIA	BONUS	MEMBERS	SCORES	BONUS	TOTAL
90–100	6 Points	Bill	93	2	95
80–89	4 Points	Juanita	85	2	87
70–79	2 Points	Sally	78	2	80

2. *Individual score plus bonus points based on lowest score.* The group members prepare each other to take an exam. Members then receive bonus points on the basis of the lowest individual score in their group. This procedure emphasizes encouraging, supporting, and assisting the low achievers in the group. The criterion for bonus points can be adjusted for each learning group, depending on the past performance of their lowest member. An example is presented in Table 7.11.

3. *Individual score plus group average.* Group members prepare each other to take an exam. Each takes the examination and receives his or her individual score. The scores of the group members are then averaged. The average is added to each member's score. An example is presented in Table 7.12.

4. *Individual score plus bonus based on improvement scores.* Members of a cooperative group prepare each other to take an exam. Each takes the exam individually and receives his or her individual grade. In addition, bonus points are awarded on the basis of whether members' percentage on the current test is higher than the average percentage on all past tests (i.e., their usual level of performance). Their percentage correct on past tests serves as the base score that they will try to improve. Every two tests or scores, the base score is updated. If a student scores within 4 points (above or below) his or her base score, all members of the group receive 1 bonus point. If they score 5 to 9 points above their base score, each group member receives 2 bonus points. Finally, if they score 10 points or above their base score, or score 100 percent correct, each member receives 3 bonus points.

5. *Totaling members' individual scores.* The individual scores of members are added together and all members receive the total. For example, if group members scored 90, 85, 95, and 90, each member would receive the score of 360.

6. *Averaging of members' individual scores:* The individual scores of members are added together and divided by the number of group members. Each member then receives the group average as their mark. For example, if the scores of members were 90, 95, 85, and 90, each group member would receive the score of 90.

TABLE 7.12

STUDENT	INDIVIDUAL SCORE	GROUP AVERAGE	FINAL SCORE
Bill	66	79	145
Juanita	89	79	168
Sally	75	79	154
Benjamin	86	79	165

7. *Group score on a single product.* The group works to produce a single report, essay, presentation, worksheet, or exam. The product is evaluated and all members receive the score awarded. When this method is used with worksheets, sets of problems, and examinations, group members are required to reach consensus on each question and be able to explain it to others. The discussion within the group enhances the learning considerably.

8. *Randomly selecting one member's paper to score.* Group members all complete the work individually and then check each other's papers and certify that they are perfectly correct. Because each paper is certified by the whole group to be correct, it makes little difference which paper is graded. The instructor picks one at random, grades it, and all group members receive the score.

9. *Randomly selecting one member's exam to score.* Group members prepare for an examination and certify that each member has mastered the assigned material. All members then take the examination individually. Because all members have certified that each has mastered the material being studied, it makes little difference which exam is scored. The instructor randomly picks one, scores it, and all group members receive that score.

10. *All members receive lowest member score.* Group members prepare each other to take the exam. Each takes the examination individually. All group members then receive the lowest score in the group. For example, if group members score 89, 88, 82, and 79, all members would receive 79 as their score. This procedure emphasizes encouraging, supporting, and assisting the low-achieving members of the group and often produces dramatic increases in performance by low-achieving students.

11. *Average of academic scores plus collaborative skills performance score:* Group members work together to master the assigned material. They take an examination individually and their scores are averaged. Concurrently, their work is observed and the frequency of performance of specified collaborative skills (such as leadership or trust-building actions) is recorded. The group is given a collaborative skills performance score, which is added to the group's academic average to determine the overall mark.

12. *Dual academic and nonacademic rewards.* Group members prepare each other for a test, take it individually, and receive an individual grade. On the basis of their group average, they are awarded free time, popcorn, extra recess time, or some other valued reward.

SUMMARY

Traditionally, assessment procedures have been quite limited. Teachers often notice the light in a student's eye, changes in voice inflections, the "aha" of discovery, the creative insight resulting from collaborating with others, the persistence and struggle of a student determined to understand complex material, the serendipitous use of skills and concepts beyond the context in which they were learned, and reports from parents and other teachers on the changes in a student resulting from a course of study. What has been lacking is a systematic way of collecting and reporting such evidence.

Times have changed. The diverse assessment procedures discussed in Johnson and Johnson (1996) and outlined in this chapter are quite developed and may be used effectively as part of any instructional program. Each has its strengths and its weaknesses. Each can be integrated into an ongoing instructional program and managed when used as part of cooperative learning. Together, they allow cooperative learning groups to engage in total quality learning and provide a comprehensive and fair means of giving grades.

In addition to cooperative learning, teachers may wish to use competitive and individualistic learning as fun changes of pace or for specific, carefully tailored instructional objectives. These methods are discussed in the next two chapters.

8

Structuring Competitive Learning

One of the most famous competitions in history is the search for a method for determining longitude (Sobel, 1995). The active search for a practical way to determine longitude was pursued throughout Europe for more than four hundred years. In the early 1700s, this problem was considered as important as discovering the formula for transforming lead into gold, the fountain of youth, and the secret of perpetual motion. The great maritime nations such as Spain, the Netherlands, and several city-states in Italy created a worldwide competition by offering large monetary rewards for a workable method. King George III of England and King Louis XIV of France spurred on the competition. Proposed methods were tested by such famous seafarers as Captain William Bligh and Captain James Cook. In 1714, the British Parliament passed its famous Longitude Act offering a prize equal to several million dollars in today's currency for a practical and useful means of determining longitude. Who would win?

_____ The most famous contenders were the astronomers, who were convinced that longitude could be determined from looking at the stars. Galileo, Cassini, Newton, and Halley all attempted to find ways of determining longitude from the clockwork universe. Great observatories were founded at Paris, London, and Berlin for the single purpose of determining longitude from the heavens. In their quest the astronomers made the first accurate determination of the weight of the Earth, the distance to the stars, and the speed of light.

_____ A second set of contenders proposed methods such as anchoring ships at strategic places on the ocean and having them fire cannon blasts at established times to tell all ships within hearing distance where they were.

——— The wounded dog theory was proposed in 1687. Sir Kenelm Digby discovered in southern France a miraculous powder of sympathy that could purportedly heal at a distance. If you sprinkled a bandage from a person's wound with the powder of sympathy, the person's wound would heal even if the person was hundreds of miles away. The healing, however, was painful so that the person would cry out. The longitude problem could be solved, therefore, by sending a wounded dog on a ship and at exactly twelve noon each day a bandage used on the dog would be dipped in the sympathy powder. The dog would then howl in pain, giving the ship's captain an accurate account of the time in the home port. The difference between the ship's time and the home port's time would allow the captain to calculate the ship's longitude accurately.

——— Another contender was an unknown, uneducated, untrained English clock maker named John Harrison. He devoted his life to inventing a clock that would carry the true time from the home port to any remote corner of the world. From knowing the difference between the current time and the time in the home port, an accurate determination of longitude could be calculated. A problem with the clock approach was that the current clocks were quickly destroyed—by marked changes in temperature (sailing from the tropics to the arctic), exposure to sea air and water, and the punishment of a ship being tossed around in storms. Harrison had no formal education and he never served an apprenticeship to any watchmaker. Yet he constructed a series of virtually friction-free clocks that operated without a pendulum. He made his clocks from materials that were impervious to rust and that required no lubrication and no cleaning. He constructed his clocks of different metals in such a way that when one component expanded or contracted with changes in temperature, the other counteracted the change and kept the clock's rate constant. He found a way to keep the moving parts perfectly balanced in relation to one another regardless of how the world pitched or tossed about them.

The winner was—John Harrison! Although Harrison clearly solved the longitude problem, the commissioners in charge of awarding the prize favored the astronomers. They kept changing the rules of the competition to deny the prize to Harrison. It took Harrison forty years of demonstrating the practical utility of his clocks before King George III took pity on the aged and exhausted Harrison and ensured that he was finally pronounced the winner in 1773.

Even more so now than in the 1700s, competition pervades our society (Johnson & F. Johnson, 1997; Johnson & R. Johnson, 1989). The language of business, politics, and even education is filled with win-lose terms. A person *wins* a promotion, *beats* the other sales clerks, *outsmarts* a teacher, becomes a *superstar, defeats* enemies, and puts other people *in their place*. Competition is so pervasive that some parents hold their children back a grade in school so that they will be bigger, stronger, and more developed cognitively and, therefore, more likely to achieve athletic and academic success. Colleges, furthermore, replace coaches who graduate all their athletes but do not achieve a winning record, even though college presidents claim that education is more important than athletics.

This chapter defines the nature of competition and its characteristics, describes its essential elements, and presents the teacher's role in using competition constructively.

NATURE OF COMPETITION

Winning isn't everything. It's the only thing!

Vince Lombardi

If you are going to use competition as part of instruction, it helps to know what it is and what its characteristics are. One would think that after about 150 years of social Darwinism and hundreds of research studies, the nature of competition would be clear. Unfortunately, that is not the case, although many different ways of defining competition have been proposed (see Table 8.1). The most commonly used definition was offered by Deutsch (1949a, 1962) who described **competition** as a negative correlation among participants' goals in a given situation. According to Deutsch, in competition an individual can attain his or her goal if and only if the other participants cannot attain their goals. Thus, individuals seek an outcome that is personally beneficial but detrimental to all others in the situation.

Johnson and Johnson (1974, 1978, 1989) developed a typology of competition based on the combination of outcome and means interdependence (see Table 8.2). **Outcome interdependence** specifies the relationship among the mutual goals and rewards the individuals are striving to achieve. **Means interdependence** specifies the actions required on the part of participants to achieve their goals. It exists when a task is structured so that two or more individuals are required to complete it, that is, no one person can complete the task without the help or involvement of another person. When the presence and absence of both outcome and means interdependence are taken into account, two types of competition can be identified: direct

TABLE 8.1   Definitions of Competition

THEORIST	DEFINITION
Social interdependence, situational: Deutsch	Competition exists when individuals' goal achievements are negatively correlated; each individual perceives that when one person achieves his or her goal, all others with whom he or she is competitively linked fail to achieve their goals (Deutsch, 1949a, 1962).
Social interdependence, situational: Johnson and Johnson	Competition exists when participants work against each other to achieve a goal that only one or a few can obtain (Johnson & Johnson, 1989).
Behavioral theory, situational: Skinner	Competition results from a reward given only to the person who achieves the highest relative to others (Skinner, 1968).
Behavioral theory, situational: Kelley and Thibaut	Competition is individuals acting in ways to maximize their own rewards and minimize their own costs relative to others (Kelley & Thibaut, 1978).
Trait: Helmreich and colleagues	Competitiveness is the desire to win in interpersonal situations (Helmreich, Beane, Lucker, & Spence, 1978).
Motive: McClintock	A competitive motive is a predisposition to act competitively in a situation that allows a choice among cooperative, competitive, and individualistic behaviors (McClintock, 1972).
Attitude: Johnson and Norem-Hebeisen	A competitive attitude is a preference for competitive over cooperative and individualistic situations (Johnson & Norem-Hebeisen, 1977).

TABLE 8.2   Outcome and Means Independence

		OUTCOME INTERDEPENDENCE	
		ABSENT	PRESENT
MEANS INTERDEPENDENCE	ABSENT	Individualistic situation	Parallel, alternating, or indirect interaction toward contrient goals
	PRESENT	Not possible	Direct oppositional interaction toward contrient goals

oppositional interaction toward contrient goals (such as a chess game) and parallel, alternating, or indirect interaction toward contrient goals (such as a race or a national test). Although negative goal interdependence is required for competition to exist, some competitions involve negative means interdependence and some do not.

In competitive situations, there is a lack of inducibility (students are closed to being influenced by each other), a lack of substitutability (the actions of competitors do not substitute for each other, so that if one member of the group has taken the action, all others still have to engage in the action even though it may be futile to do so), and negative cathexis (any action that helps another win is disliked by the other competitors). Table 8.3 lists some of the effects of a student's attempt to win. Competing, furthermore, creates motives that are contradictory and operate against each other. Affiliation needs and the desire to be involved in relationships with others may operate directly against productivity in competitive situations as someone who wins may be disliked by his or her peers. (See Table 8.4)

TABLE 8.3   In Their Attempts to Win, Students:

Recognize their negatively linked fate.	When one wins, the others lose. The more a classmate learns, the less chance of one's winning and vice versa.
Strive for differential benefit by trying to gain more than their classmates do.	Each student strives to outperform (defeat) classmates. One wins by outperforming others (offense) or by preventing others from outperforming oneself (defense). One's success creates failure for others and vice versa.
Have a short-term time perspective.	Short-term personal advantage is valued over long-term joint productivity.
Develop a relative identity based on a performance ranking within the situation.	One sees oneself as either a winner or a loser depending on how one's performance compares with the performances of others. Winning is celebrated and losing results in feeling inadequate, jealous, or angry.
Recognize the relative causation of winning or losing.	One's outcomes are caused by one's own performance and the performances of competitors. No matter how well one performs, it is of no use if someone else performs even better. No matter how poorly one performs, it does not matter if all others perform even more poorly.

TABLE 8.4   Research Outcomes

EFFORT TO ACHIEVE	INTERPERSONAL RELATIONSHIPS	PSYCHOLOGICAL HEALTH
Large proportion of students experience failure	Hostility toward competitors	Contingent self-esteem where one has value only if one wins
Extrinsic motivation: focus only on winning, not on learning	Hostility toward teachers, judges, officials	Overgeneralization of results
Low achievement motivation (low probability of success)	Low social support	General feelings of anxiety, doubt, self-centeredness
Higher achievement in simple drill review tasks		Values: Egocentrism and self-centeredness, joy in depriving others, joy in others' mistakes and failures, viewing life as rat race, a belief that cheating is legitimized if it works, a desire to win at all cost, a disregard for fairness and justice, low altruism

CHARACTERISTICS OF COMPETITION

There is more to competition than telling people to "win." At least six characteristics must be present for competition to exist. *For competition to exist, there must be negative goal interdependence.* Without negative goal interdependence, there is no competition. *For competition to exist, there must be perceived scarcity, either real or artificial.* If I must defeat you in order to reach my goal, then what I want is by definition scarce. Outcomes are restricted so that only the few who are the best performers are acknowledged as being successful. Sometimes the scarcity is based on reality. Two hungry people may compete over one loaf of bread. Sometimes the scarcity is artificially created. Individuals may compete for a limited number of A's, but how many A's there are is an arbitrary decision made by the teacher and school. Schools create artificial shortages of A's in an attempt to motivate individuals through competition. Many competitions are based on such artificial shortages created for the contest.

For competition to exist, there must be more than one party involved who may interact directly (with oppositional actions) or in parallel (with no oppositional actions), or who may not interact at all. Competitions vary as to the interaction that takes place among participants. In a boxing match there is direct interaction between the two participants who actively try to defeat each other. In a track meet there is parallel interaction (such as the 100-yard dash) or sequential interaction (for example, two javelin-throwers take turns doing the same thing). Within college admissions, participants may never see each other. **For competition to exist, there must be at least one winner.** Competitions can have one (only one baseball team can be world champions), few (10 percent of students may get A's), or many (such as national merit scholars) winners.

For competition to exist, there must be forced, salient, and obtrusive comparisons among participants. Competitions require forced social comparisons in which participants

are faced with salient and obtrusive information about their peers' performances (Levine, 1983). Competitors get the information on how they performed relative to others whether they want it or not.

For competition to exist, there must be criteria for determining the winner. Winning may be determined by subjective judgment (such as in art contests) or objective criteria (such as points in a boxing match). In either case, the criteria for success is uncertain in that what is needed for a win depends on the relative performance of the particular contestants.

Exercise 8.1 Is Competition Constructive or Destructive?

Task

Your tasks are to (a) write a group report on the issue, "Is competition constructive or destructive?" and (b) individually pass a test on the research involved in the decision. Your report should provide details of the advantages and disadvantages of competition. For the past sixty years a controversy about the value of competition has raged in our society and schools. Does competition have constructive or destructive effects? Imagine you are a committee of the top officials in the U.S. Department of Education and you are trying to decide whether or not instruction in U.S. schools should emphasize competition. To ensure that both sides get a complete and fair hearing, you have divided your group into two subgroups to present the best case possible for each side of the issue. Each subgroup will present one of the following theses:

_____ Competition is constructive and should be the dominant instructional strategy used in schools.

_____ Competition is destructive and its instructional use should be avoided in schools.

Cooperative

Write one report for the group of four. All members have to agree. Everyone has to be able to explain the choice made and the reasons why the choice is a good one. To help you write the best report possible, your group of four has been divided into two pairs. One pair has been assigned the position that competition is constructive and the other pair has been assigned the position that competition is destructive.

Procedure

1. *Research and prepare your position.* Your group of four has been divided into two pairs. Each pair is to (a) make a list of reasons supporting your position, (b) plan how to present the best case for your position to the other pair.

2. *Present and advocate your position.* Forcefully and persuasively present the best case for your list to the opposing pair. Be as convincing as possible. Take notes and clarify anything you do not understand when the opposing pair presents.

3. *Engage in an open discussion (advocate, refute, rebut).* Argue forcefully and persuasively for your advice. Critically evaluate and challenge the opposing pair's list and reasoning, and defend your reasoning from attack.

4. *Reverse Perspectives.* Reverse perspectives and present the best case for the opposing advice. The opposing pair will do the same. Strive to see the issue from both perspectives simultaneously.

5. *Enact in synthesis.* Drop all advocacy. Synthesize and integrate the best advice and reasoning from both sides into a joint position that all members can agree to. Then (a) finalize the group report, (b) present your conclusions to the class, (c) ensure that all group members are prepared to take the test, and (d) process how well you worked together as a group and how you could be even more effective next time.

Controversy Rules

1. I am critical of ideas, not people. I challenge and refute the ideas of the opposing pair, but I do not indicate that I reject them personally.

2. I remember that we are all in this together, sink or swim. I focus on coming to the best decision possible, not on winning.

3. I encourage everyone to participate and to master all the relevant information.

4. I listen to everyone's ideas, even if I don't agree.

5. I restate what someone has said if it is not clear.

6. I first bring out all ideas and facts supporting both sides, and then I try to put them together in a way that makes sense.

7. I try to understand both sides of the issue.

8. I change my mind when the evidence clearly indicates that I should do so.

Exercise 8.2   Competition Is Constructive

You represent the procompetition perspective. *Your position is that competition is constructive and should be the dominant instructional strategy used in schools.* Summarize the evidence that follows, all of which supports your position. Research your position and compile as much supporting information as possible. Arrange your information into a compelling, convincing, and persuasive argument that your position is valid and correct. Plan how to best present your assigned position to ensure it receives a fair and complete hearing. Make at least one visual to help you present a persuasive case for competition.

1. *Competition is inherent in nature (including human nature) and is, therefore, unavoidable in human society.* In 1859 Charles Robert Darwin (1809–1882) proposed the *theory of natural selection,* which posits that the better adapted a species is to its environment (and especially to changes in its environment), the greater the likelihood of its being around in the future because it will be able to procreate and thereby survive. To some authorities, natural selection involved a struggle that was competitive—to survive another day you must win over rivals. Herbert Spence coined the phrase, "survival of the fittest" and Hobbes proposed the doctrine of *bellum omnium contra omnes* (war of all against all) to describe the nature of society.

Adam Smith (1759) proposed that the business world was a "dog-eat-dog" world based on natural selection. This social Darwinism is supported by many dramatic examples in nature, usually involving competition (a) among males for females (and the right to father children) and (b) to determine territories.

2. *Competition motivates individuals to do their best.* In his retirement speech, the basketball player Magic Johnson described how much his rivalry with Larry Bird had meant to him, how it had (a) provided positive motivation to improve and refine his skills continually and (b) raised his level of play. World records are set, outstanding feats of courage and skill take place, and overachievement occurs as the result of competition. Competitiveness is a specific form of achievement motivation and an adaptive characteristic for those engaged in competitive sports and other activities (e.g., Fabian & Ross, 1984; Gill, Kelley, Martin, & Caruso, 1991; Vealey, 1988).

3. *Competition builds character.* Competition brings out the best in a person. Competitive experiences are healthy for children because they teach them to deal with a competitive society (Iso-Ahola & Hatfield, 1986) and provide them with a means for achieving recognition (Sherif, 1978). Participation in competitive sports is assumed to lead to the development of prosocial behaviors (Kleiber & Roberts, 1981).

4. *Competition is fun.* Most people voluntarily seek out competition. They play tennis or golf with friends, play cards and games at parties, seek out movies and television programs in which the good guys compete with the bad guys, and cheer on athletes at the Olympics. We seek out competition for fun, enjoyment, and amusement.

5. *Competition teaches important life values.* Competition teaches the values of playing fair, sportsmanship, winning and losing with grace and style, and striving to do your best. Many of the most important values in life are taught in competitive activities.

6. *Competition increases self-confidence and self-esteem.* Participating in competitive situations tends to give participants' the confidence to try to do their best and it increases their self-worth when participants know they have done their best.

7. *Competitiveness increases future career success.* Competition prepares students for the real world they will face in future career settings. Successful competitors will be wonderful CEOs because they will aggressively strive to outperform all others. Certain careers, such as sales, involve competition among employees, as bonuses and incentives may depend on selling more or performing higher than other employees.

Exercise 8.3   Competition Is Destructive

You represent the anticompetition perspective. *Your position is that competition is destructive and should be avoided as an instructional strategy in schools.* Summarize the evidence that follows, all of which supports your position. Research your position and compile as much supporting information as possible. Arrange your information into a compelling, convincing, and persuasive argument that your position is valid and correct. Plan how to best present your assigned position to ensure it receives a fair and complete hearing. Make at least one visual to help you present a persuasive case for competition.

1. *Social Darwinism is a cultural prejudice and a projection of a social philosophy onto the natural world.* Natural selection does not require competition, it discourages it. Natural selection usually occurs without any apparent struggle and is enhanced by a high level of cooperation (the ability to organize into groups and engage in mutual aid). Darwin (1859) himself stated that he used the term "struggle for existence" in a large and metaphorical sense that included dependence on each other. W. Edwards Deming, one of the founders of total quality management in business and industry, furthermore, describes competition as "a force for destruction."

2. *Competition motivates most individuals to exert minimal effort.* In competitions, chronic winners exert only enough effort to win and chronic losers exert little or no effort at all. Competition is based on extrinsic motivation where winning is more important than learning and where those who perceive they have no chance of winning refuse to try. Competitiveness is negatively related to group performance (Graziano, Hair, & Finch, 1997).

3. *Competition decreases character.* Highly competitive people tend to be aloof, insensitive, and do not have empathy for others (Kroll & Peterson, 1965; Loy, Birrell, & Rose, 1976; Roberts & Kleiber, 1982; Webb, 1969). They often strive to win at any cost, ignoring values of fairness and justice. They are significantly less likely to behave altruistically and significantly more likely to behave in a rivalrous manner. Losing promotes depression and aggression toward winners and judges. Participation in competitive sports may inhibit sharing (Kleiber & Roberts, 1981) and intergroup competition has been found to result in a variety of hostile and antisocial behaviors (Sherif, 1966). Stendler, Damrin, and Haines (1951) studied seven-year olds and found that destructive, boastful, and depreciatory behavior exceeded friendly conversation, sharing, and helping behavior when a task was structured competitively.

4. *Competition is stressful and anxiety provoking.* Kohn (1992), in one of the most comprehensive critiques of competition, concluded that competition poisons relationships, causes anxiety, selfishness, self-doubt, poor communication, aggression among individuals, and generally makes life unpleasant. Competition tends to increase anxiety and makes people feel less able to perform (Tseng, 1969). In competitive lessons students are more anxious, less self-assured, less secure, and engage in more incidences of self-oriented needs than students in cooperative lessons, and adults working in a large industry were more anxious when working in a competitive structure than when working in a cooperative structure (Blau, 1954; Deutsch, 1949b; Haines & McKachie, 1967; Naught & Newman, 1966). Competition creates more anxiety for students and provides a less constructive learning climate.

5. *Competition teaches dysfunctional values.* Competition teaches the values of "bettering" others, taking joy in other's mistakes and failures (because they increase one's own chances for success), and viewing life as a "rat race" aimed at outshining one's neighbors. Sport participants become increasingly committed to winning at any cost and decreasingly committed to values of fairness and justice (Kroll & Peterson, 1965; Loy, Birrell, & Rose, 1976; Roberts & Kleiber, 1982; Webb, 1969). Cheating has become a part of the school experience as the stress on grades results in

students striving for good results at all costs. High school students have declared that cheating is universal, necessary, and very easy (Jantzen, 1972). Children in the United States often believe that helping a person in distress is inappropriate and is disapproved of by others, and many children engage in irrational and self-defeating competition by reducing their own rewards in order to reduce the rewards of peers even more (Nelson & Kagan, 1972; Staub, 1971). These dysfunctional values do not just apply to students. A highly regarded school principal in Maryland was dismissed for giving his students extra time to finish segments of the Iowa Tests for Educational Development, thus artificially boosting their scores to make himself look successful. Another study found that schools in almost all of the United States cheated to increase their students' scores on standardized tests.

6. *Competition decreases self-confidence and self-esteem.* Competitive experiences result in the development of a contingent self-acceptance where one is of value only if one wins (Johnson & Johnson, 1989). Losers in a competitive learning situation tend to perceive themselves, their classmates, and school negatively (Ashmore, 1970; Blanchard, Adelman, & Cook, 1975; Crockenberg, Bryant, & Wilce, 1976) and become primarily oriented toward avoiding failure, thus becoming nonachievement oriented (Atkinson, 1965). The results of competition are overgeneralized where winning and losing are perceived to be reflective of a person's total being.

7. *Competitiveness reduces future career success.* Generally, competitiveness has been found to be detrimental to career success (Helmreich, 1982; Helmreich, Beane, Lucker, & Spence, 1978; Helmreich, Sawin, & Carsrud, 1986; Helmreich, Spence, et al., 1980). The more competitive a person is, the less chance that person has of being successful.

COMPETITIVE QUOTES

Be content with your lot; one cannot be first in everything. —*Aesop*

No man lives without jostling and being jostled; in all ways he has to elbow himself through the world, giving and receiving offence. —*Thomas Carlyle*

You can't make the world all planned and soft. The strongest and best survive—that's the law of nature after all—always has been and always will be. —*Businessman in Middletown, Lynd & Lynd*

There's no gap so large as the gap between being "first" and being "second" —*Anonymous second-place finisher*

It's not whether you win or lose, it's how you play the game. —*Unknown*

The enjoyment of competing, win or lose, encourages competition; having to win each time discourages it. —*Anonymous competitor*

A good answer may not be good enough. It has to be better than someone else's. —*R. Dreeben, in* On What Is Learned in School *(1968)*

ESTABLISHING A COMPETITIVE STRUCTURE

A science class has been working on a unit involving things that sink and float. The class is divided into cooperative learning groups and the groups have experimented with a variety of materials. One of the materials was clay. Each group was given the same weight of clay and instructed to build a clay boat. As the groups experimented with different designs, the teacher decided to have a fun change of pace by structuring a class competition to see which group could design and build the boat that would hold the most weight. Each cooperative group was told to build a boat and to ensure that all group members understood the design. The group members were then assigned to competition triads consisting of members of three different groups who were at the same achievement level. Each member was given a new lump of clay and was told to build a boat and explain its design to his or her two competitors. The boats were then placed in water and weights were placed inside each boat until it sank. The boat that supported the most weight before sinking won. The winning boat was worth six points, the second place boat was awarded four points, and the last place boat was awarded two points. After the competition, students returned to their cooperative groups and added up their points for a total group score. The winning group was announced. The class then studied the winning design and determined why it was better than the others. Each group then built a replica of the winning boat.

The essence of a competitive goal structure is to give students the individual goal of outperforming all others and to use a norm-referenced evaluation system in rewarding them. Assigning the individual goal of being the best speller in the class, giving a test, ranking students from best to worst on spelling, and distributing rewards accordingly would be an example. The teacher's role in using competition appropriately is given next. The procedures described are indebted to the teams-games-tournament (TGT) procedure pioneered by David DeVries and Keith Edwards (1974) at Johns Hopkins University.

Overall Procedure for the Competition

1. Students learn assigned material in heterogeneous cooperative learning "home" groups.
2. A competition is conducted to determine which cooperative group best learned the assigned material. Each member of the group is assigned to a homogeneous competition triad. Student receive points according to how well they know the material (compared to the other two members of their competition triad). To create equitable competition, each triad consists of students of comparable academic achievement (as determined by prior performance) from different groups.
3. The winning cooperative group is determined. Students return to their home cooperative learning groups. They sum members' scores to derive a group score. Group scores are then ranked and listed. The cooperative group with the most points "wins" the class intergroup competition.

Preinstructional Decisions

Specifying Instructional Objectives   The academic objectives include reviewing previously learned material to determine which student(s) have mastered it the best.

Assigning Students to Heterogeneous Cooperative Learning Groups   Students are assigned to cooperative learning groups of four members so that each group is balanced in academic performance (the average academic performance level of all the groups is about equal, and one high, one low, and two middle achievers are in each group) and contains a cross-section of other individual characteristics such as gender and ethnic background. The cooperative groups are given time to study together so that students can help and encourage each other to learn, and group membership is held stable for a period of time so that group cohesion and team commitment can develop.

Assigning Students to Homogeneous Competitive Triads   A class competition is structured so that each student competes in a triad as a representative of his or her cooperative learning group against students of equal performance level from other groups. Groups of three maximize the number of winners in the class (pairs tend to make the competition too personal). Rank the students in each cooperative learning group from highest to lowest on the basis of their previous achievement. Assign the three highest achieving students in the class to Table 1, the next three to Table 2, and so on until the three lowest achieving students in the class are in the bottom triad. This ensures all students have the opportunity to win within their competition. Figure 8.1 illustrates the relationship between the cooperative learning groups and the competitive triads.

Even when students are placed in a triad with classmates who achieve at the same level, if a stable pattern of who wins and who loses develops, the perceived likelihood of winning will decrease drastically for the "losers." Teachers, therefore, will wish to change the membership in each triad each time a competition is held. A pro-

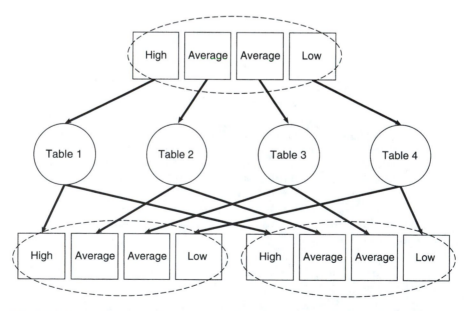

FIGURE 8.1   Assignment to Tournament Tables

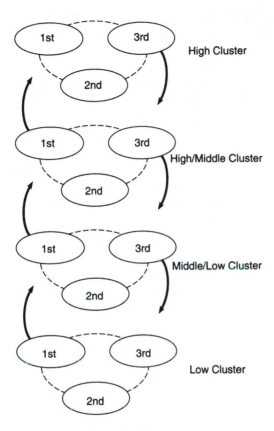

FIGURE 8.2 Bumping Process

cedure for doing so is called bumping (see Figure 8.2). Bumping involves (a) ranking the competitive triads from the highest (the three highest achievers are members) to the lowest (the three lowest achievers are members), (b) moving the winner in each triad up to the next highest triad, and (c) moving the loser down to the next lowest triad. In this way, students will always face new competitors and believe that they have a chance to win.

Planning Roles   Each competitive triad contains three roles:

1. *Reader:* Reads question card.
2. *Responder:* Answers the question.
3. *Checker:* Reads answer from book.

The roles are rotated after each question.

Arranging the Classroom   The room should be arranged so that students within each triad sit close to each other and the triads are separated from each other.

Preparing Instructional Materials   Make a question sheet consisting of about thirty items, an answer sheet, a copy of the rules, and a set of cards numbered from 1 to 30. On each card write one question from the question sheet. The questions can be either recognition or recall questions. Each competitive triad should receive one set of cards and one answer sheet. An example of the cards and answer sheet are given in Figure 8.3. The rules appear in Figure 8.4.

Explaining the Task and Goal Structure

Explaining the Academic Task   The task is to learn and demonstrate mastery of the assigned material.

Structuring Negative Goal Interdependence   Explain to students that their goal is to answer more questions correctly than the other two members of the triad so that (a) they can maximize the number of points they take back to their cooperative learning group and (b) their group can win by having more overall points than any

---

Background of the Game: Middle school students learning to be peer mediators were studying strategies for resolving conflicts. In the game they were asked to answer each of the following questions to test their understanding of the curriculum, *Teaching Students to Be Peacemakers* (Johnson & Johnson, 1995).

What is conflict?	What is negotiation?
(1)	(2)
What characterizes constructive conflicts?	What are the two types of negotiating?
(10)	(3)
What are six ways conflicts have value?	What are four criteria of a wise agreement?
(4)	(11)

Each of the following questions was placed on a card with the answer listed on an answer sheet.

1. What is conflict?
2. What is negotiation?
3. What are the two types of negotiation?
4. What are six ways conflicts have value?
5. What are two basic concerns in conflicts?
6. What are five strategies to manage conflicts?
7. What are six rules for using the five strategies?
8. What is smoothing?
9. What are problem-solving negotiations?
10. What characterizes constructive conflicts?
11. What are four criteria of a wise agreement?
12. What is a refusal skill?
13. What are the steps of negotiating?
14. What is coordinating motivation?
15. What is social perspective taking?
16. What is withdrawing?
17. What is compromising?
18. What is forcing or a win–lose negotiation?

FIGURE 8.3   Sample Game

1. To start the game, shuffle the cards and place them face down in the center of the group. Play is in a clockwise rotation. Decide who goes first.

2. Take the top card from the deck, read it aloud, and do one of two things:
   a. Say you do not know or are not sure of the answer. The two other students may then volunteer to answer the question. If no one wants to answer, place the card on the bottom of the deck.
   b. Answer the question and ask if anyone wants to challenge your answer. The player on your right has the first chance to challenge.

3. If no one challenges you, another player checks the answer on the answer sheet.
   a. If you are correct, you keep the card.
   b. If you are incorrect, the card is placed on the bottom of the deck.

4. If there is a challenge, the challenger gives an answer.
   a. If you are correct, you keep the card and the challenger must give up one of his or her cards (which is placed on the bottom of the deck).
   b. If you are incorrect and the challenger is correct, the challenger keeps the card.
   c. If both you and the challenger are incorrect, then the card is placed on the bottom of the deck.

5. The roles are rotated after each question.

6. The game ends when all of the cards have been played. Players count their cards and determine who has the most, second most, and fewest cards. The game scores are converted into points. Within each triad, the student who answers the most questions correctly receives six points, the second place student receives four points, and the last place student receives two points to take back to his or her cooperative learning group. If two students tie for first place, each receives five points. If two students tie for second place, each receives three points. In a three-way tie, each student receives four points. In a cooperative learning group of four members, the group could have between eight and twenty-four points total. The group that has the most points wins.

FIGURE 8.4   Rules of Competitive Play

Note: The game was developed by David DeVries, Keith Edwards, and Gail Fennessey with the help of Carol Hopkins.

other group in the class. Make sure the procedures, rules, criteria for winning, and the definition of what is and is not a correct answer are clearly understood by all students. Competition bogs down if there are disputes or misunderstandings over such matters.

Explaining Criteria for Success   Within each triad, the student who answers the most questions correctly receives six points, the second place student receives four points, and the last place student receives two points to take back to his or her cooperative learning group. If two students tie for first place, each receives five points. If two students tie for second place, each receives three points. In a three-way tie, each student receives four points (see Table 8.5). In a cooperative learning group of four members, the group could have between eight and twenty-four points total. The group that has the most points wins.

TABLE 8.5 Criteria for Success

PLACE	POINTS
First	6 Points
Second	4 Points
Third	2 Points
Tie: First and second	5 Points each
Tie: Second and third	3 Points each
Three-way tie	4 Points each

Specifying Desired Behaviors   Students need to know what behaviors are appropriate and desirable within a competitive learning situation. Each student should try to win in his or her triad. Students are to work alone answering each of their questions without consultation with other group members. If they need help or clarification they are to ask the teacher. They should keep track of where they stand in the competition and make adjustments in their strategy accordingly. In addition, they should

1. Seek fun and enjoyment.
2. Win with humility and pleasure.
3. Lose with dignity.
4. Recognize and deal with inappropriate anxiety.
5. Monitor the progress of competitors.
6. Form realistic perceptions of own skills.

Conducting the Competition

The competition is conducted to determine which cooperative learning group best learned the assigned material. Students receive points according to how well they mastered the material (compared with the other two members of their tournament triad).

1. To start the game, shuffle the cards and place them face down on the table. Play is in a clockwise rotation. Three rotating roles are assigned to players (roles are rotated in a clockwise direction after each question):
   a. *Question reader:* Draws a card, reads it aloud.
   b. *Answer giver:* Decides whether or not to give an answer.
   c. *Answer Checker:* If an answer is given, reads the answer to the question from the answer sheet (regardless of whether the answer is challenged).
2. To play, a student takes the top card from the deck, reads it aloud, and does one of two things:
   a. Says he or she does not know or is not sure of the answer. The two other students may then volunteer to answer the question. If no one wants to answer, the card is placed on the bottom of the deck.
   b. Answers the question and asks if anyone wants to challenge his or her answer. The player on the answer giver's right has the first right of challenge.

3. If no one challenges, another player checks the answer on the answer sheet.
   a. If correct, the answer giver keeps the card.
   b. If incorrect, the card is placed on the bottom of the deck.
4. If there is a challenge, the challenger gives an answer.
   a. If answer giver is correct, he or she keeps the card and the challenger must give up one of his or her cards (which is placed on the bottom of the deck).
   b. If the answer giver is incorrect and the challenger is correct, the challenger keeps the card.
   c. If both the answer giver and the challenger are incorrect, then the card is placed on the bottom of the deck.
5. The roles are rotated after each question.
6. The game ends when all of the cards have been played. Players count their cards and determine who has the most, second most, and fewest cards. The game scores are converted into points. Within each triad, the student who answers the most questions correctly receives six points, the second place student receives four points, and the last place student receives two points to take back to his or her cooperative learning group. If two students tie for first place, each receives five points. If two students tie for second place, each receives three points. In a three-way tie, each student receives four points. In a cooperative learning group of four members, the group could have between eight and twenty-four points total. The group that has the most points wins.

Determine the winning cooperative learning group. A team score for each cooperative group is derived by adding the scores of all the individual members. Team scores are then ranked and announced. The winning group is congratulated. When tournaments are used weekly, a *newsletter* can be used to announce the team standings. The newsletter can be distributed the day following the competition. Included in the newsletter could be the latest group standings for the grading period, the ranking of the cooperative groups on the previous day's tournament, and some commentary about the winners in each competitive triad and the performance of the members of the winning cooperative group.

Monitoring and Intervening

Monitoring Students' Behavior   After explaining the rules, procedures, and expected behaviors to students, you (the teacher) must observe to see that they are being followed. Much of the your time is spent observing students to see what problems they are having in competing appropriately. You move throughout the room, checking triads to make sure that students are understanding the process and answering questions, settling disputes over answers, and checking for the expected student behaviors. Some systematic and anecdotal record keeping will enhance the processing at the end of the lesson and is easily done by tallying on an observation sheet the number of times you see targeted desired behaviors and jotting down specific instances of appropriate behavior.

Providing Task Assistance   In monitoring the triads, you will wish to clarify instructions, review important procedures and rules, and teach task skills as necessary. As the teacher, you are the major resource for student learning and the judge and jury in settling disputes over which answer is correct. The major focus of the competitive triads should be on reviewing the previously learned material and not arguing over answers. The teacher's task assistance should focus attention on learning and minimize the importance of winning. Make sure that rules are followed, no one cheats, and disputes are settled quickly.

Intervening to Teach Competitive Skills   Students will have experience in competing but will often lack the skills to compete appropriately. Students may take the competition too seriously or feel so anxious that they do not enjoy it. Intervene to encourage the fun of competing or to de-emphasize the importance of winning when it seems necessary to do so. It is important that students learn to compete appropriately for fun and enjoyment. It strengthens cooperative learning when students can review previously learned material in a gamelike situation.

Providing Closure to the Lesson   At the end of the lesson, students should have adequately reviewed previously learned material so that they are able to contribute easily their learnings to future collaborative efforts.

Evaluating and Processing

Evaluating and Reinforcing the Quality and Quantity of Students' Learning   Within the competitive triads, students' performance needs to be evaluated by a norm-referenced procedure in which the three members are ranked from highest to lowest. Similarly, the cooperative learning groups are then evaluated by a norm-reference procedure.

Processing the Competition   It is important that competitions be discussed afterward to allow students to evaluate their skills, discuss their feelings, and realize how to behave even more appropriately next time. Processing may be done individually with students completing a questionnaire on their reactions and behavior, or it may be done in cooperative learning groups, competitive triads, or the whole class. An open and frank discussion of the competition can defuse hurt feelings and ensure increased constructiveness of future competitions.

Exercise 8.4   Teacher Role Checklist for Competitive Learning

1. What are the desired outcomes for the drill-review activity?
2. Is the classroom arranged so that
   - _____ Students are assigned to cooperative groups heterogeneous in previous performance levels?
   - _____ Students are assigned to competitive triads homogeneous in previous performance levels?
   - _____ Each triad has its set of materials (cards, answer sheet).

3. Have you effectively communicated to students that

_____ The instructional goal is relative (to win more points for one's group than competitors win for theirs)?

_____ Each student will be rewarded on the basis of how her or his work compares to the work of the other students in the competition triad?

4. Have you effectively communicated the expected patterns of student–student interaction? Do students know that they should

_____ Interact to check the progress of competitors and abide by the rules competition?

_____ Work on the assignment by trying to do the task better and faster than competitors?

_____ Perceive teacher praise or support of a competitor's work as an indication that their own work is inferior and teacher criticism of a competitor's work as an indication that their own work is superior?

_____ Ignore comments from other students?

_____ Go to the teacher for all help and assistance needed?

5. Have you effectively communicated the expected pattern of teacher–student interaction? Do students know that the teacher

_____ Wants each student to try to do better on the assignment than the other students and will evaluate students' work on the basis of how it compares with the work of other students?

_____ Will interact with each triad to clarify rules and the task without giving one student more help than another?

_____ Will praise and support students working alone and trying to do better, faster, and more work than any other student in the triad or classroom?

ESSENTIAL ELEMENTS OF COMPETITION

> *To say that "winning is everything" is ludicrous. I think it is good to lose every once in a while. I do not think there is anything wrong to having your backside handed to you every once in a while. Because you learn from it. You learn maybe you overlooked something, maybe you got carried away, maybe you were a little bit careless, maybe you did not make the commitment, or maybe someone is better than you. There is nothing wrong with that. In life you are going to find that some people are better than you.*
>
> Joe Paterno, Penn State Football Coach

When competitive situations are operationalized, eight basic elements must be included to ensure that competition is constructive (Johnson & Johnson, 1974, 1978, 1989) (also see Table 8.6).

Negative Interdependence

For competition to exist, there must be negative goal interdependence (that is, a negative correlation among participants' goals).

TABLE 8.6   Making Competition Constructive

Negative Interdependence	A negative correlation among participants' goals.
Broader context of positive interdependence	Competitions occur within a broader positive interdependence highlighting the mutual goal of conducting the competition.
Clear location	Where competition will take place.
Clear boundaries	When and how competition begins and ends (time, number of attempts, response criteria)
Clear criteria for winning	Ranking on quality or quantity of performance or time or number of attempts to reach criteria.
Clear rules of conduct	What actions are allowed or forbidden during the competition?
Intergroup competition	Intergroup (rather than interpersonal) competition provides support and assistance throughout the competition and reduces the negative effects of failure.
Appropriate tasks	Competition is appropriate when well-learned skills need to be practiced, well-learned material needs to be reviewed, or when simple, unitary/nondivisible, overlearned tasks need to be performed. When tasks are new or complex, competition is inappropriate.
Homogeneous grouping	Competitors must be carefully matched in terms of previous performance so they will believe that they have a reasonable chance of winning. If they believe that they have no chance of winning or can win with no effort, they exert little effort.
Oppositional interaction with social comparison	Competition is more fun in an ongoing relationship and where (a) participants directly interact and oppose each other's progress and (b) constant social comparisons make it clear who is winning.
Low importance of winning and losing	When competition is engaged in for fun and enjoyment, winning is incidental. When winning is considered of great importance, it generates high levels of anxiety that interfere with performance, especially when tasks are new and complex.
Appropriate use of competitive skills	Participants must play fair, be good winners and good losers, enjoy the competition (win or lose), monitor the progress of competitors, and not overgeneralize the results.

Broader Context of Positive Interdependence

The second element is a cooperative context (Johnson & Johnson, 1974, 1978, 1989). Competitions occur within a broader context of positive interdependence highlighting the mutual goal of conducting the competition. The cooperative context includes the specifics of the competition, such as where it is to take place, its boundaries (when it begins and ends), the criteria for winning, the rules of conduct, and the judges. If the underlying cooperative structure is not clearly and unambiguously established, then the competition will be destructive. Competitors must cooperate on when and where the competition is to take place, the boundaries of the competition (when it starts and ends), the criteria used to decide the winner(s), and the rules of conduct.

The *boundaries* may be specified in terms of (a) time (as in races to see how far competitors can run in twenty-four hours), (b) the number of attempts allowed to make the response (as in races where competitors are ranked on time it takes them to travel a certain distance or in golf where competitors are ranked on number of strokes required), or (c) response criteria that must be met for the contest to be concluded (as in games such as ping-pong where the first person to obtain 21 points wins). The *criteria for winning* must be clear to and accepted by all competitors so competitors can be ranked from best to worse. When competition is based on a period of time, the quantity or quality of the competitive response is used to rank competitors. If the contest ends when response criteria are met, ranking is based on time or the number of attempts required to reach the criteria. Because in a competition rewards are received only by one or a few of the participants, and the reward one receives depends on how highly one's response is ranked on a specified criterion, the criterion and the procedure for ranking must be clear, objective, and unbiased for competition to work. The *rules of conduct* must be clear to and accepted by all competitors. Rules should strictly control the interaction among competitors so competitors interact in planned ways and play fair. Ambiguity ruins competition and interferes with achievement as energy is directed toward worrying about what is fair and unfair, what the procedures actually are, and whether or not one's responses are better than those of others. This underlying foundation of cooperation keeps the competition in perspective and allows participants to enjoy the competition, win or lose. The stronger the cooperative foundation, the more constructive the competition.

Intergroup Competition

Competition may be interpersonal (individual students can compete to see who is best) or intergroup (cooperative learning groups can compete to see which group has best mastered the assigned material). *Intergroup competition, the third element, is a combination of intragroup cooperation and competition between groups.* It is important for the teacher to ensure that the intergroup competition does not become so strong that it outweighs the intragroup cooperation. Whereas interpersonal competition has many instructional drawbacks, intergroup competition can be used effectively under certain conditions. Intergroup competition provides support and assistance throughout the competition, increases the enjoyment of competition, diffuses responsibility for losing, and lowers the negative impact of failure.

Appropriate Tasks

The fourth element is an appropriate task. Competition should be used when well-learned skills need to be practiced, when well-learned material needs to be reviewed, or when simple, unitary/nondivisible (i.e., cannot be divided into subtasks), overlearned tasks need to be performed (Bond & Titus, 1983; Johnson & Johnson, 1974, 1989; Miller & Hamblin, 1963). When tasks are new or complex, competition is ineffective and inappropriate. The underlying reason that has been offered to explain why competition only enhances performance on simple, overlearned tasks is that competition increases anxiety, evaluation apprehension, and drive, which in turn increases the likelihood that the dominant or most probable response will occur. If the dominant response includes behaviors that lead to successful performance (as in the case of simple tasks), then people do better when in a high drive state. If the dominant response primarily includes behaviors that lead to poor performance (as in the case of difficult tasks), then people do worse when in a high drive state (Zajonc, 1965).

Homogeneous Matching of Participants

The fifth element is homogeneous matching in terms of ability and training. Competitors must believe that they have a reasonable chance of winning and losing. Motivation to achieve is based on the perceived likelihood of being able to achieve a challenging goal (Atkinson, 1965). Those who believe they cannot win will not try and those who believe that can win with minimal effort will not work hard (Halisch & Heckhausen, 1977; Hurlock, 1927; Lepley, 1937; Matthews, 1979; Tseng, 1969). Belief that one can win can exist only when competitors are evenly matched. Any stable pattern of winning or losing developed over time among competitors will tend to decrease the performance of all concerned (losers will give up and withdraw from the contest and winners will only work as hard as needed to win as their less effortful performances will continue to be reinforced). Competition increases concern with social comparisons of ability, especially when people perform well (Brown, 1990; Butler, 1993).

Oppositional Interaction with Monitoring of Other's Process and Social Comparison

The sixth element is ability to oppose actively and audit and monitor the relative progress of competitors. Competition is more fun when it is part of an ongoing relationship and conducted so that (a) participants directly interact and oppose each other's progress and (b) it is clear who is winning. Sports such as tennis, racketball, and soccer and games such as chess provide direct oppositional interaction that is fun and enjoyable. In competition, the only way individuals can judge their progress is by comparing themselves with their competitors. Social comparisons tend to facilitate performance on simple, unitary, nondivisible, overlearned tasks but hinder performance on complex tasks (Bond & Titus, 1983) and reduce uncertainty about one's ability and thus aid in self-evaluation (Festinger, 1954).

Low Importance of Winning

The seventh element is being relatively unimportant whether one wins or loses. When competition is engaged in for fun and enjoyment, winning is incidental. When winning is considered to be of great importance (symbolically a life or death matter), high levels of anxiety are the result (Blau, 1954; Deutsch, 1949b; Haines & McKeachie, 1967; Naught & Newman, 1966; Tseng, 1969). High anxiety tends to be beneficial when a task is extremely simple but interferes with performance when tasks are new and complex. It also contributes to a contingent process of determining self-worth. When winning becomes too important, most individuals are likely to perceive their performances as failures (Fait & Billings, 1978; Sherif, 1978) and losing promotes the development of "competition learned-helplessness" while winning can promote the development of "psychological burnout" (Roberts, 1980). Reeve and Deci

(1996) found that interpersonal pressure to win undermined intrinsic motivation. The greater the pressure to win, the more destructive the effects of competition on intrinsic motivation.

Competitive Skills

The eighth element of constructive competition is the appropriate use of competitive skills. Students in Midwest Middle School are learning how to build paper airplanes as part of a physics unit. Different designs are built and demonstrated in order for students to learn the principles of flight. As a fun change of pace, the teacher decides to have a competition to see which cooperative group can design the plane that flies the farthest, stays in the air the longest, is the most acrobatic, and is the most accurate. (Teachers who conduct such competitions may wish to add another category that brings elements of luck and humor into the competition.) The class then studies the winning designs and determines why the planes were so effective. Finally, each group has to build replicas of the winning designs.

Competition, when it is appropriate, is fun and adds spice to classroom life.[1] Because competition involves much less interaction among students and less coordination of behavior than cooperation, there are fewer skills essential to competing than to cooperating. Appropriate competition, however, does require several skills.

The first competitive skill is playing fair. This means students must understand and obey the rules. Rules should be clarified before the competition begins so students know what is and is not fair. In some competitions, for example, students are allowed to enhance their chances of winning by obstructing their opponents' progress (e.g., "sending" another player's ball away from the wicket in croquet), whereas in other competitions such disruption of opponents' progress would be declared unfair (e.g., cutting in too soon in a track race). If the rules are clear in the beginning students' actions will usually be appropriate. If any student feels it is necessary to break the rules, the situation is probably inappropriate for competition (e.g., the student perceives that the goal is too important and the situation is too serious).

A second skill is being a good winner and a good loser. This means winning with humility, pleasure, and modesty, and being gracious when you lose. Any student should be able to win or lose gracefully. Constructive competition is embodied in modesty in victory, graciousness in defeat, and the generosity of outlook that creates warm and lasting human relationships. *The third skill is enjoying the competition, win or lose.* The purpose of competition is to have an enjoyable experience drilling on previously learned material. *The fourth skill is monitoring the progress of competitors to know how one stands in the competition.* Because winning is the goal of competition,

---

[1]The two authors once decided that they had a reasonable chance to win a footrace with their father. At the time the two authors were four and five years old, and their father was twenty-seven. We decided that an old man of twenty-seven would not be very much competition! So we refused to come home for dinner, thinking he could never catch us. A short race and some swiftly administered physical aversive stimuli ended all motivation to race our father again in the future.

the only way to know where one stands is to know where the others are. Teachers can promote the development and use of monitoring skills by taking the following steps:

1. Make clear that monitoring is part of the competition and that students can watch each other's progress.
2. Set up several methods of monitoring including charting students' progress on the board, checking periodically to bring everyone up to date, and modifying the triads in which students compete.

The fifth skill is not to overgeneralize the results of the competition. Winning does not make a student a more worthwhile person and losing does not make a student less worthwhile. Being defeated in a spelling contest does not make a student a "loser." The results of any one competition provides very limited information about a student's personal worth. Clearly separating the results of competitions from one's view of oneself is an important competitive skill.

Reflection and Processing

At the end of each competition, students should reflect on their feelings and their use of competitive skills and discuss in their cooperative learning group how to behave more effectively in the next competition.

SUMMARY

Individuals should be able to cooperate, compete, and work autonomously appropriately (Johnson, 1970; Johnson & Johnson, 1989). Being able to compete for fun and enjoyment is an important competence. The major concern with the instructional use of competition is that students bring more to the competition than is intended by the teacher. Students may begin a competition with the attitude that they would "prefer to die" rather than be defeated. The anxiety produced in such students and the students around them is counterproductive. Competitions need to be kept light and fun, emphasizing review or drill, probably in a game format. Students should be homogeneously grouped so that they perceive themselves as having a chance to win, probably in threesomes to maximize the number of winners. The instructions, rules, procedures, and materials need to be clear and specific. The teacher needs to be the major resource for all students and the arbitrator of disputes. The major teacher role is to keep students focused on learning and not getting sidetracked by arguments or hurt feelings. Processing afterward is a vital part of teaching students to handle competition appropriately and enjoy it. Students need to learn how to win with enjoyment and lose with dignity. Students can be defeated, but are never "losers."

The importance of spreading an umbrella of cooperation over the class before competition is initiated cannot be overemphasized. Having students work together, get to know each other, cheer for shared successes, and develop collaborative skills, is the best foundation for making competition appropriate. In one of our teacher training sessions, a coach announced that he was not excited about cooperation. He preferred competition, believed in it, and liked to stress it with his teams. After several cooperative experiences we structured a competition involving vocabulary words, and the coach lost badly. After quiet reflection, he concluded, "I learned something about myself today. I have always hated to lose, but I found that I do not mind losing nearly as much when I lose to people I like." Building a strong cooperative learning environment may be the best way to provide a setting in which students can learn how to compete appropriately.

In addition to cooperative and competitive learning, lessons may be structured individualistically. That is the topic of the next chapter.

9

Structuring Individualistic Learning

NATURE AND APPROPRIATE USE OF INDIVIDUALISTIC LEARNING

Love many, trust few.
Learn to paddle your own canoe.

Stand on your own two feet.

Horatio Alger

You have just handed out a four-page programmed booklet on how to use a microscope. You explain, "For some of the things we are going to be doing, each student will need to know how to use a microscope. I will give each of you a microscope and the other things you will need to work through this booklet. Take your time and work carefully until you have mastered the tasks outlined in the booklet. Let me know if you need help with anything." You then see that each student has a microscope and a set of materials, and you begin to move from student to student to see how they are progressing. The goal structure described in this learning situation is individualistic. This chapter discusses the conditions under which individualistic learning can be appropriately used and details the teacher's role in structuring individualistic learning activities. Finally, the chapter examines the skills students need to function effectively in an individualistic learning situation.

Interdependence

Individualistic learning exists when the achievement of one student is unrelated to and independent from the achievement of other students; whether or not a student

TABLE 9.1   Appropriate Individualistic Learning

Interdependence	None.
Instructional tasks	Simple skill or knowledge acquisition; assignment is clear and behavior specified to avoid confusion and need for extra help.
Perception of goal importance	Goal is perceived as important for each student; students see tasks as worthwhile and relevant, and each student expects eventually to achieve the goal.
Student expectations	Each student expects to be left alone by other students, to work at own pace, to take a major part of the responsibility for completing the task, to take a major part in evaluating own progress and the quality of own efforts toward learning.
	Isolation, self-pacing, self-responsibility, self-evaluation.
Teacher–student interaction	Teacher is perceived to be the major source of assistance, feedback, reinforcement, and support.
Teacher statements	"Do not bother David while he is working." "Raise your hand if you need help." "Let me know when you are finished."
Student–student interaction	None; students work on their own with little or no interaction with classmates.
Student–materials interaction	Complete set of materials and instructions for each student. Rules, procedures, answers are clear. Adequate space for each student.
Room arrangement	Separate desks or carrels with as much space between students as can be provided.
Evaluation system	Criterion referenced.

achieves his or her goal has no bearing on whether other students achieve their goals (see Table 9.1). In other words, no interdependence results in a situation in which individuals work alone to reach a preset criteria of excellence. In such a situation, individuals

1. *Recognize they have an individual fate* unrelated to the fates of their peers.
2. *Strive for self-benefit* to do the best they can irrespective of how their peers perform.
3. *Have a short-term time perspective* focused on maximizing their performance.
4. *Recognize that their identity depends on how their performance compares* with the present criteria of excellence. Individuals expect to celebrate their individual success by themselves, with only their superiors (manager, teacher, or parent) emotionally involved in their performance. Individuals are basically indifferent to peers' successes or failures. Individuals do not cathect to their peers or the experience.
5. Recognize that their performance is *self-caused* by their own ability and effort. Individuals feel responsibility only to themselves and are invested in only their own success. They are obligated to the manager or teacher, but not to their peers. Individuals are not open to influence, are not *inducible* to their peers. Peers' actions do not substitute for individuals' actions.

Working alone does not marshal a number of motives into the service of productivity. Affiliation needs and the desire to be involved in relationships with others may operate directly against productivity in individualistic situations.

ESSENTIAL ELEMENTS OF INDIVIDUALISTIC SITUATIONS

God helps them that help themselves.

Benjamin Franklin

Individuals are more effective when they can appropriately cooperate, compete, and work autonomously on their own. Being able to work individualistically on one's own when it is appropriate is an important competence. Individualistic efforts, however, must be appropriately structured to avoid a number of problems and barriers.

Appropriate Tasks

Individualistic situations are most appropriate when unitary, nondivisible, simple tasks need to be completed, such as the learning of specific facts or the acquisition or the performance of simple skills. The directions for completing the learning task need to be clear and specific so that students do not need further clarification on how to proceed and how to evaluate their work. It is important to avoid confusion as to how the students are to proceed and the need for extra help from the teacher. If several students need help or clarification at the same time, work grinds to a halt. Finally, the learning goal must be perceived as important and students should expect to be successful in achieving those goals.

Importance of Goal: Relation to Cooperative Learning

Individualistically structured learning activities can supplement cooperative learning through a division of labor in which each student learns material or skills to be subsequently used in cooperative activities. Learning facts and simple skills to be used in subsequent cooperative learning projects increases the perceived relevance and importance of individualistic tasks. Within individualistic learning situations it is crucial that students perceive the task as relevant and worthwhile. Self-motivation is a key aspect of individualistic efforts. The more important and relevant students perceive the learning goal to be, the more motivated they will be to learn. Within classrooms, for example, students may individualistically learn facts and simple skills to be used subsequently in a cooperative project. Most divisions of labor are individualistic efforts within the context of an overall cooperative project. The goal must be perceived to be important enough so that concentrated effort is committed to achieving it. It is the overall cooperative effort that provides the meaning to individualistic work. It is contributing to the cooperative effort that makes individualistic goals important.

Be thou thine own home, and in thyself dwell. —*John Donne*

The man who goes alone can start today, but he who travels with another man must wait till the other is ready. —*Henry David Thoreau*

"If everybody minded their own business," said the Duchess in a hoarse growl, "the world would go around a deal faster than it does." —*Lewis Carroll*

God helps them that help themselves. —*Benjamin Franklin*

If a man does not keep pace with his companions, perhaps it is because he hears a different drummer. Let him step to the music he hears however measured or far away. —*Henry David Thoreau*

How many things which we cast to the ground, when others pick it up becomes a gem! —*George Meredith*

Raphael paints wisdom, Handel sings it, Phidias carves it, Shakespeare writes it, Wren builds it, Columbus sails it, Luther preaches it, Washington arms it, Watt mechanizes it. —*Ralph Waldo Emerson*

Teacher–Student Interaction

Within individualistic learning situations, the teacher is the major source of assistance, feedback, reinforcement, and support. Students should expect periodic visits from the teacher and a great deal of teacher time may be needed to monitor and assist the students.

Student–Materials Interaction

Each student needs a complete set of all necessary materials to complete the work individually. Each student has to be a separate, self-contained learner. Programmed materials, task cards, and demonstrations are among the techniques that can be used to facilitate the task. Provide separate desks or carrels, allowing as much space between students as possible.

Student-Student Interaction

No interaction should occur among students. Students should work on their own without paying attention to or interacting with classmates. Each student should have his or her own space and should be separated from other students. Since each student is working on his or her task at his or her own pace, student–student interaction is intrusive and not helpful.

Student Role Expectations

Students expect to be left alone by their classmates in order to complete the assigned task, to work at their own pace in their own space, to take responsibility for completing the task, to take a major part in evaluating their own progress and the quality of their efforts, to be successful in achieving the learning goal, and to perceive the learning goal to be important.

Evaluation System

Evaluation should be conducted on a criterion-referenced basis. Students should work on their own towards a criterion that is set so that every student could conceivably be successful. Everyone gets an A if each student earns it individually.

ESTABLISHING AN INDIVIDUALISTIC STRUCTURE

The essence of an individualistic goal structure is giving students individual goals and using a criterion-referenced evaluation system to assign rewards. In a ninth-grade English class, the students have been reading a cluster of novels centering on the building of the railroad in the western United States. The teacher has taught a unit on character analysis covering the need to find out about the appearance, personality, and perspective of major characters in a story. The teacher now explains to the class that the names of several people from the novels are in a box and each student to draw a name. The assignment is for students to spend the next few days finding out as much as possible about their characters by reading appropriate passages in the novels and by using any other resources they can find. At the end of the week, the class will have a number of discussions about the building of the railroad, and each student will be expected to introduce himself or herself and present the point of view of the selected. Until the discussion, students are to work on their own, each one gathering the necessary information on the fictional character; if students need help, they are to come to the teacher so as not to intrude on the work of classmates. The teacher will work with each student through the next few days to see that each has all the materials needed and has mastered the perspective of the character he or she has drawn so that all can each contribute to the discussions. The specific procedures for teachers to structure such an individualistic learning situation are given in the following paragraphs.

Objectives

1. Specifying instructional objectives. The academic objective needs to be specified at the correct level for each student and matched to the right level of instruction according to a conceptual or task analysis. Often the objective will be to learn specific information or a simple skill to be subsequently used in a cooperative learning situation. Examples include learning the bones and muscles of the arm and shoulder in order to teach it to classmates who are studying other parts of the body, learning the meaning of vocabulary words in order to compose a group story with more understanding, and gathering information for a section of a group report.

Decisions

2. Arranging the classroom. Adequate space must be provided for each student so that he or she can work without being interrupted by others. Examples of isolating students from looking at and being disrupted by classmates include using the perimeter of the classroom by having students face the wall, having students sit back to back, and staggering rows of seats.

3. Planning the instructional materials to promote independence. Structuring the materials to be used in the lesson is especially important for individualistic learning. Each student needs a set of self-contained materials, and usually, the materials need to contain a procedure for students to evaluate their own work. The programmed instruction format is often useful. The materials are the primary resource for learning in the individualistic situation.

Explaining the Task and Goal Structure

4. Explaining the academic task. The academic task needs to be explained in such a way that all students clearly understand what they are supposed to do, realize that they have all the materials they need, feel comfortable that they can do the task, and realize why they are doing the task. When assigning the academic task, teachers will

a. Set the task so that students are clear about the assignment. Instructions that are clear and specific are crucial in warding off student frustration.

b. Explain the objectives of the lesson and relate the concepts and information to be studied to students' past experiences and learning to maximize transfer and retention. Explaining the intended outcomes of the lesson increases the likelihood that students will focus on the relevant concepts and information throughout the lesson.

c. Define relevant concepts, explain procedures students should follow, and give examples to help students understand what they are to learn and to do in completing the assignment. To promote positive transfer of learning, point out the critical elements that separate this lesson from past learnings.

d. Ask the class specific questions to check the students' understanding of the assignment. Such questioning ensures that thorough two-way communication exists, that the assignment has been given effectively, and that the students are ready to begin completing it.

Students must perceive the task as relevant and have some idea of how the information and skills they are learning are going to be useful in future learning situations.

5. Structuring goal independence. Communicate to students that they have individual goals and must work individualistically. The basic individualistic goal is for students to work by themselves, at their own pace, to master the material specifically assigned to them, up to the preset criteria of excellence adjusted for their previous performances. Students should work by themselves without interrupting and interfering with the work of classmates. Students are to ask for assistance from the teacher, not from other students. Students who finish quickly should go beyond the specific assignment and find ways to embellish it.

6. *Structuring individual accountability.* The purpose of the individualistic goal structure is for students to attend to a specific task and master it on their own. Individual accountability may be structured by the teacher circulating through the room and randomly asking individual students to explain their work.

7. *Explaining criteria for success.* A criterion for excellence is set to orient students toward the level of mastery required in the lesson. Students need to know specifically what is an acceptable performance on the task that signifies that they have completed the task successfully. Setting a criteria ensures that students are aware that everyone who achieves up to criteria gets an "A" and, therefore, students are not in competition with each other. Whether one student does or does not learn the material does not affect the success of other students. Each student is rewarded separately on the basis of his or her own work.

8. *Specifying desired behaviors.* The word *individualistic* has different connotations and uses. Teachers need to define *individualistic* operationally by specifying the behaviors that are appropriate and desirable within the learning situation, including the following:

a. Work alone without interacting with other students.
b. Focus on the task and tune out everything else.
c. Monitor your time and pace yourself accordingly.
d. Check with the teacher for help.

Students need to know what behaviors are appropriate and desirable within an individualistic learning situation.

Monitoring and Intervening

9. *Monitoring students' behavior.* Much of the teacher's time should be spent observing students in order to see what problems they are having in completing the assignment and in working individualistically. The teacher should move throughout the room, checking students for understanding, answering questions, and checking for the expected student behaviors. The teacher needs to be active while students are working. Some teachers allow students to come to their desk for help, but some students may have to wait in line for assistance. It is more efficient for the teacher periodically to circulate through the classroom to assess the students' progress on their assigned tasks, how much the students understand, and what help each student needs to complete the assignment. This method allows teachers to work with students who are not requesting help as well as those who are. The teacher may wish to (a) observe the class as a whole to determine the number of students on task and exerting effort to achieve or (b) observe a few students intensely to obtain the data necessary for individual feedback and constructive suggestions on how to work more efficiently. Systematic observing provides feedback on how well the task is suited for individualistic work and how well students are working individualistically.

10. Providing task assistance. In monitoring individual students as they work, teachers will wish to clarify instructions, review important procedures and strategies for completing the assignment, answer questions, and teach task skills as necessary. After the materials provided, the teacher is the major resource for student learning. In discussing the concepts and information to be learned, teachers should use the language or terms relevant to the learning. Instead of saying, "Yes, that is right," teachers may wish to say something more specific to the assignment, such as, "Yes, that is the suggested way to solve for the unknown in an equation." The use of specific statements reinforces the desired learning and promotes positive transfer. Typically, considerable task assistance is required within individualistic learning situations.

11. Intervening to teach individualistic skills. Although it is likely that students have experience in working alone, many students lack some of the basic skills necessary to work well individualistically. While monitoring the class, teachers sometimes find students without the necessary individualistic skills to work effectively on their own. These skills will need to be taught. Some of the basic skills needed in an individualistic learning situation are these:

a. Clarifying the need to learn the material and making a personal commitment to learning it.
b. Tuning out extraneous noise and visual distractions and focusing in on the academic task.
c. Monitoring own progress and pacing self through the material. Charts and records are often helpful in evaluating one's progress.
d. Evaluating one's readiness to apply the material or skills being learned.

It is important that students learn to work autonomously on their own in the school setting. It strengthens cooperative learning when students can learn needed simple skills and factual information individualistically or participate successfully in a division of labor.

In an individualistic situation teachers should intervene as quickly as possible. The amount of time in which students are struggling to work more efficiently should be minimized.

12. Providing closure to the lesson. At the end of the lesson, students should be able to summarize what they have learned and to understand where they will use it in future lessons. To reinforce student learning, teachers may wish to summarize the major points in the lesson, ask students to recall ideas or give examples, and answer any final questions they may have.

Evaluation and Reinforcement

13. Evaluating and reinforcing the quality and quantity of students' learning. Student learning needs to be evaluated by a criterion-referenced system. Each student will be evaluated independently of other students. The teacher sets a standard as to how many points a student will receive for mastering the assigned material at different levels of proficiency and gives each student the appropriate grade. Having stu-

---

1. What are the desired outcomes for the activity of learning specific knowledge and noncomplex skills?

2. Is the classroom arranged so that students

   _____ Are isolated at separate desks or by a seating arrangement that separates them as much as possible?

   _____ Are arranged to do their own work without approaching or talking with each other?

   _____ Have individual sets of self-contained materials?

3. Have you effectively communicated to students that

   _____ The instructional goal is an individual goal (each student masters the material on his or her own)?

   _____ Each student will be rewarded on the basis of how his or her work meets a fixed set of standards for quality and quantity?

4. Have you effectively communicated the expected patterns of student–student interaction? Do students know that they

   _____ Should not interact with each other?

   _____ Should work on the assignment alone, trying to completely ignore the other students?

   _____ Should perceive teacher praise, support, or criticism of other students as irrelevant to their own mastery of the assigned materials?

   _____ Should go to the teacher for all help and assistance needed?

5. Have you effectively communicated the expected patterns of teacher–student interaction? Do students know that the teacher

   _____ Wants them to work by themselves and to master the assigned material without paying attention to other students, and will evaluate them on the basis of how their efforts match a fixed set of standards?

   _____ Will interact with each student individually, setting up learning contracts, viewing student progress, providing assistance, giving emotional support for effort, and answering questions individually?

   _____ Will praise and support students for working alone and ignoring other students?

FIGURE 9.1   Teacher Role Checklist for Individualistic Instruction

dents mark their progress on a chart is often helpful. Personal reinforcement needs to be given to each student. It is the teacher, not classmates, who gives praise for good work. (See Figure 9.1).

INDIVIDUALISTIC SKILLS

Because students do not interact with one another in an individualistic situation, learning under such a goal structure requires the fewest skills. Students need their own materials, enough space to be isolated from others, and a clear understanding of what they are supposed to do. The primary skill necessary is to be able to work on one's own, ignoring other students and not being distracted or interrupted by what other students are doing.

Besides being able to "tune out" noises, movement, and distractions, students need to clarify why they need to learn the information or skill, make a personal com-

mitment to do so, and assume responsibility for task completion. Each student must be motivated to complete the task and learn the assigned material on his or her own. Completing a task on one's own depends on the importance one assigns to mastering the material. The importance will probably be greatest when the results of the individualistic efforts are to be contributed to a group project in which students collaborate with each other. Having one's classmates depend on one for certain skills or facts increases one's motivation to learn them.

Third, students must be able to monitor their own progress, pace themselves through the material, and evaluate their own progress. Charts and records are often used to help students eval-

uate themselves. Self-tests are commonly used. Students must also be able to evaluate their readiness to apply the material or skills being learned.

Finally, students must take a personal pride and satisfaction from successfully completing individualistic assignments. Although teachers can provide students some recognition, support, and reinforcement for individualistic success, the students must learn to give themselves needed "pats on the back" for a job well done.

Individualistic Efforts and Personal Autonomy

Confusion often arises between individualistic efforts and personal autonomy. The admiration given to individuals who have a strong sense of personal autonomy and who are able to resist social pressure and act independently is often directed toward individualistic efforts. As will be discussed in depth in Chapter 10, individualistic efforts do not build personal autonomy. It is social support and caring personal relationships that do so. Individualistic efforts and personal autonomy are quite distinct and separate.

Problems In Implementing Individualistic Efforts

In implementing individualistic efforts there are potential problems that have to be faced and dealt with:

1. *Talking and interacting with others.* The more socializing and discussions that take place within an individualistic situation, the lower the productivity.
2. *Competing with others.* In U.S. society, persons working individualistically in the proximity of others doing similar work begin to compete.
3. *Complex or new tasks.* Individualistic work is most appropriate on simple skill- or knowledge-acquisition tasks. If the task is new or complex, individualistic efforts often are inadequate.

4. *Unimportant goal.* For many people it is hard to stay motivated while working alone. If the goal is perceived to be unimportant, attention will quickly wane, and effort will be small.

5. *Unclear rules and procedures.* Confusion leads to inaction. In individualistic situations clarification comes from authority figures who may or may not have time to explain the task and procedure again and again until it is understood.

6. *Lack of materials and resources.* In individualistic situations every person must be a self-contained unit. If needed materials and resources are lacking, then individualistic efforts grind to a halt.

7. *Lack of essential skills.*

SUMMARY

The basic elements of an individualistic goal structure include each student's working on his or her own toward a set criterion, having his or her own materials and space, perceiving the task as relevant and important, tuning out other students and distractions, and using the teacher as a resource. It is most appropriate to use the individualistic goal structure when the material to be learned is simple, straightforward, and needed for use in the near future. The jigsaw of materials in a cooperative group in which each group member is to research a different part of the topic and then help the group synthesize the different aspects of the subject into one group report is an example of where students see a need to learn material on their own. The primary skill necessary is to be able to work on one's own, ignoring other students (that is, not being distracted or interrupted by what other students are doing).

The teacher's role in an individualistic learning situation is to arrange the room so that students will not be distracted by each other, give students their individual set of materials, explain that students are to work alone and check only with the teacher when they need help, set a clear criterion for success that everyone could conceivably reach, ask students to work on their own (clarifying the relevance of the assignment for themselves, tuning out distractions, and monitoring their own progress and pacing), circulate among the students and monitor their work, intervene to teach skills or help students to refocus on their task, and give students time to evaluate how well they have learned.

10

Integrated Use of Cooperative, Competitive, and Individualistic Learning

APPROPRIATELY USING INTERDEPENDENCE

Teachers have to choose a goal structure, or a combination of goal structures, for each lesson they teach. Each goal structure has its place. In the ideal classroom all three are used. This does not mean, however, that they will all be used equally. The basic foundation of instruction is cooperation. The overall cooperative nature of instruction and learning has to be established before competitive and individualistic instruction can be used effectively. In other words, cooperation exists within the classroom on both a macro- and a microlevel.

Macro Cooperation: Classroom as Social System

On a macrolevel, instructional situations involve two complementary and interdependent roles, teacher and student. One cannot function or exist without the other. The teacher is expected to put students into contact with the subject matter, specify learning goals, create specific instructional conditions, discipline students, and evaluate students. Students are expected to be attentive, follow directions, exert effort to achieve assigned learning goals, arrive on time, and complete assignments. Successful completion of the school's objectives depends on the fulfillment of the organizational role requirements and adherence to the norms and values of the school.

When cooperation on this macrolevel breaks down, competitive and individualistic learning activities become completely ineffectual. If students refuse to be "role responsible," for example, no effective instruction can take place regardless of how interdependence among students is structured. It should also be noted that in order for competition to occur, participants must cooperate on rules, procedures, time, place, and criteria for determining the winner. Without this underlying cooperative system, no competition can take place. Skills and information learned individualistically, furthermore, must at some time be contributed to a collaborative effort. No skill is learned without being enacted within a social system such as a family or business. Nothing is produced without being part of a larger economic system. What is learned alone today is enacted in cooperative relationships tomorrow or else it has no meaning or purpose.

Microcooperation: Instructional Procedure

On the microlevel, cooperation is one of the three goal structures used to establish interdependence among students. Cooperative learning is a standard instructional practice. Of the three goal structures, it is the most complex to implement, yet it has the most powerful impact on instructional outcomes. In addition, it provides a context for the other two goal structures. Competition, as noted earlier, cannot exist without underlying cooperation concerning rules and procedures. Most competitions have referees, umpires, judges, and teachers present to ensure that the basic cooperation overrules and procedures do not break down. Individualistic activities can be effectively used as part of the division of labor in which students master certain knowledge and skills that will later be used in cooperative activities. Competitive and individualistic learning should be used to supplement the basic cooperation among students. When the three goal structures are used appropriately and in an integrated way, the combination may be more powerful than any one of them employed separately.

FREQUENCY OF USE OF EACH GOAL STRUCTURE

A teacher may wish to teach certain lessons cooperatively and others competitively or individualistically. Most teachers spend a large proportion of this time in promoting higher-level conceptual reasoning and problem-solving skills that give maximal thinking experience to the students, tasks that are best served by a cooperative goal structure. To a lesser extent, there are important and specific skills and knowledge that students may master by studying under an individualistic goal structure. Tasks calling for a drill or a review of facts may be learned under a competitive goal structure. Ideally, a cooperative goal structure may be used 60 to 70 percent of the time, an individualistic goal structure 20 percent of the time, and a competitive goal structure 10 to 20 percent of the time. With students now perceiving school as predominantly competitive, and with cooperation being used systematically in very few classrooms, your task in training students to function primarily within a cooperative goal structure and to shift quickly from one goal structure to another will not be an easy one at first.

INTEGRATED USE OF ALL THREE GOAL STRUCTURES

All three methods of structuring interdependence among students may be used in an integrated way within classrooms. A typical schedule for doing so is as follows:

1. Assign students to heterogeneous cooperative learning groups.
2. Give each member an individual assignment of learning a subsection of the material the group needs to complete its assignment.
3. Give each group a cooperative assignment of learning all of the material, with each member presenting their subsection to the entire group.
4. Conduct a competitive tournament to drill students on the material they have just learned.
5. Give a cooperative assignment to use the material learned to complete a group project.
6. Give an achievement test, which each student takes individually, and determine a group score on the basis of the performance of all group members.

EXAMPLE OF AN INTEGRATED UNIT

Tasks: Overview

1. Learn twenty-four vocabulary words.
2. Write a story using 90 percent of the assigned vocabulary words appropriately and correctly.

Cooperation

1. Students are assigned to four-person, heterogeneous, cooperative learning groups.
2. Each group is given the cooperative assignment of (a) writing one story (containing contributions from all group members) in which 90 percent of the assigned vocabulary words are used appropriately and correctly and (b) learning the assigned vocabulary words.
3. A list of twenty-four vocabulary words is given to each group. Each group member is given the assignments of (a) mastering six of the vocabulary words and planning how to teach the six words to the other group members and (b) learning all twenty-four vocabulary words.

Individualistic: Learning Subset of Vocabulary Words

Each student learns his or her assigned vocabulary words and plans how to teach them to the other members of his or her learning group.

Cooperative: Teaching and Learning Vocabulary Words

Tasks: Each group member (a) teaches his or her words to the other group members and (b) learns his or her words.

Cooperative: Ensure all group members master all vocabulary words to a recall level.

Evaluation: A 95 percent mastery to recall level by all members is considered excellent.

Individual accountability: All group members have to score 95 percent correct on the vocabulary test.

Expectations: All members will clarify definitions and assist each other's learning.

Intergroup Competition

Tasks: Review vocabulary words in a game format to increase readiness to use words properly in a story while having fun doing so.

Competitive: Students are assigned to homogeneous (in terms of the previous achievement) triads. The competitive goal is to define accurately more words than anyone else in the triad in order to gain points for one's group.

Evaluation: The student who defines the most words correctly wins in the competitive triad. The cooperative group with the most points wins the class competition.

Expected behaviors: All members will obey the rules, challenge appropriately, be a gracious winner or loser.

Cooperative

Task: Write a story using 95 percent of the assigned vocabulary words and at least three new words created from the prefixes, suffixes, and root words assigned.

Cooperative: The group will prepare one story. Members will sign off on the assignment to indicate they have contributed and are proud of the story.

Individual accountability: One member will be randomly selected to read the group's story and explain it.

Evaluation: Each story is evaluated and all group members receive the same grade based on the quality of their story. To be excellent the story has to include 95 percent of the assigned words used and three new words, it should have a planned plot and reasonable story-line flow (a beginning, plot development, and an ending), it should be entertaining to listen to, and it must not have any basic grammatical or punctuation errors.

Expectations: Everyone participates, contributes, invents at least one new word, encourages and supports each other's participation and efforts to contribute.

Individualistic

Each student takes a test on the vocabulary words. Each student receives an individual grade based on his or her mastery of the words. If everyone in the group scores 90 percent or higher on the test, each member will receive five bonus points.

Cooperative: Group Processing

Learning groups process how well they worked together and what they could do to improve.

HELPFUL HINTS FOR CONDUCTING INTEGRATED UNITS

1. *Emphasize the underlying cooperation.* The individualistic and competitive aspects of the unit are supplements to the overall cooperation among students. Individualistic and competitive learning activities should enhance but not detract from cooperative learning.

2. *Begin and end with a group meeting.* At the initial group meeting, the division of labor or "jigsaw" may be agreed on and the group's goal for success is emphasized. During the final meeting students should discuss how well the group functioned.

3. *Remember that students will bring more to the competition than you want them to.* They will want to make more of winning the competition than is appropriate. Remember to keep the reward for winning minor. In the students' past, winning has too often been viewed as a life-or-death matter. You will have to teach students to compete appropriately for fun. You may wish to have a class discussion about how enjoyable the competition was.

4. *Vary the number of instructional sessions according to the unit.* The individualistic assignments could be done as homework. Cooperative tasks could take more than one class session.

CONCLUSIONS

Competitive and individualistic learning will not reach their full potential unless they are used in a strong cooperative context. It is the integrated use of all three types of goal structures that releases their full power and makes each most effective. An essential issue that has not been fully discussed is assessment. The next chapter, therefore, examines the inherent relationship between cooperative learning and the effectiveness of assessment practices.

11

Reflections

CHANGING PARADIGM OF TEACHING

I'm just a cowhand from Arkansas, but I have learned how to hold a team together.
How to life some men up, how to calm down others, until finally they've got one heartbeat
together, a team. There's just three things I'd ever say:
If anything goes bad, I did it.
If anything goes semi-good, then we did it.
If anything goes real good, then you did it.
That's all it takes to get people to win football games for you.

Bear Bryant, former football coach for the University of Alabama

Can schools outperform the dinosaurs? Like all organizations, schools must adapt to changes in their environment or risk fading away like the dinosaurs. The dinosaurs presumably made good day-to-day adaptations to their environment. They probably made a pretty good choice of what leaves to eat from what trees and selected the most desirable swamps in which to slosh. At a tactical level of decision, we have no reason to believe that these giant beasts were not reasonably competent. But when faced with major changes in the earth's climate and the resulting changes in plant and other animal life, the dinosaurs were unable to make the fundamental changes required to adapt to the new environmental conditions. Schools may now be faced with new environmental conditions that require them to do what the dinosaurs could not. Schools need to make fundamental changes in the ways students are instructed. The changes are known as the new paradigm of teaching.

TABLE 11.1   Comparison of Old and New Paradigms of Teaching

FACTOR	OLD PARADIGM OF TEACHING	NEW PARADIGM OF TEACHING
Knowledge	Transferred from faculty to students	Jointly constructed by students and faculty
Students	Passive vessel to be filled by the faculty's knowledge	Active constructor, discoverer, transformer of own knowledge
Faculty purpose	Classify and sort students	Develop students' competencies and talents
Relationships	Impersonal relationships among students and between faculty and students	Personal transaction among students and between faculty and students
Context	Competitive/individualistic	Cooperative learning in classroom and cooperative teams among faculty
Assumption	Any expert can teach	Teaching is complex and requires considerable training

Cooperative learning is part of a broader paradigm shift that is occurring in teaching. Essential elements of this paradigm shift are presented in Table 11.1 (Johnson, Johnson, & Holubec, 1992; Johnson, Johnson, & Smith, 1991).

The *old paradigm of teaching* is based on John Locke's assumption that the untrained student mind is like a blank sheet of paper waiting for the instructor to write on it. Student minds are viewed as empty vessels into which teachers pour their wisdom. Because of these and other assumptions, teachers think of teaching in terms of these principal activities:

1. *Transferring knowledge from teacher to students.* The teacher's job is to give it; the student's job to is to get it. Teachers transmit information that students are expected to memorize and then recall.

2. *Filling passive empty vessels with knowledge.* Students are passive recipients of knowledge. Teachers own the knowledge that students memorize and recall.

3. *Classifying students by deciding who gets which grade and sorting students into categories* by deciding who does and does not meet the requirements to be graduated, go on to college, and get a good job. There is constant inspection to weed out any "defective" students. Teachers classify and sort students into categories under the assumption that ability is fixed and is unaffected by effort and education.

4. *Conducting education within a context of impersonal relationships among students and between teachers and students.* Based on the Taylor model of industrial organizations, students and teachers are perceived to be interchangeable and replaceable parts in the education machine.

5. *Maintaining a competitive organizational structure* in which students work to outperform their classmates and teachers work to outperform their colleagues.

6. *Assuming that anyone with expertise in their field can teach without training to do so.* This is sometimes known as the content premise—if you have a Ph.D. in the field, you can teach.

The old paradigm is to transfer the teacher's knowledge to a passive student so that teachers can classify and sort students in a norm-referenced, competitive way. The assumption was that if you have content expertise, you can teach. Many teachers consider the old paradigm the only alternative. Lecturing while requiring students to be passive, silent, isolated, and in competition with each other seems the only way to teach. The tradition of the old paradigm is carried forward by sheer momentum, while almost everyone persists in the hollow pretense that all is well. All is not well. Teaching is changing. The old paradigm of teaching is being dropped for a new paradigm.

The *new paradigm of teaching* is based on the theory and research that have clear applications to instruction. Educators perhaps should think of teaching in terms of several principal activities.

First, knowledge is constructed, discovered, transformed, and extended by students. Teachers create the conditions within which students can construct meaning from the material studied by processing it through existing cognitive structures and then retaining it in long-term memory where it remains open to further processing and possible reconstruction.

Second, students actively construct their own knowledge. Learning is conceived of as something a learner does, not something that is done to a learner. Students do not passively accept knowledge from the teacher or curriculum. Students activate their existing cognitive structures or construct new ones to subsume the new input.

Third, teacher effort is aimed at developing students' competencies and talents. Student effort should be inspired and secondary schools must add value by cultivating talent. A "cultivate and develop" philosophy must replace a "select and weed out" philosophy. Students' competencies and talents are developed under the assumption that with effort and education, any student can improve.

Fourth, education is a personal transaction among students and between the teachers and students as they work together. All education is a social process that cannot occur except through interpersonal interaction (real or implied). Learning is a personal but social process that results when individuals cooperate to construct shared understandings and knowledge. Teachers must be able to build positive relationships with students and to create the conditions within which students build caring and committed relationships with each other. The school then becomes a learning community of committed scholars in the truest sense. The more difficult and complex the learning, the harder students have to struggle to achieve, the more important the social support students need. There is a general rule of instruction: The more pressure placed on students to achieve and the more difficult the material to be learned, the more important it is to provide social support within the learning situation. Challenge and social support must be balanced if students are to cope successfully with the stress inherent in learning situations.

Fifth, all of the above can only take place within a cooperative context. When students interact within a competitive context, communication is minimized, misleading and false information often is communicated, helping is minimized and viewed as cheating, and classmates and faculty tend to be disliked and distrusted. Competitive and individualistic learning situations, therefore, discourage the active construction of knowledge and the development of talent by isolating students and creating negative relationships among classmates and with teachers. Classmates and teachers need to be viewed as collaborators rather than as obstacles to the student's own academic and personal success. Teachers, therefore, structure learning situations so that students work together cooperatively to maximize each other's achievement. Ideally, administrators would in turn create a cooperative, team-based organizational structure within which faculty work together to ensure each other's success (Johnson & Johnson, 1994).

Sixth, teaching is assumed to be a complex application of theory and research that requires considerable teacher training and continuous refinement of skills and procedures. Becoming a good teacher takes at least one lifetime of continuous effort to improve.

The primary means of achieving the new paradigm of teaching is to use cooperative learning. Cooperative learning provides the means of operationalizing the new paradigm of teaching and provides the context within which the development of student talent is encouraged. Carefully structured cooperative learning ensures that students are cognitively, physically, emotionally, and psychologically actively involved in constructing their own knowledge and is an important step in changing the passive and impersonal character of many classrooms. Cooperative learning may be used in three ways: formally, informally, and in base groups (see Figure 11.1). In addition, the power of cooperative learning may be enhanced by the appropriate use of competitive and individualistic learning activities.

USING COOPERATIVE LEARNING APPROPRIATELY

The appropriate use of cooperative learning involves implementing the five basic elements into formal and informal cooperative learning and cooperative base groups. The five basic elements are positive interdependence so that students believe in their hearts that they are responsible for each other's learning as well as their own, individual accountability so that students do their fair share of the work, face-to-face interaction in which students promote each other's learning by assisting and encouraging, appropriately using the interpersonal and small-group skills needed to work together effectively, and processing how well they are working together and what they could do to improve. These basic elements are what separates cooperative learning from traditional learning groups.

The *first step* in mastering the use of cooperative learning is to gain expertise in using formal cooperative learning. The *second step* is gaining expertise in using informal cooperative learning and cooperative base groups.

Formal Cooperative Learning

Formal cooperative learning groups may last for several minutes to several class sessions to complete a specific task or assignment (such as solving a set of problems,

SOCIAL INTERDEPENDENCE

Cooperative	Competitive	Individualistic

RESEARCH: WHY USE COOPERATIVE LEARNING

Effort to Achieve	Positive Relationships	Psychological Health

FIVE BASIC ELEMENTS

Positive Interdependence	Individual Accountability	Promotive Interaction	Social Skills	Group Processing

COOPERATIVE LEARNING

FORMAL COOP LEARNING	INFORMAL COOP LEARNING	COOP BASE GROUPS
Make preinstructional decisions	Conduct introductory focused discussion	Opening class meeting to check homework, ensure members understand academic material, complete routine tasks such as attendance
Explain task and cooperative structure	Conduct intermittent pair discussions every ten or fifteen minutes	Ending class meeting to ensure members understand academic material, homework assignment
Monitor learning groups and intervene to improve taskwork and teamwork	Conduct closure-focused discussion	Members help and assist each other, learn in between classes
Assess student learning and process group effectiveness		Conduct semester or year–long school or class service projects

COOPERATIVE SCHOOL

Teaching Teams	Site-Based Decision Making	Faculty Meetings

CONSTRUCTIVE CONFLICT

STUDENTS			FACULTY	
Academic Controversy	Negotiating, Mediating		Decision-Making Controversy	Negotiating, Mediating

CIVIC VALUES

Work for Mutual Benefit, Common Good	Equality of All Members	Trusting, Caring Relationships	View Situations from All Perspectives	Unconditional Worth of Self, Diverse Others

FIGURE 11.1 Cooperative Learning

completing a unit, writing a report or theme, conducting an experiment, and reading and comprehending a story, play, chapter, or book). Any course requirement or assignment may be reformulated to be cooperative rather than competitive or individualistic through the use of formal cooperative learning groups. The teacher's role in using formal cooperative learning includes the following:

1. Making preinstructional decisions.
2. Explaining the instructional task and the cooperative structure.
3. Monitoring the learning groups and intervening when necessary to improve students' teamwork and taskwork.
4. Assessing the quality and quantity of student learning, evaluating periodically, and ensuring the learning groups process how well they are working together and how they could improve their effectiveness.

Gaining expertise in using formal cooperative learning groups provides the foundation for gaining expertise in using informal cooperative learning and cooperative base groups.

Informal Cooperative Learning

Informal cooperative learning groups are temporary, ad hoc groups that last for only one discussion or one class period. Their *purposes* are to focus student attention on the material to be learned, to create an expectation set and mood conducive to learning, to help organize in advance the material to be covered in a class session, to ensure that students cognitively process the material being taught, and to provide closure to an instructional session. They may be used at any time, but they are especially useful during a lecture or direct teaching.

During direct teaching the instructional challenge for the teacher is to ensure that students do the intellectual work of organizing material, explaining it, summarizing it, and integrating it into existing conceptual networks. This may be achieved by having students do the advance organizing, use cognitive processes to better understand what they are learning, and provide closure to the lesson. Breaking up lectures with short cooperative processing times will reduce lecture time, but it will enhance what is learned and build relationships among the students in your class. It will help counter what is proclaimed as the main problem of lectures: "The information passes from the notes of the teacher to the notes of the student without passing through the mind of either one."

1. *Focused Discussion 1:* Direct teaching begins with a focused discussion aimed at promoting *advance organizing* of what the students know about the topic to be presented and creates an *expectation set* and a learning mood conducive to learning. The lecture should be planned around a series of questions that students discuss in triads or pairs.
2. *Turn-to-Your-Partner Discussions:* The lecture is divided into ten to fifteen minute segments. A short discussion task is given to pairs of students after each segment. The task needs to be short enough for students to complete it within three or four minutes. Its purpose is to ensure that students actively think about the material being presented.

Each discussion task has four components: *formulating* an answer to the question being asked, *sharing* your answer with your partner, *listening* carefully to his or her answer, and to *creating* a new answer that is superior to each member's initial formulation through the processes of association, building on each other's thoughts, and synthesizing. Students will need to gain some experience with this procedure to become skilled in doing it within a short period of time.

3. *Focused Discussion 2:* At the end of the lecture a student discussion provides closure. Students have four or five minutes to summarize and discuss the material covered in the lecture. The discussion (a) requires students to integrate what they have just learned into existing conceptual frameworks and (b) prepares students for the homework and what will be presented in the next class session.

Informal cooperative learning gets students actively involved in processing what they are learning. It also provides time for you as their teacher to gather your wits, reorganize your notes, take a deep breath, and move around the class listening to what students are saying. Listening to student discussions provides you with direction and insight into (a) students' levels of reasoning and (b) how the concepts you are teaching are being grasped by your students.

Base Groups

Base groups are long-term, heterogeneous cooperative learning groups with stable membership. *The primary responsibility of members is to provide each other with the support, encouragement, and assistance they need to make academic progress.* The base group verifies that each member is completing the assignments and progressing satisfactorily through the academic program. Base groups may be given the task of letting absent group members know what went on in the class when they miss a session and bring them up to date. The use of base groups tends to improve attendance, personalize the work required and the school experience, and improve the quality and quantity of learning. The base group provides permanent and caring peer relationships in which students are committed to and support each other's educational success. Long-term caring and committed relationships provide students with the support, help, encouragement, and assistance they need to make academic progress and develop cognitively and socially in healthy ways.

Summary

When used in combination, formal and informal cooperative learning and cooperative base groups provide an overall structure to classroom life. Additional variety can be instituted by occasionally using competitive and individualistic learning.

INTEGRATED USE OF ALL THREE GOAL STRUCTURES

The *third step* in increasing your expertise in using cooperative learning is to supplement it occasionally with appropriate competitive and individualistic learning.

Besides structuring learning cooperatively (so that students work in small groups to ensure that all members master the assigned material), teachers may periodically have students compete (so students engage in win–lose activities to see who is best) or work individualistically (so that each student works on his or her own to achieve his or her own learning goals). For each lesson taught, teachers must decide which goal structure or which combination of goal structures to use. Teachers full instructional potential is released when they use all three goal structures in an integrated way. Although the dominant goal structure within any classroom should be cooperation (which ideally would be used about 60 to 70 percent of the time), competitive and individualistic efforts are useful supplements. Competition may be used as a fun change of pace during an instructional unit that is predominantly structured cooperatively, and individualistic learning is often productive when the information learned is subsequently used in a cooperative activity.

Competitive Learning

Competition exists when an individual can attain his or her goal if and only if the other participants cannot attain their goals. This negative goal interdependence causes individuals to seek an outcome that is personally beneficial but detrimental to all others in the situation. Competition is based on perceived scarcity and requires social comparisons. Competitions vary as to how many winners will result, the criteria used to select a winner, and the way contestants interact. In the 1930s, 1940s, 1950s, and even during most of the 1960s, competitive learning was seen as the answer to education's problems. Lessons were supposed to pit students against each other with the intensity of a 100-yard dash, each class was supposed to be normatively evaluated on a normal curve, and class rank was the total summary of a student's academic performance. In addition to its advocates, however, competition has its critics. Many of the critics, such as John Holt, disagreed on philosophical grounds. Michaels (1977) concluded that competitive learning produced superior achievement when compared to cooperative learning. Alphie Kohn (1992) concluded that all competition is destructive and should never be used in instructional situations. W. Edwards Demming labeled competition as a "force for destruction" that must be eliminated in all its forms in organizations (Walton, 1986). There are numerous destructive outcomes of traditional competition in schools: students can become highly anxious about whether they will be perceived as winners or losers, they can become overly focused on extrinsic rewards and motivation to the exclusion of learning, and they can become involved in negative relationships with classmates and faculty.

Competition in learning situations is constructive only under a set of very narrow conditions:

1. Clear negative goal interdependence.
2. Context of strong positive goal interdependence, which means that the location of the competition, the competition's boundaries (when it will begin and end), the criteria for winning, and the rules of conduct are all clear and unambiguous.

3. The task involves practicing well-learned skills, reviewing well-learned material, or performing simple, unitary/nondivisible, overlearned tasks. When tasks are new or complex, competition is inappropriate.

4. Competitors are carefully matched in terms of previous performance so they believe they have a reasonable chance of winning.

5. There is oppositional interaction with social comparisons. Competition is more fun in an ongoing relationship and in which (a) participants directly interact and oppose each other's progress and (b) constant social comparisons make it clear who is winning.

8. Competitive skills are used appropriately. Participants must play fair, be good winners and good losers, enjoy the competition (win or lose), monitor the progress of competitors, and not overgeneralize the results.

The importance of spreading an umbrella of cooperation over the class before competition is initiated cannot be overemphasized. Having students work together, get to know each other, cheer for shared successes, and develop collaborative skills, is the best foundation for making competition appropriate. Building a strong cooperative learning environment may be the best way to provide a setting in which students can learn how to compete appropriately. Students need to develop the important competence of being able to compete for fun and enjoyment.

Individualistic Learning

Individualistic learning exists when the achievement of one student is unrelated to and independent from the achievement of other students; whether or not a student achieves his or her goal has no bearing on whether other students achieve their goals. Individualistic efforts are based on independence and isolation from others.

The use of competitive and individualistic efforts has been controversial. In the 1960s, 1970s, and early 1980s, individualistic learning had numerous advocates, including B. F. Skinner. Individualistic learning was seen as a way to correct the faults of competition and to apply behavioral psychology to learning situations. Slavin (1977) concluded individualistic learning promoted higher achievement than did cooperative learning. There were also critics (such as Urie Bronfrenbrenner [1970]) who labeled individualistic and competitive learning as "forces for isolation and alienation" that cause, reinforce, and perpetuate psychological pathology.

Individualistic learning is appropriate under the following conditions:

1. When no interdependence is structured among students.

2. When unitary, nondivisible, simple tasks need to be completed, such as the learning of specific facts or the acquisition or performance of simple skills.

3. When material to be learned is for use in the near future in a cooperative assignment. An example is the jigsaw of materials in a cooperative group in which each group mem-

ber is to research a different part of the topic and then help the group synthesize the different aspects of the subject into one group report.

4. When learning goals are important. For many students, it is hard to stay motivated while working alone. If the goal is perceived to be unimportant, attention will quickly wane and effort will be small.

5. When rules and procedures are clear. Confusion leads to inaction. Because the teacher is the single source of clarification of the task and procedures, the initial instructions need to be clear.

6. When enough materials and resources are available for each student. In individualistic situations, every person must be a self-contained unit. If needed materials and resources are lacking, then individualistic efforts grind to a halt.

7. When individuals can learn from working alone, without interacting or monitoring other students.

8. When the use of individualistic skills is appropriate. These skills include (a) being able to work on one's own by ignoring other students without being distracted or interrupted by what other students are doing, (b) monitoring one's own progress, pacing oneself through the material, and evaluating one's own progress, (c) taking personal pride and satisfaction from successfully completing the assignments.

Summary

The conditions under which competitive and individualistic learning may be constructive are best met when they are within the context of cooperation. What is learned cooperatively can be reviewed in a fun and energetic competition. When students need simple skills and knowledge to contribute to a cooperative effort, individualistic learning may be helpful. The format for integrating the three goal structures is as follows. Students meet in cooperative learning groups and begin working on a task. The simple skills and knowledge needed to complete the assignment are identified and assigned to different group members. Each member works individualistically to learn his or her part of the material. The group then continues the cooperative work with members contributing their resources to the joint effort. As a fun change of pace an intergroup competition is conducted in which students compete with members of other groups in a gamelike, tournament format. Winning or losing does not affect their grades. Finally, the cooperative group completes the assignment, hands it in, and the overall learning of members is assessed and evaluated. Lessons always begin and end with cooperative efforts.

Exercise 11.1   *Conditions for Effective Learning*

Given below is a list of conflicts for effective learning. Working in pairs, decide whether each is a condition for effective

    1. Cooperative learning   2. Competitive learning   3. Individualistic learning

_____ Students exhibit clear, positive interdependence.

_____ Students exhibit clear, negative interdependence.

_____   Student behavior is clear, showing no interdependence.

_____   The task is unitary, nondivisible, simple.

_____   The task is complex, difficult.

_____   Students practice well-learned skills and review well-learned material.

_____   Individuals are accountable for doing their work.

_____   Students are grouped with classmates who have achieved the same level.

_____   Individuals work alone, interacting with or monitoring others.

_____   Students use interpersonal and small-group skills appropriately.

_____   Students monitor and compare their progress with others' progress.

_____   Students ignore others.

_____   Students promote each other's progress and learning.

_____   Students obstruct each other's progress and learning.

_____   Each student has a self-contained set of materials and instructions.

TEACHING STUDENTS SOCIAL SKILLS

In addition to using cooperative, competitive, and individualistic learning in competent ways, teachers will wish to teach students social skills. There are many sources for teaching further social skills to students, including *Learning to Lead Teams* (Johnson & Johnson, 1997), *Advanced Cooperative Learning* (Johnson, Johnson, & Holubec, 1992), *Reaching Out* (Johnson, 1997), and *Joining Together* (Johnson & F. Johnson, 1997).

UTILIZING CREATIVE CONFLICT

A cooperative foundation for learning cannot be maintained unless conflicts are encouraged and managed constructively. Cooperation and conflict go hand in hand. The more group members care about achieving the group's goals, and the more they care about each other, the more likely they are to have conflicts with each other. How conflict is managed largely determines how successful cooperative efforts tend to be. To ensure that conflicts are managed constructively, students must be taught two procedures and sets of skills:

1. *Use academic controversies to facilitate achievement and cognitive and social development* (Johnson & Johnson, 1995b). To maximize academic learning and higher-level reasoning, engage students in intellectual conflicts. Organize students into cooperative learning groups of four. Divide them into two pairs. Give one pair the pro position and the other the con position on the issue being studied. Students research and prepare positions, make a persuasive presentation of their position, refute the opposing position while rebutting attacks on their own position, view the issue from both perspectives, and create a synthesis or integration of the best reasoning on both sides.

2. *Implement the peacemaker program* (Johnson & Johnson, 1995a). First, you teach students what is and is not a conflict. Second, you teach students how to engage in problem-solving negotiations. Students are taught to state what they want and how they feel, explain why they want and feel as they do, accurately understand the opposing perspective, create a number of optional agreements that maximize joint outcomes, and reach an agreement as to which option to adopt. Third, you teach students how to mediate. When students cannot successfully negotiate a constructive resolution to their conflicts, mediators are available to end hostilities, ensure commitment to the mediation process, facilitate negotiations, and formalize the agreement.

The combination of knowing how to manage intellectual disagreements and how to negotiate or mediate conflicts among students' wants, needs, and goals ensures that the power of cooperative efforts will be maximized. The productivity of learning groups increases dramatically when members are skilled in how to manage conflicts constructively.

EMPOWERING STAFF THROUGH COOPERATIVE TEAMS

Once skillful cooperation and constructive conflict resolution are pervasive, teachers need to create a cooperative school. What is good for students is even better for staff. A cooperative school is one in which cooperative learning dominates the classroom and cooperative teams dominate staff efforts (Johnson & Johnson, 1994). It is social support from and accountability to valued peers that motivates committed efforts to succeed. Empowering individuals through cooperative teams is done in three ways: (a) **colleagial teaching teams** (to increase teachers' instructional expertise and success), (b) **task forces** (to plan and implement solutions to schoolwide issues and problems such as curriculum adoptions and lunchroom behavior), and (c) **ad hoc decision-making groups** (to use during faculty meetings to involve all staff members in important school decisions). How to structure and use these three types of cooperative teams may be found in Johnson and Johnson (1994).

CREATING A LEARNING COMMUNITY

Frances Hodgson Burnett, in her book *The Secret Garden,* stated, "Where you tend a rose, a thistle cannot grow." Schools should tend roses. They do so by creating a learning community characterized by cooperative efforts to achieve meaningful goals. In a recent review of the research (*Within Our Reach: Breaking the Cycle of Disadvantage*), Lisbeth Schorr concluded that the most important attribute of effective schools is caring. Educational historians David Tyack and Elizabeth Hansot (1985) concluded that the theme that runs through all successful schools is that students, teachers, administrators, and parents share a sense of community and a "socially integrating sense of purpose."

A *community* is a limited number of people who share common goals and a common culture. The smaller the community, the more personal the relationships, and the greater the personal accountability. Everyone knows everyone else. Relationships are long-term and have a future rather than being temporary brief encounters. Instruction becomes personalized. The students are thought of as citizens, whereas the teachers are thought of as the community leaders. A sense of belonging tends to boost the desire to learn. The learning community becomes an extended family where mutual achievement and caring for one another are important. With citizenship in the community comes an ethical code that includes certain rules, such as (a) be prepared for classes each day, (b) pay attention in class, (c) be your personal best, and (d) respect other people and their property. To create a learning community, students (and teachers) need to be organized into cooperative teams.

At the end of this book you are at a new beginning. The next step in increasing your teaching expertise is to gain experience using formal and informal cooperative learning as well as cooperative base groups and supplementing their use with appropriate competitive and individualistic activities. Such expertise is difficult to attain without the help of a colleagial teaching team. Through implementing cooperative learning in your classes and building cooperative relationships with members of your teaching team, a true learning community of scholars may be created for both your students and yourself.

IN RETROSPECT

Cooperation is the air of society that we constantly breathe—it is completely necessary but relatively unnoticed. It is cooperation that provides the medium in which joint actions, relationships, families, communities, and societies thrive. This is not to say that the skills of competitive and individualistic efforts are unimportant. They are important, but only within the larger context of cooperation with others. All students need to learn how to cooperate effectively, how to compete for fun and enjoyment, and how to work autonomously on their own. Unfortunately, instruction in schools often stresses competitive and individualistic efforts without much attention to cooperation. To encourage a positive learning environment and maximize the positive outcomes of schools, we must realize that *cooperation is the forest—competitive and individualistic efforts are but trees.*

As we (the authors) look back on the aspects of our growing up together, we realize that we may have misled you. We developed as quite different, distinct individuals who value our autonomy and individuality. The competition between us was a rather small part of the time we spent together. What made our individuality and the instances of competition livable were our partnership and the constant supportive cooperation within our family. It is the foundation of cooperation that provided the context within which we could grow into quite different, autonomous individuals who frequently compete to add spice and fun to our lives.

Appendix A: Goal Structures, Interaction among Students, and Instructional Outcomes

No logic or wisdom or will-power could prevail to stop the sailors. Buffeted by the hardships of life at sea, the voices came out of the mist to the ancient Greek sailors like a mystical, ethereal love song with tempting and seductive promises of ecstasy and delight. The voices and the song were irresistible. The mariners helplessly turned their ships to follow the Siren's call with scarcely a second thought. Lured to their destruction, the sailors crashed their ships on the waiting rocks and drowned in the tossing waves, struggling with their last breath to reach the source of that beckoning song.

Centuries later, the Sirens still call. Educators seem drawn to competitive and individualistic learning, crashing their teaching on the rocks due to the seductive and tempting attractions of explicating knowledge to an adoring audience and teaching as they were taught. Yet if you ask individuals who have made remarkable achievements during their lifetimes, they typically say their success came from cooperative efforts (Kouzes & Posner, 1987). Not only is cooperation connected with success, competitiveness has been found to be detrimental to career success (Kohn, 1992). The more competitive a person is, the less chance that person has of being successful. Perhaps the most definitive research on this issue has been conducted by Robert L. Helmreich and his colleagues (Helmreich, 1982; Helmreich, Beane, Lucker, & Spence, 1978; Helmreich, Sawin, & Carsrud, 1986; Helmreich, Spence, et al., 1980). They first determined that high achievers, such as scientists, MBAs, and pilots, tend *not* to be very competitive individuals. Then Helmreich and his associates examined the relationship between the competitive drive within individuals and career success. They conceptualized the desire to achieve consisting of competitiveness (desire to win in interpersonal situations, in which one tends to see that success depends on another's failure), mastery (desire to take on challenging tasks), and work (positive attitudes toward hard work). A sample of 103 male Ph.D. scientists was rated on the three factors based on a questionnaire. Achievement was defined as the number of times their work was cited by colleagues. The result was that the most citations were obtained by those high on the work and mastery scale but low on the competitiveness scale. Startled by these results, Helmreich and his associates conducted follow-up studies with academic psychologists, businesspeople working in "cut-throat" big business (measuring achievement by their salaries), undergraduate male and female students (measuring achievement by grade-point average), fifth- and sixth-grade students (measuring achievement by performance on standardized achievement tests), airline pilots (measuring achievement by performance ratings), airline reservation agents (measuring achievement by performance ratings), and super-tanker crews. In all cases they found a negative correlation between achievement and competitiveness. With regard to the faculty members, the researchers proposed that competitive individuals focus so heavily on outshining others and putting themselves forward that they lose track of the scientific issues and produce research that is more superficial and less sustained in direction. As yet Hemreich and his colleagues have not been able to identify a single professional arena where highly competitive individuals tended to be more successful.

Given that competitiveness seems to be detrimental to career success, why has it been so prevalent in classrooms? One answer may be that the evidence cited is not enough—Interesting, but not conclusive. This appendix, therefore, reviews the research that directly compares the relative effects of competitive, individualistic, and cooperative efforts.

> "Let us put our minds together . . . and see what life we can make for our children."
> —*Sitting Bull*

HISTORY OF COOPERATIVE LEARNING

> *Two are better than one, because they have a good reward for toil. For if they fall, one will lift up his fellow; but woe to him who is alone when he falls and has not another to lift him up. . . . And though a man might prevail against one who is alone, two will withstand him. A threefold cord is not quickly broken.*
>
> Ecclesiastics 4:9–12

Cooperative learning has been around a long time. It will probably never go away. Its rich history of theory, research, and actual use in the classroom makes it one of the most distinguished of all instructional practices (see Table A.1). Theory, research, and practice all interact and enhance each other. Theory both guides and summarizes research. Research validates or disconfirms theory, thereby leading to its

TABLE A.1   Time-Line: History Of Cooperative Learning

Given below is a partial time-line on the history of cooperative learning. In limited space it is not possible to list all the people and events important to the history of cooperative learning. The absence of anyone or any event that should be listed is unintended.

DATE	EVENT
B.C.	Talmud
First century	Quintillion, Seneca (*Qui Docet Discet*)
1600s	Johann Amos Comenius of Moravia
1700s	Joseph Lancaster, Andrew Bell
1806	Lancaster School Established in the United States
Early 1800s	Common School Movement in the United States
Late 1800s	Colonel Frances Parker
Early 1900s	John Dewey, Kurt Lewin, Jean Piaget, Lev Vygotsky
1929–1930s	Books on Cooperation and Competition by Maller, Mead, May, and Dobb Liberty League and National Association of Manufacturers Promoted Competition
1940s	
1940s	World War II, Office of Strategic Services, Military-Related Research
1949	Morton Deutsch, Theory and Research on Cooperation and Competition
1950s	
1950s	Applied Group Dynamics Movement, National Training Laboratories Deutsch Research on Trust, Individualistic Situations Naturalistic Studies
1960s	
1960s	Stuart Cook (1969) Research on Cooperation Madsen (Kagan) Research on Cooperation and Competition in Children Inquiry (Discovery) Learning Movement: Bruner, Suchman, B. F. Skinner, Programmed Learning, Behavior Modification
1962	Morton Deutsch Nebraska Symposium, Cooperation and Trust, Conflict Robert Blake and Jane Mouton, Research on Intergroup Competition
1966	David Johnson, University of Minnesota, Began Training Teachers in Cooperative Learning
1969	Roger Johnson Joined David Johnson at University of Minnesota
1970s	
1970	David W. Johnson, *Social Psychology of Education*
1971	Robert Hamblin: Behavioral Research on Cooperation/Competition
1973	David DeVries and Keith Edwards, Combined Instructional Games Approach With Intergroup Competition, Teams-Games-Tournament
1974–1975	David and Roger Johnson Research Review on Cooperation/Competition, David and Roger Johnson, *Learning Together and Alone*
Mid 1970s	Annual Symposium at APA Began (David DeVries and Keith Edwards, David and Roger Johnson, Stuart Cook, Elliot Aronson, Elizabeth Cohen, Others) Robert Slavin Began Development of Cooperative Curricula Spencer Kagan Continued Research on Cooperation among Children
1976	Shlomo and Yael Sharan, *Small Group Teaching* (Group Investigation)
1978	Elliot Aronson, *Jigsaw Classroom Journal of Research and Development in Education*, Cooperation Issue Jeanne Gibbs, *Tribes*
1979	First IASCE Conference in Tel Aviv, Israel

(continued)

TABLE A.1   *(continued)*

DATE	EVENT
1980s	
1981, 1983	David and Roger Johnson, Meta-Analyses of Research on Cooperation
1985	Elizabeth Cohen, *Designing Groupwork*
	Spencer Kagan Developed Structures Approach to Cooperative Learning
	AERA and ASCD Special Interest Groups Founded
1989	David and Roger Johnson, *Cooperation and Competition: Theory and Research*
1990s	
Early 1990s	Cooperative Learning Gains Popularity among Educators
1996	First Annual Cooperative Learning Leadership Conference, Minneapolis

refinement and modification. Practice is guided by validated theory, and applications of the theory reveal inadequacies that lead to refining the theory, conducting new research studies, and modifying the application. A review of the history of cooperative learning emphasizes the theories that have guided the development of cooperative learning and the research they have generated.

Where We Have Been: Theoretical Roots

Theories are causal explanations of how things work. Theory guides and improves practice. Theory is to practice what the soil is to plants. If the soil is appropriate, the plant will grow and flourish. If the theory is appropriate, the practice will grow and continuously improve. Without an appropriate theory, practice is static and stagnant. At least three general theoretical perspectives have guided research on and practice of cooperative learning—social interdependence, cognitive-developmental, and behavioral learning theories.

Social Interdependence Theory   The most influential theorizing on cooperative learning focused on **social interdependence.** In the early 1900s, one of the founders of the gestalt school of psychology, Kurt Koffka, proposed that groups were dynamic wholes in which the interdependence among members could vary. One of his colleagues, Kurt Lewin (1935) refined this notion in the 1920s and 1930s while stating that (a) the essence of a group is the interdependence among members (created by common goals), which results in the group being a "dynamic whole" so that a change in the state of any member or subgroup changes the state of any other member or subgroup, and (b) an intrinsic state of tension within group members motivates movement toward the accomplishment of the desired common goals. One of Lewin's graduate students, Morton Deutsch, refined Lewin's notions and formulated a theory of cooperation and competition in the late 1940s (Deutsch, 1949a, 1962), noting that interdependence can be positive (cooperation) or negative (competition). One of Deutsch's graduate students, David Johnson (working with his brother Roger Johnson), extended Deutsch's work into social interdependence theory (Johnson & Johnson, 1974, 1989).

Social interdependence theory posits that the way social interdependence is structured determines how individuals interact which, in turn, determines outcomes. Positive interdependence (cooperation) results in **promotive interaction** as individuals encourage and facilitate each other's efforts to learn. Negative interdependence (competition) typically results in **oppositional interaction** as individuals discourage and obstruct each other's efforts to achieve. In the absence of interdependence (individualistic efforts) there is *no interaction* as individuals work independently without any interchange with each other. Promotive interaction leads to increased efforts to achieve, positive interpersonal relationships, and psychological health. Oppositional and no interaction leads to decreased efforts to achieve, negative interpersonal relationships, and psychological maladjustment.

Cognitive-Developmental Theory   The **cognitive developmental perspective** is largely based on the theories of Piaget (1950), Vygotsky (1978), cognitive science, and academic controversy (Johnson & Johnson, 1979, 1995). To Jean Piaget, **cooperation** is the striving to attain common goals while coordinating one's own feelings and perspective with a consciousness of others' feelings and perspectives. From Piaget and related theories comes the premise that when individuals cooperate on the environment, socio-cognitive conflict occurs that creates cognitive disequilibrium, which in turn stimulates perspective-taking ability and cognitive development. Cooperative learning in the Piagetian tradition is aimed at accelerating a student's intellectual development by forcing him or her to reach consensus with other students who hold opposing points of view about the answer to the school task.

Lev Semenovich Vygotsky and related theorists claim that our distinctively human mental functions and accomplishments have their origins in our social relationships. Mental functioning is the internalized and transformed version of the accomplishments of a group. Knowledge is social, constructed from cooperative efforts to learn, understand, and solve problems. A central concept is the **zone of proximal development,** which is the zone between what a student can do on his or her own and what the student can achieve while working under the guidance of instructors or in collaboration with more capable peers. Unless students work cooperatively, they will not grow intellectually and, therefore, the time students work alone on school tasks should be minimized.

From the cognitive science viewpoint, cooperative learning involves modeling, coaching, and scaffolding (conceptual frameworks provided for understanding what is being learned). The learner must cognitively rehearse and restructure information for it to be retained in memory and incorporated into existing cognitive structures (Wittrock, 1978). An effective way of doing so is explaining the material being learned to a collaborator. Tutoring, when it is viewed from the perspective of the benefits that accrue to the tutor, is also a form of cooperative learning.

Controversy theory (Johnson & Johnson, 1979, 1995c) posits that being confronted with opposing points of view creates uncertainty or conceptual conflict, which creates a reconceptualization and an information search, which results in a more refined and thoughtful conclusion. The key steps are organizing what is known into a position, advocating that position to someone who is advocating the opposing position, attempting to refute the opposing position while rebutting the attacks on one's own position, reversing perspectives so that the issue may be seen from both points of view simultaneously, and creating a synthesis to which all sides can agree.

Behavioral Learning Theory The **behavioral learning perspective** assumes that students will work hard on those tasks for which they secure a reward of some sort and will fail to work on tasks that yield no reward or yield punishment (Bandura, 1977; Skinner, 1968). Cooperative learning is designed to provide incentives for the members of the group to participate in a group effort since it is assumed that students will not intrinsically help their classmates or work toward a common goal. Skinner focused on group contingencies, Bandura focused on imitation, and Homans as well as Thibaut and Kelley focused on the balance of rewards and costs in social exchange among interdependent individuals.

Differences among Theories These three theories provide a classic triangulation of validation for cooperative learning. Social interdependence theory, behavioral learning theory, and cognitive-developmental theory all predict that cooperative learning will promote higher achievement than would competitive or individualistic learning. Each theory has generated considerable research, which is reviewed here. However, basic differences among the theoretical perspectives exist. Social interdependence theory assumes that cooperative efforts are based on intrinsic motivation generated by interpersonal factors in working together and joint aspirations to achieve a significant goal. Behavioral learning theory assumes that cooperative efforts are powered by extrinsic motivation to achieve rewards. Social interdependence theory is made up of relational concepts dealing with what happens among individuals (e.g., cooperation is something that exists only among individuals, not within them), whereas the cognitive-developmental perspective focuses on what happens within a single person (e.g., disequilibrium, cognitive reorganization). The differences in basic assumptions among the theoretical perspectives have yet to be fully explored or resolved (see Figure A.1).

Usefulness of Theories Although all three theories have inspired research on cooperation, the most fully developed, the most clearly related to practice, and the greatest inspiration of research is social interdependence theory. Besides giving the clearest and most precise definitions of cooperative, competitive, and individualistic efforts, social interdependence theory specifies (a) the conditions under which cooperation is most effective, (b) the outcomes most effected by cooperation, and (c) the procedures teachers should use in implementing cooperative learning (Deutsch, 1949b, 1962; Johnson, 1970; Johnson & Johnson, 1974, 1989; Johnson, Johnson, & Holubec, 1998).

Where We Have Been: Research

We know a lot about cooperation and we have known it for some time. In the late 1800s, Triplett (1898) in the United States, Turner (1889) in England, and Mayer (1903) in Germany conducted a series of studies on the factors associated with competitive

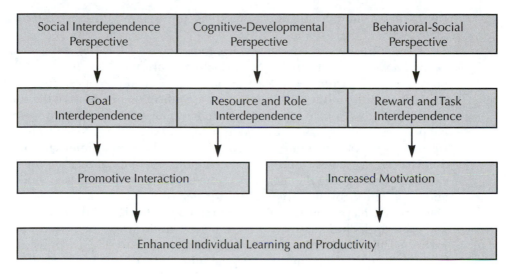

FIGURE A.1 A General Theoretical Framework

performance. Since then we have found out a lot about cooperation. In 1929 Maller wrote a book about it (*Cooperation and Competition: An Experimental Study in Motivation*). In 1936 Margaret Mead (*Cooperation and Competition among Primitive Peoples*) and in 1937 May and Doob (*Competition and Cooperation*) wrote research reviews on it. In 1949 Deutsch published a research study and a theory on it. In the 1950s Muzafer Sherif (Sherif & Hovland, 1961) conducted his famous studies on three summer camps in which he engineered intense intergroup competition and studied its resolution. Stuart Cook (1969), in collaboration with Shirley and Larry Wrightsman, conducted a study on the impact of cooperative interaction on relationships between black and white college students. James Coleman (1961) published an observational study of schools in the United States in which a pervasive competitiveness was documented. In 1963 Miller and Hamblin reviewed twenty-four studies on cooperation and competition. From an anthropological perspective, Millard C. Madsen (1967) and his associates developed a series of dyadic games that allowed comparison of children's preferences for competitive and cooperative interaction across ages and various cultures. One of Madsen's students, Spencer Kagan, began a series of studies on cooperation and competition in children. The research of Madsen and Kagan presents a consistent picture of rural children collaborating more than urban children, and middle-class urban children in the United States being most strongly motivated to compete.

In 1970 (*The Social Psychology of Education*), 1974, and 1975 (*Learning Together and Alone,* first edition), the authors of this book published comprehensive research reviews on cooperation and competition. From then on the research review articles are too many to mention. Since 1898 more than 550 experimental and 100 correlational research studies have been conducted on cooperative, competitive, and individualistic efforts (see Johnson & Johnson, 1989 for a complete review of these studies).

The effectiveness of cooperative learning has been confirmed by both theoretical and demonstration research. There is a "scientific" literature and a "professional" literature on cooperative learning. The scientific literature is made up of carefully controlled research studies conducted to validate or disconfirm theory. Most of the studies are either laboratory or field experimental studies. The vast majority of the research on cooperative learning was conducted to validate or disconfirm theory. The theoretical studies typically are carefully controlled and have high internal validity, randomly assigning subjects to conditions, carefully operationalizing the independent variable, ensuring that the measures of the dependent variables were both reliable and valid. The theoretical studies have focused on a wide variety of dependent variables from achievement to higher-level reasoning to friendships between majority and minority individuals to accuracy of perspective taking to self-esteem to psychological health. The results of these theoretical studies are highly consistent in supporting the use of cooperative over competitive and individualistic learning. It is this combination of hundreds of studies producing validated theory that could be operationalized into practice that has created such interest in cooperative learning.

There are problems with theoretical studies. They lack credibility with many practitioners. Most of the theoretical studies on cooperative learning were conducted in social psychology laboratories using college students as subjects. Although they clarified the power of cooperative efforts, they did not in fact demonstrate that cooperative learning could work in the real world.

The professional literature is made up of field quasi-experimental or correlational studies demonstrating that cooperative learning works in real classrooms for a prolonged period of time. Demonstration studies have tended to focus on external validity. The demonstration studies may be grouped into four categories:

1. *Summative evaluations.* By far the largest category of demonstration studies is straightforward summative evaluation in which the central question is whether a particular cooperative learning program produces beneficial results. The comparison is typically between a cooperative learning method and traditional classroom learning. The Johns Hopkins research on specific cooperative learning programs (teams-games-tournaments, student team achievement divisions [STAD], team-assisted individualization) are examples that focused achievement primarily on lower-level learning tasks. The reviews of these studies (Slavin, 1983, 1991) are organized around a particular method, not a particular skill or knowledge to be learned. This serves the advocates of the method, but users of cooperative learning may not be so concerned with whether STAD works or does not work, but instead would like to know the best procedures for maximizing learning or higher-level reasoning. Although these evaluation studies are of interest, the information value of their conclusions is limited for designing effective instructional programs.

2. *Comparative summative evaluations.* Less research attention has been devoted to the comparative question of which of two or more cooperative learning methods produces the most beneficial effects when compared on the same criterion measures. The jigsaw method, for example, might be compared with team-assisted individualization. An

inherent problem with such studies, is that it is difficult if not impossible to tell if both methods have been implemented at the same strength. The results can be easily biased through carefully implementing one method at full strength and implementing the other method at partial strength.

3. *Formative evaluations.* Very little research focused on where a cooperative learning program went wrong and how it could be improved makes its way into the literature. Formative evaluations are aimed at improving ongoing implementations of cooperation learning. The critical incident method seems well suited to the diagnosis of training deficiencies or unintended consequences, as does a combination of surveys with follow-up interviews of a representative subsample of respondents.

4. *Survey studies.* A few studies have conducted large-scale surveys of the impact of cooperation on students (Johnson & Johnson, 1991b). These studies have (a) correlated attitudes toward cooperative, competitive, and individualistic learning with such variables as perceived social support, self-esteem, and attitudes learning and (b) compared the responses of students in high-use classrooms (where cooperative learning was frequently used) with the responses of students in low-use classrooms (where cooperative learning was never or rarely used) on a number of learning climate variables (e.g., Johnson & Johnson, 1983b; Johnson, Johnson, & Anderson, 1983; Johnson, Johnson, Buckman, & Richards, 1986). Although these studies are not direct evaluations of cooperative learning procedures, they do provide interesting data about the long-term impact of cooperative learning on a variety of attitudinal and learning climate outcomes.

Demonstration studies have both weaknesses and strengths. *First,* like all case studies, demonstration studies simply indicate that a certain method worked at that time in those circumstances. *Second,* demonstration studies are always in danger of being biased because the researchers are typically evaluating programs they have developed themselves and have a professional and sometimes a financial stake in their success. By definition, such researchers favor cooperative learning. Reviews of demonstration studies, furthermore, suffer the same limitation as they are most often conducted by the researchers who invented the cooperative learning programs. The *third* problem with demonstration studies is that what is labeled as cooperative learning is not always cooperation. In many cases, the cooperative learning method being evaluated was only one element of a broader educational package and, therefore, cooperative learning was confounded with other variables. The original jigsaw procedure (Aronson, 1978), for example, is a combination of resource interdependence (cooperative) and the individual reward structure (individualistic). Teams-games-tournaments (DeVries & Edwards, 1974) and student teams achievement divisions (Slavin, 1980) are mixtures of cooperation and intergroup competition. Team-assisted instruction (Slavin, Leavey, & Madden, 1982) is a mixture of individualistic and cooperative learning. It is difficult to interpret the results of studies evaluating the effectiveness of such mixtures as it is impossible to know which elements contributed which part of the found effects.

Fourth, demonstration studies often lack methodological rigor, focusing far more on external validity (such as length of study) than on internal validity (such as experimental control). In many demonstration studies, the comparison has been with an ambiguous and unknown form of traditional classroom learning. When differences are found, it is not clear what has been compared with what. The lack of methodological quality to most demonstration studies adds further doubts as to how seriously their results can be taken. *Finally,* most demonstration studies have been conducted in elementary schools. Very few have been conducted at the secondary and college levels. This reduces their relevance.

> A human being is a part of the whole, called by us "Universe," a part limited in time and space. He experiences himself, his thoughts and feelings as something separated from the rest—a kind of optical delusion of consciousness. This delusion is a kind of prison for us, restricting us to our personal desires and to affection for a few persons nearest to us. Our task must be to free ourselves from this prison by widening our circle of compassion to embrace all living creatures, and the whole nature in its beauty. —*Albert Einstein*

Demonstration studies have at least two strengths. *First,* there is a clear value to demonstration studies when their results are viewed in combination with more controlled and more theoretical studies. When the results of the demonstration studies agree with and support the results of the theoretical studies, the demonstration studies strengthen the validity of the theory and make it more credible. *Second,* demonstration studies provide a model for teachers who wish to implement identical programs.

Cooperative learning can be used with some confidence at every grade level, in every subject area, and with any task. Research participants have varied as to economic class, age, sex, nationality, and cultural background. A wide variety of research tasks, ways of structuring cooperation, and measures of the dependent variables have been used. The research has been conducted by many different researchers with markedly different orientations working in different settings, countries, and decades. The research on cooperative learning has a validity and a generalizability rarely found in the educational literature.

Cooperation is a generic human endeavor that affects many different instructional outcomes simultaneously. Over the past ninety years researchers have focused on such diverse outcomes as achievement, higher-level reasoning, retention, achievement motivation, intrinsic motivation, transfer of learning, interpersonal attraction, social support, friendships, prejudice, valuing differences, social support, self-esteem, social competencies, psychological health, and moral reasoning, among many others. These numerous outcomes may be subsumed within three broad categories (Johnson & Johnson, 1989): effort to achieve, positive interpersonal relationships, and psychological health (see Figure A.2 and Table A.2).

Research in Different Cultures Part of the generalizability of the research on cooperation is the diversity of settings in which the research has been conducted. Research on cooperation has been conducted in numerous countries and cultures. In North America (the United States, Canada, and Mexico), for example, research has been

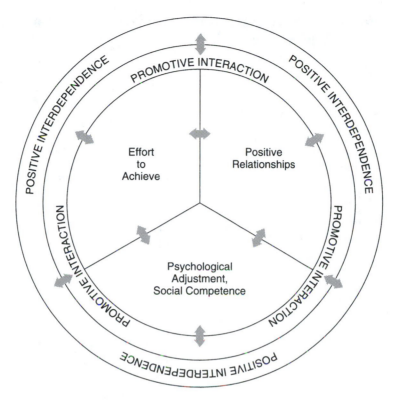

FIGURE A.2 Outcomes of Social Interdependence (*Source:* D. W. Johnson & R. Johnson, (1989), *Cooperation and competition: Theory and research.* Edina, MN: Interaction Book Company. Reprinted with permission.)

conducted with Caucasian, African American, Native American, and Hispanic subject populations. In addition, cooperation has been researched in Asia (Japan), Southeast Asia (Australia and New Zealand), the Middle East (Israel), Africa (Nigeria and South Africa), Europe (Greece, Norway, Sweden, Finland, Germany, France, the Netherlands, and England), and other parts of the world. Essentially, the findings have been consistent. Higher productivity, more positive relationships, and increased social adjustment and competencies are found more in cooperative than in competitive or individualistic situations. The robustness of the research in a wide variety of cultures adds to the validity and generalizability of the theory. The critical research, however, has yet to be conducted. It seems reasonable that different cultures have different definitions of (a) what is cooperative and competitive and (b) where each is appropriate. Within the United States, for example, different Native American tribes have quite different views of cooperation and competition and different ways of expressing them. Given the hundreds of studies that have established the basic theory of cooperation and competition, considerable more research is needed to establish the cultural nuances of how cooperative efforts are conducted.

TABLE A.2   Mean Effect Sizes for Impact of Social Interdependence on Dependent Variables

CONDITIONS	ACHIEVEMENT	INTERPERSONAL ATTRACTION	SOCIAL SUPPORT	SELF-ESTEEM
Total Studies				
Coop vs. Comp	0.67	0.67	0.62	0.58
Coop vs. Ind	0.64	0.60	0.70	0.44
Comp vs. Ind	0.30	0.08	–0.13	–0.23
High Quality Studies				
Coop vs. Comp	0.88	0.82	0.83	0.67
Coop vs. Ind	0.61	0.62	0.72	0.45
Comp vs. Ind	0.07	0.27	–0.13	–0.25
Mixed Operationalizations				
Coop vs. Comp	0.40	0.46	0.45	0.33
Coop vs. Ind	0.42	0.36	0.02	0.22
Pure Operationalizations				
Coop vs. Comp	0.71	0.79	0.73	0.74
Coop vs. Ind	0.65	0.66	0.77	0.51

Note: Coop = Cooperation, Comp = Competition, Ind = Individualistic

Source: D. W. Johnson & R. Johnson, (1989), *Cooperation and competition: Theory and research.* Edina, MN: Interaction Book Company. Reprinted with permission.

History of Practical Use of Cooperative Learning

The practical use of cooperative learning has a rich and long history. Thousands of years ago the *Talmud* stated that in order to understand the Talmud, one must have a learning partner. As early as the first century, *Quintillion* argued that students could benefit from teaching one another. The Roman philosopher *Seneca* advocated cooperative learning through such statements as, *"Qui Docet Discet"* (when you teach, you learn twice). *Johann Amos Comenius* (1592–1679) believed that students would benefit both by teaching and being taught by other students. In the late 1700s *Joseph Lancaster* and *Andrew Bell* made extensive use of cooperative learning groups in England, and the idea was brought to the United States when a Lancastrian school was opened in New York City in 1806. Within the *Common School Movement* in the United States in the early 1800s there was a strong emphasis on cooperative learning. Certainly, the use of cooperative learning is not new to U.S. education. There have been periods in which cooperative learning had strong advocates and was widely used to promote the educational goals of that time.

One of the most successful advocates of cooperative learning in the United States was *Colonel Francis Parker.* In the last three decades of the nineteenth century, Colonel Parker brought to his advocacy of cooperative learning enthusiasm, idealism, practicality, and an intense devotion to freedom, democracy, and individuality in the public schools. His fame and success rested on the vivid and regenerating spirit that he brought into the schoolroom and on his power to create a classroom atmosphere that was truly cooperative and democratic. When he was superintendent of the public schools at Quincy, Massachusetts (1875–1880), he averaged more than 30,000 visitors a year to examine his use of cooperative learning procedures (Campbell, 1965). Parker's instructional methods of structuring cooperation among students dominated U.S. education through the turn of the century. Following Parker, John Dewey promoted the use of cooperative learning groups as part of his famous project method in instruction (Dewey, 1924). In the late 1930s, however, interpersonal competition began to be emphasized in public schools (Pepitone, 1980).

In the mid-1960s, the authors began training teachers on how to use cooperative learning at the University of Minnesota. *The Cooperative Learning Center* resulted from our efforts to (a) synthesize existing knowledge concerning cooperative, competitive, and individualistic efforts (Johnson, 1970; Johnson & Johnson, 1974, 1978, 1983a, 1989), (b) formulate theoretical models concerning the nature of cooperation and its essential components, (c) conduct a systematic program of research to test our theorizing, (d) translate the validated theory into a set of concrete strategies and procedures for using cooperation in classrooms, schools, and school districts (Johnson, Johnson, & Holubec, 1992a, 1992c, 1994, 1998), and (e) build and maintain a network of schools and colleges implementing cooperative strategies and procedures throughout North America and a variety of other countries. Related to cooperative learning was the development of academic controversy (Johnson & Johnson, 1995c) and conflict resolution and peer mediation programs (Johnson & Johnson, 1995a).

In the 1970s David DeVries and Keith Edwards at Johns Hopkins University developed teams-games-tournaments (TGT) and Sholmo and Yael Sharan in Israel developed the group investigation procedure for cooperative learning groups. Robert Slavin extended Devries and Edward's work at Johns Hopkins University by modifying TGT into student team achievement divisions (STAD) and modifying computer-assisted instruction into team-assisted instruction (TAI). Concurrently, Spencer Kagan developed the co-op co-op procedure. In the 1980s, Donald Dansereau developed a number of cooperative scripts and many other individuals worked out further cooperative procedures. In the 1990s, cooperative learning was extended into conflict resolution and peer mediation programs (Johnson & Johnson, 1995a, 1995b).

RESEARCH ON SOCIAL INTERDEPENDENCE

Learning together to complete assignments can have profound effects. Building on the theorizing of Kurt Lewin and Morton Deutsch, the premise may be made that the type of interdependence structured among students determines how they interact with each other, which, in turn, largely determines instructional outcomes. Structuring situations cooperatively results in promotive interaction, structuring situations competitively results in oppositional interaction, and structuring situations individualistically results in no interaction among students. These interaction patterns affect numerous variables, which may be subsumed within the three broad and interrelated outcomes: effort exerted to achieve, quality of relationships among participants, and participants' psychological adjustment and social competence (see Figure A.1) (Johnson & Johnson, 1989). In most cases, references to individual studies are not included in this chapter. Rather, the reader is referred to the reviews that contain the references to the specific studies that corroborate the point being made.

INTERACTION PATTERNS

Two heads are better than one.

Heywood

Simply placing students near each other and allowing interaction to take place does not mean that learning will be maximized, high-quality peer relationships will result, or student psychological adjustment, self-esteem, and social competencies will be maximized. Students can obstruct as well as facilitate each other's learning. Or they can ignore each other. The way students interact depends on how faculty members structure interdependence in the learning situation.

Positive interdependence results in students promoting each other's learning and achievement. **Promotive interaction** may be defined as individuals encouraging and facilitating each other's efforts to achieve, complete tasks, and produce in order to reach the group's goals. Although positive interdependence in and of itself may have some effect on outcomes, it is the face-to-face promotive interaction among individuals fostered by the positive interdependence that most powerfully influences efforts to achieve, caring and committed relationships, psychological adjustment, and social competence. Students focus both on increasing their own achievement *and* on increasing the achievement of their groupmates. Promotive interaction by individuals is characterized by the following (Johnson & Johnson, 1989):

1. Providing each other with efficient and effective help and assistance.
2. Exchanging needed resources such as information and materials and processing information more efficiently and effectively.
3. Providing each other with feedback in order to improve the subsequent performance of their assigned tasks and responsibilities.
4. Challenging each other's conclusions and reasoning in order to promote higher-quality decision making and greater insight into the problems being considered.
5. Advocating the exertion of effort to achieve mutual goals.
6. Influencing each other's efforts to achieve the group's goals.
7. Acting in trusting and trustworthy ways.
8. Being motivated to strive for mutual benefit.
9. Having a moderate level of arousal characterized by low anxiety and stress.

Negative interdependence typically results in students opposing each other's success. Oppositional interaction occurs as students discourage and obstruct each other's efforts to achieve. Students focus both on increasing their own achievement and on preventing any classmate from achieving higher than they do. No interaction exists when students work independently without any interaction or interchange with each other. Students focus only on increasing their own achievement and ignore as irrelevant the efforts of others.

Giving and Receiving Assistance and Help

Within most task situations, productivity is enhanced when individuals give each other relevant task-related help and assistance (see Johnson & Johnson, 1989). There are consistent perceptions of more frequent helping and tutoring (including cross-ethnic and cross-disability helping) in cooperative than in competitive or individualistic situations. In both social-psychological and applied behavior research, cooperative structures have enhanced helping and assistance among group members, whereas competitive structures have resulted in individuals obstructing each other's efforts to achieve, refusing to help and share, and engaging in antisocial behaviors. These effects of competition are exacerbated by losing. Observational studies of actual learning groups consistently find more giving and receiving of help in cooperative than in competitive or individualistic situations.

Information Exchange and Cognitive Processes

More efficient and effective exchange and processing of information takes place in cooperative than in competitive or individualistic situations (Johnson, 1974; Johnson & Johnson, 1989). Although a wide variety of material resources may need to be exchanged in order to complete tasks and accomplish goals, the most common resource shared and exchanged within cooperative efforts is information.

Compared with competitive and individualistic situations, students working cooperatively (Johnson & Johnson, 1989) exhibit the following traits:

1. Seek significantly more information from each other than do students working within a competitive goal structure.
2. Are less biased and have fewer misperceptions in comprehending the viewpoints and positions of other individuals.
3. More accurately communicate information by verbalizing ideas and information more frequently, attending to others' statements more carefully, and accepting others' ideas and information more frequently.
4. Are more confident about the value of their ideas.
5. Make optimal use of the information provided by other students.

In **cooperative situations,** students are bound by their mutual fate, shared identity, and mutual causation and, therefore, celebrate (and feel benefited by) each other's successes. Relevant ideas, information, conclusions, and resources tend to be made available, exchanged, and utilized in ways that promote collective and individual insights and increase energy to complete the task. Such oral discussion of relevant information has at least two dimensions: oral explanation and listening. Both benefit the giver and receiver. The giver benefits from the cognitive organizing and processing, higher-level reasoning, insights, and personal commitment to achieving the group's goals derived from orally explaining, elaborating, and summarizing information and teaching one's knowledge to others. The receiver benefits from the opportunity to utilize others' resources in their goal accomplishment efforts.

Information exchange and stimulation of cognitive processes may not occur in competitive or individualistic situations. In **competitive situations** communication and information exchange tends to be nonexistent or misleading and competition biases a person's perceptions and comprehension of viewpoints and positions of other individuals. **Individualistic situations** are usually deliberately structured to ensure that individuals do not communicate or exchange information at all.

Survey research indicates that fear of public speaking is quite common among the general population of adolescents and adults (Motley, 1988). College students, in particular, frequently experience communication apprehension in the classroom (Bowers, 1986). Such speech anxiety, however, can be significantly reduced if students are given the opportunity to first express themselves in the more comfortable social context of a small group of peers (Neer, 1987). Students whose primary language is not English may especially find their anxiety reduced by working in cooperative learning groups.

Peer Feedback

An important aspect of promotive interaction is the opportunity for group members to provide each other with feedback as to how they are fulfilling their responsibilities and completing their work. **Feedback** is information made available to individuals that makes possible the comparison of actual performance with some standard of performance. **Knowledge of results** is information provided to the person about his or her performance on a given effort. It may be in the form of qualitative information in which the person is informed that a performance is either correct or incorrect, or it may be in the form of quantitative information about how much discrepancy exists between the person's response and the correct response. Usually, quantitative information (i.e., process feedback) about (a) the size of the discrepancy existing between actual performance and some standard of performance or (b) how to improve one's reasoning or performance promotes achievement more effectively than does qualitative information (i.e., terminal feedback) about being right or wrong or what the correct answer is. Receiving personalized feedback from another person increases performance to a greater extent than does receiving impersonal feedback, and peer feedback from collaborators may be especially vivid and personalized. Frequent and immediate feedback serves to increase a student's motivation to learn (Mackworth, 1970).

Challenge and Controversy

An important aspect of promotive interaction is **controversy,** the conflict that arises when involved group members have different information, perceptions, opinions, reasoning processes, theories, and conclusions, and they must reach agreement. When controversies arise, they may be dealt with constructively or destructively, depending on how they are managed and the level of interpersonal and small-group skills of the participants. When managed constructively, controversy promotes uncertainty about the correctness of one's views, an active search for more information, a reconceptualization of one's knowledge and conclusions and, consequently, greater mastery and retention of the material being discussed. Individuals working alone in competitive and individualistic situations do not have the opportunity for such a process and therefore their productivity, quality of decision making, and achievement suffer.

Public Advocacy and Commitment

Promotive interaction includes advocating that cooperators increase their efforts to accomplish the group's goals and publicly committing oneself to do the same. **Commitment** may be defined as the binding or pledging of the individual to an act or decision. To the extent that people act in the absence of coercion, commit themselves to act in front of others, or invest time, money, or personal prestige in an activity, they come to see themselves as believers in that sort of activity and develop a personal interest in it. Individuals become more committed to attitudes that are made public than to attitudes that remain private. People are particularly prone to increase their commitment to actions that they have attempted to persuade another to adopt.

Mutual Influence

During the information-exchange process, individuals share ideas and information and utilize each other's resources in order to maximize their productivity and achievement. This entails mutual influence in which cooperators consider each other's ideas and conclusions and coordinate their efforts. Participants must be open to influence attempts aimed at facilitating the accomplishment of shared goals, must trust each other not to use the resources being shared in detrimental ways, and must form emotional bonds that result in commitment to each other's welfare and success. Influence takes place within social situations in one of three ways: direct influence, social modeling, and group norms. Students will be receptive to the *direct influence* attempts of others to the extent that they perceive a cooperative relationship among goal attainments. In cooperative situations, students benefit from groupmates' *modeling* effective and committed behaviors, skills, and attitudes. Visible and credible models who demonstrate the recommended attitudes and behavior patterns and who directly discuss their importance are powerful influences. Finally, achievement is influenced by whether or not *group norms* favor high performance. Within cooperative situations everyone benefits from the efforts of cooperators and, therefore, group norms support efforts to achieve. Evidence furthermore indicates that in the generally competitive climate of most schools, success at academic tasks has little value for many individuals and may even be a deterrent to popularity with peers (see Johnson & Johnson, 1989).

Achievement Motivation

> *Achievement is a we thing, not a me thing, always the product of many heads and hands.*
>
> J. W. Atkinson

Motivation to achieve is reflected in the effort individuals commit purposely to acquire increased understandings and skills they perceive as being meaningful and worthwhile. Although humans may be born with a motivation to increase their competencies, achievement motivation is basically induced through interpersonal processes, either through internalized relationships or current interaction patterns within the learning situation. Depending on whether interaction takes place within a context of positive, negative, or no interdependence, different interaction patterns result, causing different motivational systems, which in turn affect achievement differently, which determines expectations for future achievement. The motivational system promoted within *cooperative situations* includes intrinsic motivation, high expectations for success, high incentive to achieve based on mutual benefit, high epistemic curiosity and continuing interest in achievement, high commitment to achieve, and high persistence. The motivational system promoted within *competitive situations* includes extrinsic motivation to win, low expectations for success by all but the highest ability individuals, an incentive to learn based on differential benefit, low epistemic curiosity and a lack of continuing interest to achieve, a lack of commitment to achieving, and low task persistence by most individuals. The motivational system promoted within *individualistic situations* includes extrinsic motivation to meet preset criteria of excellence, low expectations for success by all but the highest ability individuals, an incentive to achieve based on self-benefit, low epistemic curiosity and continuing interest to achieve, low commitment to achieving, and low task persistence by most individuals.

Motivation is most commonly viewed as a combination of the perceived likelihood of success and the perceived incentive for success. The greater the likelihood of success and the more important it is to succeed, the higher the motivation. Success that is intrinsically rewarding is usually seen as being more desirable for learning than is having students believe that only extrinsic rewards are worthwhile. There is greater perceived likelihood of success and success is viewed as more important in cooperative than in competitive or individualistic learning situations (Johnson & Johnson, 1989). Striving for mutual benefit results in an emotional bonding with collaborators liking each other, wanting to help each other succeed, and committing to each other's well-being. These positive feelings toward the group and the other members may have a number of important influences on one's *intrinsic motivation to achieve* and actual productivity. In many cases, the relationships among group members may become more important than the actual rewards given for the work being done. Consequences provided by group members (e.g., respect, liking, blame, or rejection) may supplement or replace those produced by task performance (e.g., salary or grades). Such consequences might be important in sustaining behavior during periods in which students receive no task-based reinforcement.

Interpersonal Trust

To disclose one's reasoning and information, one must trust the other individuals involved in the situation to listen with respect. Trust is a central dynamic of promotive interaction. Trust tends to be developed and maintained in cooperative situations and it tends to be absent and destroyed in competitive and individualistic situations (Deutsch, 1958, 1960, 1962; Johnson, 1971, 1973a, 1974; Johnson & Noonan, 1972). Trust includes the following elements (Deutsch, 1962):

1. Risk—the anticipation of beneficial or harmful consequences.
2. Realization that others have the power to determine the consequences of one's actions.
3. Expectation that the harmful consequences are more serious than are the beneficial consequences.
4. Confidence that the others will behave in ways that ensure beneficial consequences for oneself.

Interpersonal trust is built by placing one's consequences in the control of others and by having one's confidence in the others confirmed. Interpersonal trust is destroyed by placing one's consequences in the hands of others and by having one's confidence in the others disconfirmed because of their behaving in ways that ensure harmful consequences for oneself. Thus, trust is composed of two sets of behaviors. **Trusting behavior** is the willingness to risk beneficial or harmful consequences by making oneself vulnerable to another person. **Trustworthy behavior** is the willingness to respond to another person's risk taking in a way that ensures that the other person will experience beneficial consequences. To establish trust, two or more people must be trustworthy and trusting. Within cooperative situations, individuals tend to be both trusting and trustworthy. Within competitive situations, individuals tend to be distrusting and untrustworthy as they use information to promote their own success and the other's failure.

Anxiety and Performance

Cooperation typically produces (a) less anxiety and stress and (b) more effective coping strategies used to deal with the anxiety than does competition. Anxiety is one of the most pervasive barriers to productivity and positive interpersonal relationships. Anxiety generally leads to an egocentric preoccupation with oneself, disruption of cognitive reasoning, and an avoidance of the situation one fears. This can mean skipping school or work, cutting classes or taking long breaks, or avoiding challenging learning and work situations. A continued experience of even moderate levels of anxiety over a number of years, furthermore, can produce psychological and physiological harm. Especially for individuals with a chronically high state of anxiety, cooperation promotes a better learning and work climate.

Summary of Promotive Interaction

Positive interdependence results in promotive interaction which, in turn, promotes efforts to achieve, positive interpersonal relationships, and psychological health. **Promotive interaction** may be defined as individuals encouraging and facilitating each other's efforts to achieve, complete tasks, and produce in order to reach the group's goals. Promotive interaction is characterized by individuals providing each other with efficient and effective help and assistance, exchanging needed resources such as information and materials and processing information more efficiently and effectively, providing each other with feedback in order to improve their subsequent performance of their assigned tasks and responsibilities, challenging each other's conclusions and reasoning in order to promote higher-quality decision making and greater insight into the problems being considered, advocating the exertion of effort to achieve mutual goals, influencing each other's efforts to achieve the group's goals, acting in trusting and trustworthy ways, being motivated to strive for mutual benefit, and maintaining a moderate level of arousal characterized by low anxiety and stress. Oppositional and no interaction results in the opposite pattern of interaction. Promotive interaction results in a number of important outcomes.

> Cooperation, not conflict, was evidently the selectively most valuable form of behavior for man taken at any stage of his evolutionary history, and surely, quite as evident never more so than today. . . . It is essentially the experience, the means, that fits human beings not to their external environment so much as to one another. It must never be forgotten that society is fundamentally, essentially, and in all ways a cooperative enterprise, an enterprise designed to keep men in touch with one another. Without the cooperation of its members society cannot survive, and the society of man has survived because the cooperativeness of its members made survival possible—it was not an advantageous individual here and there who did so, but the group. In human societies the individuals who are most likely to survive are those who are best enabled to do so by their group.
> —Asley Montagu (1965)

LEARNING OUTCOMES

Different learning outcomes result from the student–student interaction patterns promoted by the use of cooperative, competitive, and individualistic goal structures (Johnson & Johnson, 1989). The numerous outcomes of cooperative efforts may be subsumed within three broad categories: effort to achieve, positive interpersonal relationships, and psychological adjustment. Because research participants have varied as to economic class, age, sex, and cultural background, because a wide variety of research tasks and measures of the dependent variables have been used, and because the research has been conducted by many different researchers with markedly different orientations working in different settings and in different decades, the overall body of research on social interdependence has considerable generalizability.

EFFORT TO ACHIEVE

More than 375 studies have been conducted over the past ninety years to give an answer to the question of how successful competitive, individualistic, and cooperative efforts are in promoting productivity and achievement (Johnson & Johnson, 1989). The results are summarized in Table A.1. When all of the studies were included in the analysis, the average student cooperating performed at about two-thirds of a standard deviation above the average student learning within a competitive (effect size = 0.67) or individualistic situation (effect size = 0.64). When only high-quality studies were included in the analysis, the effect sizes were 0.88 and 0.61, respectively. Cooperative learning, furthermore, resulted in more higher-level reasoning, more frequent generation of new ideas and solutions (i.e., process gain), and greater transfer of what is learned from one situation to another (i.e., group to individual transfer) than did competitive or individualistic learning.

> The highest and best form of efficiency is the spontaneous cooperation of a free people.
> *—Woodrow Wilson*

Some cooperative learning procedures contained a mixture of cooperative, competitive, and individualistic efforts whereas others were "pure." The original jigsaw procedure (Aronson, 1978), for example, is a combination of resource interdependence (cooperative) and the individual reward structure (individualistic). Teams-games-tournaments (DeVries & Edwards, 1974) and student teams achievement divisions (Slavin, 1980) are mixtures of cooperation and intergroup competition. Team-assisted instruction (Slavin, Leavey, & Madden, 1982) is a mixture of individualistic and cooperative learning. When the results of pure and mixed operationalizations of cooperative learning were compared, the pure operationalizations produced higher achievement (cooperative versus competitive, pure = 0.71 and mixed = 0.40; cooperative versus individualistic, pure = 0.65 and mixed = 0.42).

The potential value of cooperative learning in large classes is highlighted by a recent study designed to identify what specific factors contributed to student learning in large classes. Wulff, Nyquist, and Abbott (1987) surveyed 800 college students and found that the second most frequently cited factor contributing to their learning in large classes was other students. The researchers concluded that faculty may wish to use cooperative learning within the large-class context. Levin, Glass, and Meister (1984) concluded from a comparison of the cost-effectiveness of four academic strategies that working with classmates is the most cost-effective support system for increasing student achievement.

That working together to achieve a common goal produces higher achievement and greater productivity than does working alone is so well confirmed by so much research that it stands as one of the strongest principles of social and organizational psychology. Cooperative learning is indicated whenever the learning goals are highly important, mastery and retention is important, the task is complex or conceptual, problem solving is desired, divergent thinking or creativity is desired, quality of performance is expected, and higher-level reasoning strategies and critical thinking are needed.

Why does cooperation result in higher achievement—what mediates? The critical issue in understanding the relationship between cooperation and achievement is specifying the variables that mediate the relationship. Simply placing students in groups and telling them to work together does not in and of itself promote higher achievement. It is only under certain conditions that group efforts may be expected to be more productive than individual efforts. Those conditions are clearly perceived positive interdependence, considerable promotive (face-to-face) interaction, felt personal responsibility (individual accountability) to achieve the group's goals, frequent use of relevant interpersonal and small-group skills, and periodic and regular group processing (Johnson & Johnson, 1989).

Critical Thinking Competencies

In many subject areas the teaching of facts and theories is considered to be secondary to the development of students' critical thinking and use of higher-level reasoning strategies. The aim of science education, for example, has been to develop individuals "who can sort sense from nonsense" or who have the critical thinking abilities of grasping information, examining it, evaluating it for soundness, and applying it appropriately. The application, evaluation, and synthesis of knowledge and other higher-level reasoning skills, however, are often neglected. *Cooperative learning promotes a greater use of higher level reasoning strategies and critical thinking than do competitive or individualistic learning strategies* (Gabbert, Johnson, & Johnson, 1986; Johnson & Johnson, 1981; Johnson, Skon, & Johnson, 1980; Skon, Johnson, & Johnson, 1981). Cooperative learning experiences, for example, promote more frequent insight into and use of higher-level cognitive and moral reasoning strategies than do competitive or individualistic learning experiences (effect sizes = 0.93 and 0.97, respectively).

Studies conducted by Laughlin and his colleagues (Laughlin, 1965, 1973; Laughlin & Jaccard, 1975; Laughlin, McGlynn, Anderson, & Jacobson, 1968; McGlynn, 1972) found more frequent use of a focusing strategy (used to figure out a concept underlying a set of numbers or words) in cooperative than in competitively or individualistically situations and, therefore, cooperators solved the problems faster. Studies conducted by Dansereau and his colleagues (Spurlin, Dansereau, Larson, & Brooks, 1984; Larson, Dansereau, O'Donnell, Hythecker, Lambiotte, & Rocklin, 1984) found that an elaboration strategy (integrating new information being learned with prior knowledge) was used more frequently by cooperators than by students working individualistically and, therefore, the cooperators performed at a higher level.

In addition to the research directly relating cooperative learning with critical thinking, lines of research link critical thinking and cooperative learning. McKeachie (1988) concluded that at least three elements of teaching make a difference in improving students' thinking skills: (1) student discussion, (2) explicit emphasis on problem-solving procedures and methods using varied examples, and (3) verbalization of methods and strategies to encourage development of metacognition. He stated,

> Student participation, teacher encouragement, and student-to-student interaction positively relate to improved critical thinking. These three activities confirm other research and theory stressing the importance of active practice, motivation, and feedback in thinking skills as well as other skills. This confirms that discussions, especially in small classes, are superior to lectures in improving thinking and problem solving.

Ruggiero (1988) argued that the explicit teaching of higher-level reasoning and critical thinking does not depend on what is taught, but rather on how it is taught. He stated, "The only significant change that is required is a change in teaching methodology" (p. 12). Cooperative learning is such a methodological change.

Research conducted by Schoenfeld (1985, 1989), Brown, Collins and Duguid (1989), Lave (1988), and others indicates that cooperative learning is an important procedure for involving students in meaningful activities in the classroom and engaging in situated cognition. Higher-level writing assignments may also best be done by cooperative peer response groups (DiPardo and Freedman, 1988).

Attitudes toward Subject Area

Cooperative learning experiences, compared with competitive and individualistic ones, promote more positive attitudes toward the subject area, more positive attitudes toward the instructional experience, and more continuing motivation to learn more about the subject being studied (Johnson & Johnson, 1989). Guetzkow, Kelley, and McKeachie (1954) and McKeachie (1951) found in a study comparing group discussion and lecturing that students in discussion sections were significantly more favorable than the other groups in attitude toward psychology, and a follow-up of the students three years later revealed that seven men each from the tutorial and discussion groups majored in psychology, whereas none of those in the recitation group did so. Bligh (1972) found that students who had in-class opportunities to interact actively with classmates and the teacher were more satisfied with their learning experience than were students who were taught exclusively by the lecture method. Kulik and Kulik (1979) reported from their comprehensive literature review on college teaching that students who participated in discussion groups in class were more likely to develop positive attitudes toward the course's subject matter. One of the major conclusions of the Harvard Assessment Seminars was that the use of cooperative learning groups resulted in a large increase in satisfaction with the class (Light, 1990). These findings have important implications for influencing female and minority students to enter science- and math-oriented careers.

Time on Task

Achievement consists of never giving up. . . . If there is no dark and dogged will, there will be no shining accomplishment; if there is no dull and determined effort, there will be no brilliant achievement.

Hsun Tzu, Chinese Confucian Philosopher

One explanation for why cooperation promoted greater productivity than did competitive or individualistic efforts is that members of cooperative groups may have spent more time on task. More than thirty studies did in fact measure time on task (see Johnson & Johnson, 1989). They found that cooperators spent more time on task than did competitors (effect size = 0.76) or students working individualistically (effect size = 1.17). Competitors spent more time on task than did students working individualistically (effect size = 0.64). These effect sizes are quite large, indicating that members of cooperative learning groups do seem to spend considerable more time on task than do students working competitively or individualistically.

INTERPERSONAL RELATIONSHIPS

Interpersonal Attraction and Cohesion

The degree of emotional bonding that exists among students has a profound effect on the quality of the work performed. Although evidence from a variety of fields links caring relationships and productivity, one of the most dramatic examples comes from the sport of sled-dog racing. The most grueling and longest sled race in the world is the Alaskan Iditarod, a 1,500-mile race from Anchorage to Nome that winds its way across frozen mountain paths and cuts across long open stretches of land subject to blinding snowstorms. The race was won by a woman in 1985, 1986, 1987, and 1990. When asked if they had any special advantage over men in this race, the winning women said that they developed a closer bond with their dogs and, consequently, their dogs worked harder. A second example may be found in the world of business. When asked about their success, the chief executives of the companies that have the best track records in North America state that they have been successful because they are able to create teams in which members care about each other on a personal as well as a professional level (Kouzes & Posner, 1987). The successful chief executives create a family within which members care deeply about each other and the mutual goals they are striving to achieve. Secondary schools should do likewise.

Cooperative learning experiences, compared with competitive, individualistic, and traditional instruction, promote considerably more liking among students (effect sizes = 0.66 and 0.60, respectively) (Johnson & Johnson, 1989; Johnson, Johnson, & Maruyama, 1983) (see Table A.2). This is true regardless of individual differences in ability level, sex, disabling conditions, ethnic membership, social class differences, or task orientation. Students who studied cooperatively, compared with those who studied competitively or individualistically, developed considerably more commitment and caring for each other no matter what their initial impressions of and attitudes toward each other were. When only the high-quality studies were included in the analysis the effect sizes were 0.82 (cooperative vs. competitive) and 0.62 (cooperative vs. individualistic), respectively. The effect sizes are higher for the studies using pure operationalizations of cooperative learning than for studies using mixed operationalizations (cooperative versus competitive, pure = 0.79 and mixed = 0.46; cooperative versus individualistic, pure = 0.66 and mixed = 0.36). Students learning cooperatively also liked the teacher better and perceived the teacher as being more supportive and accepting academically and personally.

To be productive, a class of students has to cohere and have a positive emotional climate. As relationships within the class or school become more positive, absenteeism decreases, and increases may be expected in student commitment to learning, feelings of personal responsibility to do the assigned work, willingness to take on difficult tasks, motivation and persistence in working on learning tasks, satisfaction and morale, willingness to endure pain and frustration to succeed, willingness to defend the school against external criticism or attack, willingness to listen to and be influenced be peers, commitment to peers' success and growth, and productivity and achievement (Johnson, & F. Johnson, 1997; Johnson & Johnson, 1989; Watson & Johnson, 1972).

In addition, when students are heterogeneous with regard to ethnic, social class, language, and ability differences, cooperative learning experiences are a necessity for building positive peer relationships. Studies on desegregation indicated that cooperation promoted more positive cross-ethnic relationships than did competition (effect size = 0.54) or individualistic (effect-size = 0.44) learning experiences (Johnson & Johnson, 1989). Cross-disability relationships were also more positive in cooperative than in competitive (effect size = 0.70) or individualistic (effect size = 0.64) learning experiences.

Social Support

A friend is one to whom one may pour out all the contents of one's heart,
chaff and grain together knowing that the gentlest of hands will take and sift it,
keep what is worth keeping and with a breath of kindness blow the rest away.

Arabian Proverb

Social support may be defined as the existence and availability of people on whom one can rely for emotional, instrumental, informational, and appraisal aid. More specifically, social support involves the following:

1. Emotional concern, such as attachment, reassurance, and a sense of being able to rely on and confide in a person, all of which contribute to the belief that one is loved and cared for.
2. Instrumental aid, such as direct aid, goods, or services.
3. Information, such as facts or advice that may help to solve a problem.
4. Appraisal, such as feedback about degree to which certain behavioral standards are met (information relevant to self-evaluation).

A **social support system** consists of significant others who collaboratively share people's tasks and goals and who provide individuals with resources (such as money, materials, tools, skills, information, and advice) that enhance their well-being or help people mobilize their resources in order to deal with the particular stressful situation to which they are exposed. Social support is most often reciprocated, and if reciprocity is prevented, then the relationship is weakened. Because not all interpersonal interactions are positive, it is assumed that social support is intended by the giver and perceived by the recipient as beneficial to the recipient. Social support may be given by peers or by authority figures. It may be focused on encouraging and assisting efforts to achieve goals (i.e., productivity or achievement support) or it may be focused on personal caring and liking (i.e., personal support).

Social support involves the exchange of resources intended to enhance mutual well-being and the existence and availability of people on whom one can rely for assistance, encouragement, acceptance, and caring. By providing emotional concern, instrumental aid, information, and feedback, supportive people directly and indirectly promote the following:

1. Academic achievement and productivity.
2. Physical health as individuals involved in close relationships live longer, get sick less often, and recover from illness faster than do isolated individuals.
3. Psychological health, adjustment, and development by preventing neuroticism and psychopathology, reducing distress, and providing resources such as confidants.
4. Constructive management of stress by providing the caring, resources, information, and feedback needed to cope with stress and by buffering the impact of stress on the individual.

Since the 1940s, 106 studies have compared the relative impact of cooperative, competitive, and individualistic efforts on social support. Cooperative experiences tended to promote greater social support than did competitive (effect-size = 0.62) or individualistic (effect-size = 0.70) efforts. Stronger effects were found for peer support than for superior (teacher) support. For methodologically higher-quality studies, the effect sizes for cooperation compared with competition and individualistic efforts are even stronger (effect sizes = 0.83 and 0.71, respectively). The pure cooperative operationalizations promoted significantly higher levels of social support than did the mixed operationalizations (competitive: mixed = 0.45 and pure = 0.73; individualistic: mixed = 0.02 and pure = 0.77).

Social support is perceived to extend to personal commitment and caring as well as task encouragement. Caring about how much a person achieves and wanting to be the person's friend were perceived to go hand in hand. There was little difference between the levels of task and personal support perceived from peers and superiors (teachers).

The importance of social support has been ignored within education over the past thirty years. *A general principle is that the pressure to achieve should always be matched with an equal level of social support.* Challenge and security must be kept in balance (Pelz & Andrews, 1976). Whenever increased demands and pressure to be productive are placed on students (and faculty), a corresponding increase in social support should be structured. Social support and stress are related in that the greater the social support individuals have, the less the stress they experience and the better able they are to manage the stresses involved in their lives. Whenever pressure is placed on individuals to achieve higher and challenge their intellectual capacities, considerable social support should be provided to buffer the individuals from the stress inherent in the situation and to help individuals cope constructively with the stress.

Student Retention

Traditional classroom teaching practices in higher education favor the assertive student. But our analysis indicates that instructors should give greater attention to the passive or reticent student. . . . Passivity is an important warning sign that may reflect a lack of involvement that impedes the learning process and leads to unnecessary attrition.

National Institute of Education (1984)

Tinto (1975, 1987), synthesizing the retention research, concluded that the greater the degree of students' involvement in their learning experience, the more likely they were to persist to graduation. The social-networking processes of social involvement, integration, and bonding with classmates are strongly related with higher rates of student retention. Astin (1985), on the basis of research conducted over ten years, found that student involvement academically and socially in the school experience was the cornerstone of persistence and achievement. Astin and his associates (1972) had earlier concluded that active involvement in the learning experience was especially critical for withdrawal-prone students, such as disadvantaged minorities, who have been found to be particularly passive in academic settings.

Cooperative learning experiences tend to lower attrition rates in schools. Students working on open-ended problems in small groups of four to seven members were more likely to display lower rates of attrition and higher rates of academic achievement than those not involved in the group learning approach (Wales & Stager, 1978). Treisman (1985) found that the five-year retention rate for black students majoring in math or science at Berkeley who were involved in cooperative learning groups was 65 percent (compared to 41 percent for black students not involved). The percentage of black students involved in cooperative learning experiences who graduated in mathematics-based majors was 44 percent (compared to only 10 percent for a control group of black students not participating in cooperative learning groups).

College students report greater satisfaction with courses that allow them to engage in group discussion (Bligh, 1972; Kulik & Kulik, 1979). Students are more likely to stay in school if they are satisfied with their learning experiences (Noel, 1985). Cooperative learning allows for significant amounts of meaningful student discussion that enhances students' satisfaction with the learning experience and, in so doing, promotes student retention.

Importance of Peer Relationships

Peer relationships contribute to (a) social and cognitive development and (b) socialization in numerous ways. Some of the more important consequences correlated with peer relationships are as follows (the specific supporting evidence may be found in Johnson, 1980, and Johnson & Johnson, 1989).

1. *In their interaction with peers, individuals directly learn attitudes, values, skills, and information unobtainable from adults.* In their interaction with each other, individuals imitate each other's behavior and identify with friends possessing admired competencies. By providing models, reinforcement, and direct learning, peers shape a wide variety of social behaviors, attitudes, and perspectives.

2. *Interaction with peers provides support, opportunities, and models for prosocial behavior.* It is within interactions with peers that one helps, comforts, shares with, takes care of, assists, and gives to others. Without peers with whom to engage in such behaviors, many forms of prosocial values and commitments could not be developed. Conversely, whether individuals engage in problem or transition behavior, such as the use of illegal drugs and delinquency, is related to the perceptions of their friends' attitudes toward such behaviors. Being rejected by one's peers tends to

result in antisocial behavioral patterns characterized by aggressiveness, disruptiveness, and other negatively perceived behaviors.

3. *Individuals frequently lack the time perspective needed to tolerate delays in gratification.* As they develop and are socialized, the focus on their own immediate impulses and needs is replaced with the ability to take longer time perspectives. Peers provide models of, expectations of, directions for, and reinforcements of learning to control impulses. Aggressive impulses provide an example. Peer interaction involving such activities as rough-and-tumble play promotes the acquisition of a repertoire of effective aggressive behaviors and helps establish the necessary regulatory mechanisms for modulating aggressive affect.

4. *Students learn to view situations and problems from perspectives other than their own through their interaction with peers.* Such perspective taking is one of the most critical competencies for cognitive and social development. All psychological development may be described as a progressive loss of egocentrism and an increase in ability to take wider and more complex perspectives. It is primarily in interaction with peers that egocentrism is lost and increased perspective taking is gained.

5. *Autonomy* is the ability to understand what others expect in any given situation and to be free to choose whether to meet their expectations. Autonomous people are independent of both extreme inner or outer directness. When making decisions concerning appropriate social behavior, autonomous people tend to consider both their internal values and the situational requirements and then respond in flexible and appropriate ways. Autonomy is the result of (a) the internalization of values (including appropriate self-approval) derived from caring and supportive relationships and (b) the acquisition of social skills and sensitivity. *Relationships with peers are powerful influences on the development of the values and the social sensitivity required for autonomy.* Individuals with a history of isolation from or rejection by peers often are inappropriately other directed. They conform to group pressures even when they believe the recommended actions are wrong or inappropriate.

6. Although adults can provide certain forms of companionship, students need close and intimate relationships with peers with whom they can share their thoughts and feelings, aspirations and hopes, dreams and fantasies, and joys and pains. They need constructive peer relationships to avoid the pain of loneliness.

7. Throughout infancy, childhood, adolescence, and early adulthood, a person moves though several successive and overlapping identities. The physical changes involved in growth, the increasing number of experiences with other people, increasing responsibilities, and general cognitive and social development all cause changes in self-definition. The final result should be a coherent and integrated identity. In peer relationships children and adolescents become aware of the similarities and differences between themselves and others. They experiment with a variety of social roles that help them integrate their own sense of self. In peer relationships values and attitudes are clarified and integrated into an individual's self-definition. *It is through peer relationships that a frame of reference for perceiving oneself is developed.* Gender typing and its impact on one's identity is an example.

8. *Coalitions formed during childhood and adolescence provide help and assistance throughout adulthood.* Friends provide entry into new relationships, pooling of resources, career boosts, and all sorts of unforeseen opportunities.

9. *The ability to maintain independent, cooperative relationships is a prime manifestation of psychological health.* Poor peer relationships in elementary school predict psychological disturbance and delinquency in high school, and poor peer relationships in high school predict adult pathology. The absence of any friendships during childhood and adolescence seems to increase the risk of mental disorder.

10. *In both educational and work settings, peers have a strong influence on productivity.* Greater achievement is typically found in collaborative situations where peers work together than in situations where individuals work alone.

11. *Student educational aspirations may be more influenced by peers than by any other social influence.* Similarly, ambition in career settings is greatly influenced by peers. Within instructional settings, peer relationships can be structured to create meaningful interdependence by learning cooperatively. Within cooperative learning situations, students experience feelings of belonging, acceptance, support, and caring, and the social skills and social roles required for maintaining interdependent relationships can be taught and practiced.

Through repeated cooperative experiences students can develop the social sensitivity of what behavior is expected from others and the actual skills and autonomy to meet such expectations if they so desire. Through holding each other accountable for appropriate social behavior, students can greatly influence the values they internalize and the self-control they develop. It is through a series of interdependent relationships that values are learned and internalized. It is through prolonged cooperative interaction with other people that healthy social development with the overall balance of trust rather than distrust of other people, the ability to view situations and problems from a variety of perspectives, a meaningful sense of direction and purpose in life, an awareness of mutual interdependence with others, and an integrated and coherent sense of personal identity takes place (Johnson, 1979; Johnson & Matross, 1977).

For peer relationships to be constructive influences, they must promote feelings of belonging, acceptance, support, and caring, rather than feelings of hostility and rejection (Johnson, 1980). Being accepted by peers is related to willingness to engage in social interaction, utilizing abilities in achievement situations, and providing positive social rewards for peers. Isolation from peers is associated with high anxiety, low self-esteem, poor interpersonal skills, emotional handicaps, and psychological pathology. Rejection by peers is related to disruptive classroom behavior, hostile behavior and negative affect, and negative attitudes toward other students and school. To promote constructive peer influences, therefore, teachers first must ensure that students interact with each other and, second, must ensure that the interaction takes place within a cooperative context.

PSYCHOLOGICAL HEALTH AND PSYCHOLOGICAL ADJUSTMENT

When students leave school, they need the psychological health and stability required to build and maintain career, family, and community relationships, to establish a basic and meaningful interdependence with other people, and to participate effectively in society. We have conducted a series of studies on the relationship between cooperation and psychological health. Our studies (see Johnson & Johnson, 1989) indicate that *cooperativeness* is positively related to a number of indices of psychological health, namely, emotional maturity, well-adjusted social relations, strong personal identity, and basic trust in and optimism about people. *Competitiveness* also seems to be related to a number of indices of psychological health, whereas *individualistic attitudes* tend to be related to a number of indices of psychological pathology, such as emotional immaturity, social maladjustment, delinquency, self-alienation, and self-rejection. Schools should be organized cooperatively to reinforce those traits and tendencies that promote students' psychological well-being.

Accuracy of Perspective Taking

Social perspective taking is the ability to understand how a situation appears to another person and how that person is reacting cognitively and emotionally to the situation. The opposite of perspective taking is **egocentrism,** the embeddedness in one's own viewpoint to the extent that one is unaware of other points of view and of the limitation of one's perspective. Cooperative learning experiences tend to promote greater cognitive and affective perspective taking than do competitive or individualistic learning experiences (Johnson & Johnson, 1989). Bovard (1951a, 1951b) and McKeachie (1954) found that students participating in class discussions (as opposed to listening to lectures) showed greater insight (as rated by clinical psychologists) into problems of the young women depicted in the film *The Feeling of Rejection.*

Self-Esteem

> *We must see our own goodness, appreciate our assets and abilities, and celebrate our humanness.*
>
> Dennis Wholey

A person is not born with a sense of self. It is during the first two or three years that a kind of crude self-awareness develops, such as being able to make distinctions between what is part of his or her body and what is part of something else. It takes many years of maturation before full adult self-awareness comes into being. As people develop self-awareness, they formulate a self-conception and build processes through which they derive conclusions about their self-worth. *Self-esteem* is a judgment about one's self-worth, value, and competence based on a process of conceptualizing and gathering information about oneself and one's experiences (Johnson & Norem-Hebeisen, 1981). It has two components: the level of worth a person places on himself or herself and the processes through which individuals derive conclusions about their self-worth. Conclusions about self-esteem may be derived through at least five processes (Johnson, 1979; Norem-Hebeisen, 1976; Norem-Hebeisen & Johnson, 1981): *basic self-acceptance,* (the perceived intrinsic acceptability of oneself), *conditional self-acceptance,* (the perceived acceptability of oneself resulting from outperforming others and meeting external standards and expectations), *comparative self-evaluation,* (the estimate of how positively one's attributes compare with those of peers), *reflected self-acceptance,* (the seeing oneself as others see one), and *real-ideal self-esteem,* (the correspondence between what one thinks one is and what one thinks one should be). The latter has not been studied in connection with social interdependence. Many studies, furthermore, used *academic self-esteem* (the self-perception of being a capable, competent, and successful student) as a dependent measure.

Since the 1950s more than 80 studies have compared the relative impact of cooperative, competitive, and individualistic experiences on self-esteem. Cooperative efforts promoted higher self-esteem than did competitive (effect-size = 0.58) or individualistic (effect-size = 0.44) efforts (Johnson & Johnson, 1989). These findings are consistent across high-, medium-, and low-quality studies. The pure operationalizations of cooperation had a significantly stronger impact on self-esteem than did the mixed operationalizations (competitive: mixed = 0.33 and pure = 0.74; cooperative versus individualistic: mixed = 0.22 and pure = 51). A similar pattern of findings was found for academic self-esteem and reflected self-esteem. Our own research demonstrated that cooperative experiences tended to be related to beliefs that one is intrinsically worthwhile, believing that others see one in positive ways, comparing one's attributes favorably with those of one's peers, and judging that one is a capable, competent, and successful person (Johnson, 1979; Norem-Hebeisen, 1974, 1976; Norem-Hebeisen & Johnson, 1981). In cooperative efforts, students (a) realized that they are accurately known, accepted, and liked by their peers (basic self-acceptance), (b) knew that they have contributed to their own, others, and group success (reflected self-esteem), and (c) perceived themselves and others in a differentiated and realistic way that allowed for multidimensional comparisons based on complementarity of one's own and others' abilities (comparative self-evaluation). In cooperative situations, individuals tend to interact, promote each other's success, form multi-dimensional and realistic impressions of each other's competencies, and give accurate feedback. Such interaction tends to promote a basic self-acceptance of oneself as a competent person. Competitive experiences tended to be related to conditional self-esteem based on whether one wins or loses. Competitors' self-esteem tends to be based on the contingent view of one's competence that "If I win, then I have worth as a person, but if I lose, then I have no worth." Winners attribute their success to superior ability and attribute the failure of others to lack of ability, both of which contribute to self-aggrandizement. Losers, who are the vast majority, defensively tend to be self-disparaging, apprehensive about evaluation, and tend to withdraw psychologically and physically. Individualistic experiences tended to be related to basic self-rejection. In individualistic situations, students are isolated from one another, receive little direct comparison with or feedback from peers, and perceive evaluations as inaccurate and unrealistic. A defensive avoidance, evaluation apprehension, and distrust of peers results.

SOCIAL SKILLS

> *If you want one year of prosperity, grow grain.*
> *If you want ten years of prosperity, grow trees.*
> *If you want one hundred years of prosperity, grow people.*

Chinese Proverb

Most people realize that education or vocational training improves their career opportunities. Many people are less aware that interpersonal skills may be the most important set of skills to their employability, productivity, and career success. A recent national survey found that employers value five types of skills: verbal communication skills, responsibility, interpersonal skills, initiative, and decision-making skills. In 1982, the Center for Public Resources published *Basic Skills in the U.S. Workforce,* a nationwide survey of businesses, labor unions, and educational institutions. The study found that 90 percent of the people fired from their jobs were fired for poor job attitudes, poor interpersonal relationships, inappropriate behavior, and inappropriate dress. Being fired for lack of basic and technical skills was infrequent. Even in high-tech careers, the ability to work effectively with other high-tech personnel is essential, and so is the ability to communicate and work with people from other professions to solve interdisciplinary problems. In the real world of work, the heart of most jobs, especially the higher-paying, more interesting jobs, is getting others to cooperate, leading others, coping with complex power and influence issues, and helping solve people's problems in working with each other (Johnson & Johnson, 1989).

Social competence is an essential aspect of psychological health. We are not born instinctively knowing how to interact effectively with others. Interpersonal and group skills do not magically appear when they are needed. Many individuals lack basic interpersonal skills, such as correctly identifying the emotions of others and appropriately resolving a conflict, and often their social ineptitude seems to persist as they get older. Their lives typically do not go well. Individuals who lack social skills find themselves isolated, alienated, and at a disadvantage in vocational and career settings. The relationships so essential for living productive and happy lives are lost when the basic interpersonal skills are not learned.

Generally, students may be more effectively taught social skills in work contexts than in isolation from actually completing a meaningful task. Working together to learn increases students' social skills. To coordinate efforts to achieve mutual goals students must (1) get to know and trust each other, (2) communicate accurately and unambiguously, (3) accept and support each other, and (4) resolve conflicts constructively (Johnson, 1997; Johnson & F. Johnson, 1997). Interpersonal and small-group skills form the basic nexus among individuals, and if individuals are to work together productively and cope with the stresses and strains of doing so, they must have a modicum of these skills.

A number of studies have examined the impact of cooperative learning experiences on the mastery and use of social skills. Lew, Mesch, Johnson, and Johnson (1986a, 1986b) found that socially isolated and withdrawn students learned more social skills and engaged in them more frequently within cooperative than within individualistic situations, especially when the group was rewarded for their doing so. Slavin (1977) found that emotionally disturbed adolescents who experienced cooperative learning were more likely than traditionally taught students to interact appropriately with other students, and this effect was still present five months after the end of the project. Janke (1980) found enhancing effects of cooperative learning on appropriate interactions among emotionally disturbed students and also found the program improved these students' attendance. More generally, cooperative situations promote more frequent, effective, and accurate communication than do competitive and individualistic situations (Johnson, 1973a, 1974). Within cooperative situations communication is more open, effective, and accurate, whereas in competitive situations communication will be closed, ineffective, and inaccurate (Bonoma, Tedeschi, & Helm, 1974; Crombag, 1966; Deutsch, 1949b, 1962; Deutsch & Krauss, 1962; Fay, 1970; French, 1951; Grossack, 1953; Johnson, 1971, 1973a, 1974; Krauss & Deutsch, 1966).

One of the most important sets of social skills to master is conflict resolution. Involved participation in cooperative efforts inevitably produces conflicts. The more caring and committed the relationships, furthermore, the more intense conflicts tend to be (Johnson & Johnson, 1991a, 1992a). Cooperative efforts provide a context in which the structures and skills for managing conflicts constructively may be successfully implemented and learned. Cooperation, furthermore, promotes more constructive management of conflicts than do competitive and individualistic efforts (Deutsch, 1962, 1973; Johnson, 1971, 1973a, 1974).

Inculcating Constructive Attitudes

From the standpoint of everyday life . . . there is one thing we do know; that man is here for the sake of other men—above all, for those upon whose smile and well-being our own happiness depends, and also for the countless unknown souls with whose fate we are connected by a bond of sympathy. Many times a day I realize how much my own outer and inner life is built upon the labors of my fellow men, both living and dead, and how earnestly I must exert myself in order to give in return as much as I have received.

Albert Einstein

Certain attitudes and behavioral patterns are essential to psychological health, and schools may wish to inculcate them in students. Students need to develop a love of learning, curiosity, the desire to distinguish between sense and nonsense, and the ability to use higher-level reasoning to solve problems. Students also need to develop a desire to do high-quality work, a desire to improve continuously, and a sense of pride and accomplishment in doing a good job. Students need to develop self-respect, respect for other people, and respect for property. They need to learn how to fulfill assigned roles reliably. Students need to develop a meaningful purpose and direction in life, develop a desire to achieve, and wish to contribute to making the world a better place. Students need to develop a love of democracy, liberty, and freedom, a high level of patriotism, and a desire to be a good citizen. Students need to learn to value the diversity of people within our society. Students, furthermore, need to develop lifelong good health habits such as nutritious eating patterns, adequate sleep each night, and regular exercise.

In many subject areas (such as health, art, or music), educators have designed instructional programs aimed at promoting a lifelong pattern of attitudes and behavior. Yet the issues of creating enduring conceptual frameworks, positive attitudes, and behavioral habits have been slighted in most discussions of educational practice.

It is through interpersonal influences that attitudes are acquired and behavioral patterns are changed, and it is through the cognitive processing resulting from interpersonal interaction that conceptual frameworks are developed and retained over long periods of time. The factors involved in promoting learning, developing desirable attitudes, and establishing lifelong behavioral patterns are as follows (Johnson & Johnson, 1985):

1. Adopting and conforming to the norms of the reference groups to which one belongs and aspires to belong and with which one identifies.
2. Publicly committing oneself to adopt desired attitudes and behavior and being held accountable by peers to fulfill one's public commitments.
3. Being exposed to visible and credible social models.
4. Being confronted with vivid and personalized information and appeals.
5. Discussing information with peers in ways that promote active cognitive processing and the development of enduring conceptual frameworks.
6. Teaching others the information one has learned.
7. Acquiring continuing motivation to learn.
8. Framing information received as a gain or a loss.

RECIPROCAL RELATIONSHIPS AMONG THE THREE OUTCOMES

The reason we were so good, and continued to be so good, was because he (Joe Paterno [the team coach]) forces you to develop an inner love among the players. It is much harder to give up on your buddy, than it is to give up on your coach. I really believe that over the years the teams I played on were almost unbeatable in tight situations. When we needed to get that six inches we got it because of our love for each other. Our camaraderie existed because of the kind of coach and kind of person Joe was.

Dr. David Joyner

Efforts to achieve, positive interpersonal relationships, and psychological health are reciprocally related (see Figure A.2). Within cooperative situations, the three outcomes are all bidirectional. Each induces and is induced by the others.

Joint efforts to achieve mutual goals create caring and committed relationships; caring and committed relationships among group members increase their joint effort to achieve (Johnson & Johnson, 1989). From working together to accomplish academic tasks students develop camaraderie and friendships. As students strive together, helping each other, sharing materials, exchanging ideas and information, and encouraging each other's efforts they get to know each other, become committed to each other, and develop friendships. Caring relationships come from mutual accomplishment, mutual pride in joint work, and the bonding that results from joint efforts. At the same time, caring and committed relationships promote joint efforts to achieve mutual goals. Individuals seek out opportunities to work with those they care about. As caring increases, so does regular attendance, commitment to learning and achievement, personal responsibility to do one's share of the work, willingness to take on difficult tasks, motivation and persistence in working toward goal achievement, willingness to listen to and be influenced by groupmates, and willingness to endure pain and frustration on behalf of the group (Johnson & F. Johnson, 1997; Johnson & R. Johnson, 1989; Watson & Johnson, 1972). All these contribute to group productivity. The most successful leaders in business and industry are ones that build teams with such personal closeness that team members feel like a family (Kouses & Posner, 1987).

Joint efforts to achieve mutual goals promote psychological health and social competence; the more healthy psychologically group members are, the more able they are to contribute to the joint effort (Johnson & Johnson, 1989). Cooperating involves contributing to other's success and well-being, knowing there are others who contribute to your success and well-being, and being involved in a joint effort greater than oneself. Working together to complete academic tasks increases a person's social competencies, success, sense of meaning and purpose, ability to cope with failure and anxiety, self-esteem, and self-efficacy. Contributing to others' success has been found to cure the blues (i.e., decrease depression). Knowing that one's efforts contribute to the success of others as well as oneself gives added meaning and value to academic work. At the same time, the healthier psychologically individuals are, the better able they are to work with others to achieve mutual goals. States of depression, anxiety, guilt, shame, and fear interfere with ability to cooperate and decrease the energy a person has to devote to a cooperative effort. Joint efforts require coordination, effective communication, leadership, and conflict management that, in turn, require social competencies.

The more caring and committed the relationships among group members, the greater their psychological health and social competencies tend to be; the healthier members are psychologically, the more able they are to build and maintain caring and committed relationships (Johnson & Johnson, 1989). Psychological health is built on the internalization of the caring and respect received from loved ones. Through the internalization of positive relationships, direct social support, shared intimacy, and expressions of caring, psychological health and the ability to cope with stress are built. Friendships are developmental advantages that promote self-esteem, self-efficacy, and general psychological adjustment. Destructive relationships, and even the absence of caring and committed relationships, tend to increase psychological pathology. At the same time, the healthier people are psychologically (i.e., free of psychological pathologies such as depression, paranoia, anxiety, fear of failure, repressed anger, hopelessness, and meaninglessness), the more able they are to initiate, build, and maintain caring and committed relationships.

> The fundamental facts that brought about cooperation, society, and civilization and transformed the animal man into a human being are the facts that work performed under the division of labor is more productive than isolated work and that man's reason is capable of recognizing this truth. But for these facts men would have forever remained deadly foes of one another, irreconcilable rivals in their endeavors to secure a portion of the scarce supply of means of sustenance provided by Nature. Each man would have been forced to view all other men as his enemies; his craving for the satisfaction of his own appetites would have brought him into an implacable conflict with all his neighbors. No sympathy could possibly develop under such a state of affairs. . . .We may call consciousness of kind, sense of community, or sense of belonging together the acknowledgement of the fact that all other human beings are potential collaborators in the struggle for survival because they are capable of recognizing the mutual benefits of cooperation. —*Ludwig Von Mises (1949)*

REDUCING THE DISCREPANCY

The research results consistently indicate that cooperative learning will promote higher achievement, more positive interpersonal relationships, and greater psychological health than will competitive or individualistic efforts. Although competitive and individualistic efforts may have a place in classrooms, there are those who believe that competition is inherently destructive (Kohn, 1992). From his review of the research, Kohn concluded that making others fail is not only an unproductive way to work and learn but also is devastating to individuals and society as competition (a) causes anxiety, selfishness, self-doubt, and poor communication, (b) poisons relationships among individuals thereby making life more unpleasant than it needs to be, and (c) often results in outright aggression. Kohn (1990) also noted that competitive structures create a negative view of human nature as solitary individuals striving to maximize personal gain. He has presented evidence that there is a brighter side to human nature based on our relationships with others characterized by altruism, empathy, caring, and commitment. Kohn would replace all competition in higher education with cooperative efforts.

With the amount of research evidence available, it is surprising that classroom practice is so oriented toward competitive and individualistic learning and schools are so dominated by competitive and individualistic organizational structures. *It is time for the discrepancy to be reduced between what the research indicates is effective in teaching and what faculty actually do.* To do so, faculty must understand the role of the teacher in implementing cooperative learning experiences. This text has focused on the essential elements of cooperative lessons and the teacher's role in using formal cooperative learning groups, informal cooperative learning groups, and cooperative base groups.

References

ARMENTO, B. (1977). Teacher behaviors related to student achievement on a social science concept test. **Journal of Teacher Education, 28,** 46–52.

ASHMORE, R. (1970). Solving the problems of prejudice. In B. E. Collins (Ed.), **Social psychology.** Reading, MA: Addison-Wesley Publishing Co.

ARCHER–KATH, J., JOHNSON, D. W., & JOHNSON, R. (1994) Individual versus group feedback in cooperative groups. **Journal of Social Psychology, 134** (5), 681–694.

ARONSON, E. (1978). **The jigsaw classroom.** Beverly Hills, CA: Sage Publications.

ASTIN, A. (1985). **Achieving educational excellence.** San Francisco: Jossey-Bass.

ASTIN, A. (1993). **What matters in college?** San Francisco: Jossey-Bass.

ASTIN, H., ASTIN, A., BISCONTI, A., & FRANKEL, H. (1972). **Higher education and the disadvantaged student.** Washington, DC: Human Science Press.

ASTIN, A., GREEN, K., & KORN, W. (1987). **The American freshman: Twenty year trends.** Los Angeles: University of California at Los Angeles, Higher Education Research Institute.

ASTIN, A., GREEN, K., KORN, W., & SHALIT, M. (1986). **The American freshman: National norms for fall 1986.** Los Angeles: University of California at Los Angeles, Higher Education Research Institute.

ATKINSON, J. (1965). The mainsprings of achievement-oriented activity. In J. D. Krumholtz (Ed.), **Learning and the educational process** (pp. 25–66). Chicago: Rand McNally.

BLANCHARD, F., ADELMAN, L., & COOK, S. (1975). The effect of group success and failure upon interpersonal attraction in cooperating interracial groups. **Journal of Personality and Social Psychology, 32,** 519–530.

BLAU, P. (1954). Co-operation and competition in a bureaucracy. **American Journal of Sociology, 59,** 530–535.

BLIGH, D. (1972). **What's the use of lectures.** Harmondsworth, England: Penguin.

BLUMBERG, A., MAY, J., & PERRY, R. (1974). An inner-city school that changed—and continued to change. **Education and Urban Society, 6,** 222–238.

BOND, C. & TITUS, L. (1993). Social facilitation: A meta-analysis of 241 studies. **Psychological Bulletin, 94,** 265–292.

BONOMA, T., TEDESCHI, J., & HELM, B. (1974). Some effects of target cooperation and reciprocated promises on conflict resolution. **Sociometry, 37,** 251–261.

BOVARD, E. (1951a). Group structure and perception. **Journal of Abnormal and Social Psychology, 46,** 398–405.

BOVARD, E. (1951b). The experimental production of interpersonal affect. **Journal of Abnormal Psychology, 46,** 521–528.

BOWERS, J. (1986). Classroom communication apprehension: A survey. **Communication Education, 35**(4), 372–378.

BRONFRENBRENNER, U. (1970). **Two worlds of childhood.** New York: Russell Sage.

BROWN, J. (1990). Evaluating one's abilities: Shortcuts and stumbling blocks on the road to self-knowledge. **Journal of Experimental Social Psychology, 26,** 149–167.

BROWN, J., COLLINS, A., & DUGUID, P. (1989). Situated cognition and the culture of learning. **Educational Researcher, 18**(1), 32–42.

BUTLER, R. (1993). Effects of task- and ego-achievement on information-seeking during task engagement. **Journal of Personality and Social Psychology, 65,** 18–31.

CAMPBELL, J. (1965). **The children's crusader: Colonel Francis W. Parker.** PhD dissertation, Teachers College, Columbia University.

COHEN, E. (1994). **Designing groupwork** (2nd ed.). New York: Teachers College Press.

COLEMAN, J. (1961). **The adolescent society.** New York: Macmillan.

COLLINS, B. (1970). **Social Psychology.** Reading, MA: Addison-Wesley.

CONGER, J. (1981). Freedom and commitment: Families, youth, and social change. *American Psychologist, 36,* 1475–1484.

CONGER, J. (1988). Hostages to fortune: Youth, values, and the public interest. **American Psychologist, 43,** 291–300.

COOK, S. (1969). Motives in a conceptual analysis of attitude-related behavior. In W. Arnold and D. Levine (Eds.), **Nebraska symposium on motivation** (Vol. 17). Lincoln: University of Nebraska Press.

COSTIN, F. (1972, January). Lecturing versus other methods of teaching: A review of research. **British Journal of Educational Technology, 3**(1), 4–30.

CROCKENBERG, S., BRYANT, B., & WILCE, L. (1976). The effects of cooperatively and competitively structured learning environments on inter- and intrapersonal behavior. **Child Development, 47,** 386–396.

DALOZ, L. (1987). **Effective teaching and mentoring.** San Francisco: Jossey-Bass.

DANSEREAU, D. (1985). Learning strategy research. In J. Segal, S. Chipman, and R. Glaser (Eds.). **Thinking and learning skills, Vol. 1: Relating instruction to research.** Hillsdale, NJ: Lawrence Erlbaum.

DARWIN, C. (1859). **The origin of species.** London: John Murray.

DEUTSCH, M. (1949a). An experimental study of the effects of cooperation and competition upon group processes. **Human Relations, 2,** 199–232.

DEUTSCH, M. (1949b). A theory of cooperation and competition. **Human Relations, 2,** 129–152.

DEUTSCH, M. (1958). Trust and suspicion. **Journal of Conflict Resolution, 2,** 25–279.

DEUTSCH, M. (1960). The effects of motivational orientation upon trust and suspicion. **Human Relations, 13,** 123–139.

DEUTSCH, M. (1962). Cooperation and trust: Some theoretical notes. In M. R. Jones (Ed.), **Nebraska symposium on motivation** (pp. 275–319). Lincoln, NE: University of Nebraska Press.

DEUTSCH, M. (1973). **The resolution of conflict.** New Haven, CT: Yale University Press.

DEUTSCH, M. (1985). **Distributive justice.** New Haven, CT: Yale University Press.

DEUTSCH, M., & KRAUSS, R. (1962). Studies of interpersonal bargaining. **Journal of Conflict Resolutions, 6,** 52–76.

DEVRIES, D., & EDWARDS, K. (1973). Learning games and student teams: Their effects on classroom process. **American Educational Research Journal, 10,** 307–318.

DEVRIES, D., & EDWARDS, K. (1974). Student teams and learning games: Their effects on cross-race and cross-sex interaction. **Journal of Educational Psychology, 66**(5), 741–749.

DEVRIES, D., MUSE, D., & WELLS, E. (1971). **The effects of working in cooperative groups: An exploratory study.** Baltimore: Johns Hopkins University, Center for Social Organization of Schools, Report #120.

DeVries, D., Slavin, R., Fennessey, G., Edwards, K., & Lombardo, M. (1980). **Teams-Games-Tournament: The team learning approach.** Englewood Cliffs, NJ: Educational Technology Publications.

Dewey, J. (1924). **The school and society.** Chicago: University of Chicago Press.

Diamond, J. (1989, May). The great leap forward. **Discover, 10,** 50–60.

DiPardo, A., & Freedman, S. (1988). Peer response groups in the writing classroom: Theoretic foundations and new directions. **Review of Educational Research, 58,** 119–150.

Dreeben, R. (1968). **On what is learned in school.** Reading, MA: Addison-Wesley.

Ebel, K. (1983). **The aims of college teaching.** San Francisco: Jossey-Bass.

Fait, H., & Billings, J. (1978). Reassessment of the value of competition. In R. Martens (Ed.), **Joy and sadness in children's sports (pp. 98–103).** Champaign IL: Human Kinetics.

Farb, P. (1963). **Ecology.** New York: Time.

Fay, A. (1970). **The effects of cooperation and competition on learning and recall.** Unpublished master's thesis, George Peabody College.

Frank, M. (1984). **A comparison between an individual and group goal structure contingency that differed in the behavioral contingency and performance-outcome components.** Unpublished Ph.D. dissertation, University of Minnesota.

French, J. (1951). Group productivity. In H. Guetzkow (Ed.), **Groups, leadership, and men** (pp. 44–55). Pittsburgh: Carnegie Press.

Gabbert, B., Johnson, D. W., & Johnson, R. (1986). Cooperative learning, group-to-individual transfer, process gain and the acquisition of cognitive reasoning strategies. **Journal of Psychology, 120**(3), 265–278.

Gould, S. (1988). Kropotkin was no crackpot: Understanding the spell of his homeland, a peace-loving Russian anarchist argued cogently against a narrow Darwinian view of evolution. **Natural History, 97,** 12–21.

Graziano, W., Hair, E., & Finch, J. (1997). Competitiveness mediates the link between personality and group performance. **Journal of Personality and Social Psychology, 73**(6), 1394–1408.

Green, D. (1977). The immediate processing of sentences. **Quarterly Journal of Experimental Psychology, 29,** 135–146.

Grossack, M. (1953). Some effects of cooperation and competition upon small group behavior. **Journal of Abnormal and Social Psychology, 49,** 341–348.

Guetzkow, H., Kelly, E., & McKeachie, W. (1954). An experimental comparison of recitation, discussion, and tutorial methods in college teaching. **Journal of Educational Psychology, 45,** 193–209.

Halisch, F., & Heckhausen, H. (1977). Search for feedback information and effort regulation during task performance. **Journal of Personality and Social Psychology, 35,** 724–733.

Haines, D., & McKeachie, W. (1967). Cooperative versus competitive discussion methods in teaching introductory psychology. **Journal of Educational Psychology, 58**(6), 386–390.

Harkins, S., & Petty, R. (1982). The effects of task difficulty and task uniqueness on social loafing. **Journal of Personality and Social Psychology, 43,** 1214–1229.

Hartup, W. (1976). Peer interaction and the behavioral development of the individual child. In E. Schloper & R. Reicher (Eds.), **Psychology and child development.** New York: Plenum Press.

Hartup, W., Glazer, J., & Charlesworth, R. (1967). Peer reinforcement and sociometric status. **Child Development, 38,** 1017–1024.

Helmreich, R. (1982, August). **Pilot selection and training.** Paper presented at the annual meeting of the American Psychological Association, Washington, DC.

HELMREICH, R., BEANE, W., LUCKER, W., & SPENCE, J. (1978). Achievement motivation and scientific attainment. **Personality and Social Psychology Bulletin, 4,** 222–226.

HELMREICH, R., SAWIN, L., & CARSRUD, A. (1986). The honeymoon effect in job performance: Temporal increases in the predictive power of achievement motivation. **Journal of Applied Psychology, 71,** 185–188.

HELMREICH, R., SPENCE, J., BEANE, W., LUCKER, W., & MATTHEWS, K. (1980). Making it in academic psychology: Demographic and personality correlates of attainment. **Journal of Personality and Social Psychology, 39,** 896–908.

HILL, G. (1982). Group versus individual performance: Are N + 1 heads better than one? **Psychological Bulletin, 91,** 517–539.

HOLT, J. (1964). **How children fail.** New York: Dell Publishing.

HUNT, P., & HILLERY, J. (1973). Social facilitation in a coaction setting: An examination of the effects over learning trials. **Journal of Experimental Social Psychology, 9,** 563–571.

HURLOCK, E. (1927). Use of group rivalry as an incentive. **Journal of Abnormal and Social Psychology, 22,** 278–290.

HWONG, N., CASWELL, A., JOHNSON, D. W., & JOHNSON, R. (1993). Effects of cooperative and individualistic learning on prospective elementary teachers' music achievement and attitudes. **Journal of Social Psychology, 133** 53–64.

HENRY, J. (1963). **Culture against man.** New York: Random House.

HILL, G. (1982). Group versus individual performance: Are N + 1 heads better than one? **Psychology Bulletin, 91,** 517–539.

HWONG, N., CASWELL, A., JOHNSON, D. W., & JOHNSON, R. (1993). Effects of cooperative and individualistic learning on prospective elementary teachers' music achievement and attitudes. **Journal of Social Psychology, 133,** 53–64.

ILLICH, J. (1971). **Deschooling society.** New York: Harrow Books.

INGHAM, A., LEVINGER, G., GRAVES, J., & PECKHAM, V. (1974). The Ringelmann effect: Studies of group size and group performance. **Journal of Personality and Social Psychology, 10,** 371–384.

ISO-AHOLA, S., & HATFIELD, B. (1986). **Psychology of sports: A social psychological approach.** Dubuque, Iowa: Wm. C. Brown.

JACKSON, P. (1968). **Life in classrooms.** New York: Holt, Rinehart & Winston.

JANKE, R. (1980). Computational errors of mentally retarded students. **Psychology in the Schools, 17,** 30–32.

JOHNSON, D. W. (1970). **The social psychology of education.** New York: Holt, Rinehart & Wilson.

JOHNSON, D. W. (1971). Role reversal: A summary and review of the research. **International Journal of Group Tensions, 111,** 318–334.

JOHNSON, D. W. (1973a). Communication in conflict situations: A critical review of the research. **International Journal of Group Tensions, 3,** 46–47.

JOHNSON, D. W. (Ed.). (1973b). **Contemporary Social Psychology.** Philadelphia: Lippincott.

JOHNSON, D. W. (1974). Communication and the inducement of cooperative behavior in conflicts: A critical review. **Speech Monographs, 41,** 64–78.

JOHNSON, D. W. (1979). **Educational psychology.** Englewood Cliffs, NJ: Prentice-Hall.

JOHNSON, D. W. (1980). Constructive peer relationships, social development, and cooperative learning experiences: Implications for the prevention of drug abuse. **Journal of Drug Education, 10,** 7–24.

JOHNSON, D. W. (1991). **Human relations and your career** (3rd ed.). Englewood Cliffs, NJ: Prentice-Hall.

JOHNSON, D. W. (1997). **Reaching out: Interpersonal effectiveness and self-actualization** (6th ed.). Needham Heights, MA: Allyn & Bacon.

JOHNSON, D. W., & JOHNSON, F. (1997). **Joining together: Group theory and group skills** (6th ed.). Boston: Allyn & Bacon.

JOHNSON, D. W., & JOHNSON, R. (1974). Instructional goal structure: Cooperative, competitive, or individualistic. **Review of Educational Research, 44,** 213–240.

JOHNSON, D. W., & JOHNSON, R. (1977). **Controversy in the classroom** (Video). Edina, MN: Interaction Book Company.

JOHNSON, D. W., & JOHNSON, R. (1978). Cooperative, competitive, and individualistic learning. **Journal of Research and Development in Education, 12,** 3–15.

JOHNSON, D. W., & JOHNSON, R. (1979). Conflict in the classroom: Controversy and learning. **Review of Educational Research, 49,** 51–70.

JOHNSON, D. W., & JOHNSON, R. (1981). Effects of cooperative and individualistic learning experiences on interethnic interaction. **Journal of Educational Psychology, 73**(3), 454–459.

JOHNSON, D. W., & JOHNSON, R. (1983a). The socialization and achievement crisis: Are cooperative learning experiences the solution? In L. Bickman (Ed.), **Applied Social Psychology Annual 4** (pp. 119–164). Beverly Hills, CA: Sage.

JOHNSON, D. W., & JOHNSON, R. (1983b). Social interdependence and perceived academic and personal support in the classroom. **Journal of Social Psychology, 120, 77–82.**

JOHNSON, D. W., & JOHNSON, R. (1985a). The internal dynamics of cooperative learning groups. In Slavin, R., Sharan, S., Kagan, S., Lazarowitz, R., Webb, C., & Schmuck, R. (Eds.). (1985). **Learning to cooperate, cooperating to learn** (pp. 103–124). New York: Plenum.

JOHNSON, D. W., & JOHNSON, R. (1985b). Classroom conflict: Controversy vs. debate in learning groups. **American Educational Research Journal, 22,** 237–256.

JOHNSON, D. W., & JOHNSON, R. (1985c). Motivational processes in cooperative, competitive, and individualistic learning situations. In C. Ames and R. Ames (Eds.), **Research on Motivation in Education, Vol. 2, The Classroom Milleu** (pp. 249–286). New York: Academic Press.

JOHNSON, D. W., & JOHNSON, R. (1986). Impact of classroom organization and instructional methods on the effectiveness of mainstreaming. In C. Meisel (Ed.), **Mainstreaming handicapped children: Outcomes, controversies, and new directions** (pp. 219–250). Hillsdale, NJ: Lawrence Erlbaum.

JOHNSON, D. W., & JOHNSON, R. (1987). **Creative Conflict.** Edina, MN: Interaction Book Company.

JOHNSON, D. W., & JOHNSON, R. (1989). **Cooperation and competition: Theory and research.** Edina, MN: Interaction Book Company.

JOHNSON, D. W., & JOHNSON, R. (1991a). **Teaching students to be peacemakers** (Video). Edina, MN: Interaction Book Company.

JOHNSON, D. W., & JOHNSON, R. (1991b). Cooperative learning and classroom and school climate. In B. Fraser & H. Walberg (Eds.), **Educational environments: Evaluation, antecedents and consequences** (pp. 55–74). New York: Pergamon Press.

JOHNSON, D. W., & JOHNSON, R. (1992a). **Positive interdependence: The heart of cooperative learning.** Edina, MN: Interaction Book Company.

JOHNSON, D. W., & JOHNSON, R. (1992b). **Positive interdependence: The heart of cooperative learning** (Videotape). Edina, MN: Interaction Book Company.

JOHNSON, D. W., & JOHNSON, R. (1992c). **Advanced cooperative learning** (2nd ed.). Edina, MN: Interaction Book Company.

JOHNSON, D. W., & JOHNSON, R. (1994). **Leading the cooperative school** (2nd ed). Edina, MN: Interaction Book Company.

JOHNSON, D. W., & JOHNSON, R. (1995a). **Teaching students to be peacemakers** (3rd ed.). Edina, MN: Interaction Book Company.

JOHNSON, D. W., & JOHNSON, R. (1995b). **My mediation notebook** (3rd ed.). Edina, MN: Interaction Book Company.

JOHNSON, D. W., & JOHNSON, R. (1995c). **Creative controversy: Intellectual challenge in the classroom.** Edina, MN: Interaction Book Company.

JOHNSON, D. W., & JOHNSON, R. (1996). **Meaningful and manageable assessment through cooperative learning.** Edina, MN: Interaction Book Company.

JOHNSON, D. W., & JOHNSON, R. (1997). **Learning to lead teams: Developing leadership skills.** Edina, MN: Interaction Book Company.

JOHNSON, D. W., & JOHNSON, R. (1998). Cooperative learning, values, and culturally plural classrooms. In M. Leicester, C. Modgill, & S. Modgil (Eds.). **Values, the classroom, and cultural diversity.** London: Cassell PLC.

JOHNSON, D. W., & JOHNSON, R. (1998). The three Cs of school and classroom management. In H. Freiberg (Ed.), **Beyond behaviorism: Changing the classroom management paradigm.** Boston: Allyn & Bacon.

JOHNSON, D. W., JOHNSON, R., & ANDERSON, D. (1978). Relationship between student cooperative, competitive, and individualistic attitudes toward schooling. **Journal of Psychology, 100,** 183–199.

JOHNSON, D. W., JOHNSON, R., & ANDERSON, D. (1983). Social interdependence and classroom climate. **Journal of Psychology, 114,** 135–142.

JOHNSON, D. W., JOHNSON, R., BUCKMAN, L., & RICHARDS, P. (1986). The effect of prolonged implementation of cooperative learning on social support within the classroom. **Journal of Psychology, 119,** 405–511.

JOHNSON, D. W., JOHNSON, R., & HOLUBEC, E. (Eds.). (1987). **Stucturing cooperative learning: Lesson plans for teachers.** Edina, MN: Interaction Book Company.

JOHNSON, D. W., JOHNSON, R., & HOLUBEC, E. (1992). **Advanced cooperative learning.** Edina, MN: Interaction Book Company.

JOHNSON, D. W., JOHNSON, R., & HOLUBEC, E. (1993). **Circles of learning: Cooperation in the classroom** (4th ed.). Edina, MN: Interaction Book Company.

JOHNSON, D. W., JOHNSON, R., & HOLUBEC, E. (1993). **Cooperation in the classroom** (6th ed.). Edina, MN: Interaction Book Company.

JOHNSON, D. W., JOHNSON, R., & HOLUBEC, E. (1998). **Cooperation in the classroom** (7th ed.). Edina, MN: Interaction Book Company.

JOHNSON, D. W., JOHNSON, R., & MARUYAMA, G. (1983). Interdependence and interpersonal attraction among heterogeneous and homogeneous individuals: A theoretical formulation and a meta-analysis of the research. **Review of Educational Research, 53,** 5–54.

JOHNSON, D. W., JOHNSON, R., ORTIZ, A., & STANNE, M. (1991). Impact of positive goal and resource interdependence on achievement, interaction and attitudes. **Journal of General Psychology, 118,** 341–347.

JOHNSON, D. W., JOHNSON, R., & SMITH, K. (1986). Academic conflict among students: Controversy and learning. In R. Feldman, (Ed.). **Social psychological applications to education.** New York: Cambridge University Press.

JOHNSON, D. W., JOHNSON, R., & SMITH, K. (1991). **Active learning: Cooperative in the college classroom.** Edina, MN: Interaction Book Company.

JOHNSON, D. W., JOHNSON, R., & SMITH, K. (1997). **Academic controversy: Encriching college instruction through intellectual conflict.** ASHE-ERIC Higher Education Report Volume 25, No.3. Washington, DC: The George Washington University, Graduate School of Education and Human Development.

JOHNSON, D. W., JOHNSON, R., STANNE, M., & GARIBALDI, A. (1990). The impact of leader and member group processing on achievement in cooperative groups. **The Journal of Social Psychology, 130,** 507–516.

JOHNSON, D. W., MARUYAMA, G., JOHNSON, R., NELSON, D., & SKON, L. (1981). Effects of cooperative, competitive, and individualistic goal structures on achievement: A meta-analysis. **Psychological Bulletin, 89,** 47–62.

JOHNSON, D. W., & MATROSS, R. (1977). The interpersonal influence of the psychotherapist. In A. Gurman & A. Razin (Eds.), **The effective therapist: A handbook.** Elmsford, NY: Pergamon Press.

JOHNSON, D. W., & NOONAN, P. (1972). Effects of acceptance and reciprocation of self-disclosures on the development of trust. **Journal of Counseling Psychology, 19**(5), 411–416.

JOHNSON, D. W., & NOREM-HEBEISEN, A. (1977). Attitudes toward interdependence among persons and psychological health. **Psychological Reports, 40,** 843–850.

JOHNSON, D. W., & NOREM-HEBEISEN, A. (1981). Relationships between cooperative, competitive, and individualistic attitudes and differentiated aspects of self-esteem. **Journal of Personality, 49,** 415–426.

JOHNSON, D. W., SKON, L., & JOHNSON, R. (1980). Effects of cooperative, competitive, and individualistic conditions on children's problem-solving performance. **American Educational Research Journal, 17**(1), 83–94.

JOHNSON, R., & JOHNSON, D. W. (1985). **Warm-ups, grouping strategies, and group activities.** Edina, MN: Interaction Book Company.

KAGAN, J. (1965, Summer). Personality and the learning process. **Daedalus,** 553–563.

KAGAN, S. (1991). **Cooperative learning.** San Juan Capistrano, CA: Resources for Teachers.

KAGAN, S., & MADSEN, M. (1972). Experimental analyses of cooperation and competition of Anglo-American and Mexican children. **Developmental Psychology, 6**(1), 49–59.

KARP, D., & YOELS, W. (1987). The college classroom: Some observations on the meanings of student participation. **Sociology and Social Research, 60,** 421–439.

KATZENBACH, J., & SMITH, D. (1993). **Wisdom of teams.** Boston: Harvard Business School Press.

KEPPEL, G., & UNDERWOOD, B. (1962). Proactive inhibition in short-term retention of single items. **Journal of Verbal Learning and Verbal Behavior, 1,** 153–161.

KERR, N., & BRUUN, S. (1983). The dispensability of member effort and group motivation losses: Free-rider effects. **Journal of Personality and Social Psychology, 44,** 78–94.

KERR, N. (1981). Ringelmann revisited: Alternative explanations for the social loafing effects. **Personality and Social Psychology Bulletin, 7,** 224–231.

KERR, N., & BRUUN, S. (1983). The dispensability of member effort and group motivation losses: Free-rider effects. **Journal of Personality and Social Psychology, 44,** 78–94.

KIEWRA, K. (1985a). Investigating notetaking and review: A depth of processing alternatives. **Educational Psychologist, 20**(1), 23–32.

KIEWRA, K. (1985b). Providing the instructor's notes: An effective addition to student learning. **Educational Psychologist, 20**(1), 33–39.

KIEWRA, K. (1987). Notetaking and review: The research and its implications. **Instructional Science, 16,** 233–249.

KIEWRA, K., & BENTON, S. (1988). The relationship between information-processing ability and notetaking. **Contemporary Educational Psychology, 13,** 33–44.

KLEIBER, D., & ROBERTS, G. (1981). The effects of experience in the development of social character: An exploratory investigation. **Journal of Sport Psychology, 3,** 114–122.

KLINGER, E. (1977). **Meaning and void: Inner experiences and the incentives in people's lives.** Minneapolis: University of Minnesota Press.

KOHL, H. (1969). **The open classroom.** New York: Vintage Books.

KOHN, A. (1990). **The brighter side of human nature.** New York: Basic Books.

KOHN, A. (1992). **No contest** (2nd ed.). Boston: Houghton Mifflin.

KOUZES, J., & POSNER, B. (1987). **The leadership challenge.** San Francisco: Jossey-Bass.

KROLL, W., & PETERSON, K. (1965). Study of values test and collegiate football teams. **Research Quarterly, 36,** 441–447.

KROPOTKIN, P. (1914). **Mutual aid: A factor of evolution.** London: Heinemann.

KUHN, T. (1962). **The structure of scientific revolutions.** Chicago: University of Chicago Press.

KULIK, J., & KULIK, C. L. (1979). College teaching. In P. L. Peterson & H. J. Walberg (Eds.), **Research on teaching: Concepts, findings, and implications.** Berkeley, CA: McCutcheon.

LAMM, H., & TROMMSDORFF, G. (1973). Group verses individual performance on tasks requiring ideational proficiency (Brainstorming): A review. **European Journal of Social Psychology, 3,** 361–388.

LANGER, E., & BENEVENTO, A. (1978). Self-induced dependence. **Journal of Personality and Social Psychology, 36,** 886–893.

LARSON, C., DANSEREAU, D., O'DONNELL, A., HYTHECKER, V., LAMBIOTTE, J., & ROCKLIN, T. (1984). Verbal ability and cooperative learning: Transfer of effects. **Journal of Reading Behavior, 16**(4), 280–296.

LATANE, B., WILLIAMS, K., & HARKINS, S. (1979). Many hands make light the work: The causes and consequences of social loafing. **Journal of Personality and Social Psychology, 37,** 822–832.

LAUGHLIN, P. (1965). Selection strategies in concept attainment as a function of number of persons and stimulus display. **Journal of Experimental Psychology, 70**(3), 323–327.

LAUGHLIN, P. (1973). Selection strategies in concept attainment. In R. Solso (Ed.), **Contemporary issues in cognitive psychology: The Loyola symposium.** Washington, DC: V. H. Winston.

LAUGHLIN, P., & BARTH, J. (1981). Group-to-individual and individual-to-group problem-solving transfer. **Journal of Personality and Social Psychology, 41**(6), 1087–1093.

LAUGHLIN, P., BRANCH, L., & JOHNSON H. (1969). Individual versus triadic performances on a unidimensional complementary task as a function of initial ability level. **Journal of Personality and Social Psychology, 12**(2), 144–150.

LAUGHLIN, P., & JACCARD, J. (1975). Social facilitation and observational learning of individuals and cooperative pairs. **Journal of Personality Social Psychology, 32**(5), 873–879.

LAUGHLIN, P., & McGLYNN, R. (1967). Cooperative versus competitive concept attainment as a function of sex and stimulus display. **Journal of Personality and Social Psychology, 7**(4), 398–402.

LAUGHLIN, P., McGLYNN, R., ANDERSON, J., & JACOBSON, E (1968). Concept attainment by individuals versus cooperative pairs as a function of memory, sex, and concept rule. **Journal of Personality and Social Psychology, 8**(4), 410–417.

LAVE, J. (1988). **Cognition in practice: Mind, mathematics and culture in everyday life.** Cambridge: Cambridge University Press.

LAWRENCE, G. (1974). **Patterns of effective inservice education: A state of the art summary of research on materials and procedures for changing teacher behaviors in inservice education.** Tallahassee: Florida State Department of Education.

LEPLEY, W. (1937). Competitive behavior in the albino rat. **Journal of Experimental Psychology, 21,** 194–201.

LEVIN, H., GLASS, G., & MEISTER, G. (1984). **Cost-effectiveness of educational interventions.** Stanford, California: Institute for Research on Educational Finance and Governance.

LEVINE, J. (1983). Social comparison and education. In J. Levine & M. Wang (Eds.), **Teacher and student perceptions: Implications for learning.** New York: Erlbaum.

LEW, M., MESCH, D., JOHNSON, D. W., & JOHNSON, R. (1986a). Positive interdependence, academic and collaborative-skills group contingencies and isolated students. **American Educational Research Journal, 23,** 476–488.

LEW, M., MESCH, D., JOHNSON, D. W., & JOHNSON, R. (1986b). Components of cooperative learning: Effects of collaborative skills and academic group contingencies on achievement and main streaming. **Contemporary Educational Psychology, 11,** 229–239.

LEWIN, K. (1935). **A dynamic theory of personality.** New York: McGraw-Hill.

LEWIN, K. (1948). **Resolving social conflicts.** New York: Harper.

LIGHT, R. (1990). **The Harvard assessment seminars.** Cambridge, MA: Harvard University Press.

LIPPITT, R., & GOLD, M. (1959). Classroom social structure as a mental health problem. **Journal of Social Issues, 15,** 40–58.

LITTLE, J. (1981). **School success and staff development in urban desegregated schools.** Paper presented at the American Educational Research Association, Los Angeles, April.

LITTLE, J. (1990). The persistence of privacy: Autonomy and initiative in teachers' professional relations. **Teacher's College Record, 9,** 509–536.

LOY, J., BIRRELL, S., & ROSE, P. (1976). Attitudes held toward agnostic activities as a function of selected social identities. **Quest, 26,** 81–95.

MCCLINTOCK, C. (1972). Social motives: A set of propositions. **Behavioral Science, 17,** 438–454.

MCGLYNN, R. (1972). Four-person group concept attainment as function of interaction format. **Journal of Social Psychology, 86,** 89–94.

MCKEACHIE, W. (1951). Anxiety in the college classroom. **Journal of Educational Research, 45,** 153–160.

MCKEACHIE, W. (1954). Individual conformity to attitudes of classroom groups. **Journal of Abnormal and Social Psychology, 49,** 282–289.

MCKEACHIE, W. (1967). Research in teaching: The gap between theory and practice. In C. Lee (Ed.), **Improving college teaching** (pp. 211–239). Washington, DC: American Council of Education.

MCKEACHIE, W. (1986). **Teaching Tips: A guidebook for the beginning college teacher** (8th ed.). Boston: D.C. Heath.

MCKEACHIE, W. (1988). Teaching thinking. **Update, 2**(1), 1.

MCKEACHIE, W., & KULIK, J. (1975). Effective college training. In F. Kerlinger (Ed.), **Review of Research in Education.** Itasca, IL: Peacock.

MCKEACHIE, W., PINTRICH, P., YI-GUANG, L., & SMITH, D. (1986). **Teaching and learning in the college classroom: A review of the research literature.** Ann Arbor, MI: The Regents of the University of Michigan.

MACKWORTH, J. (1970). **Vigilance and habituation.** Harmondsworth, England: Penguin.

MADSEN, M. (1967). Cooperative and competitive motivation of children in three Mexican subcultures. **Psychological Reports, 20,** 1307–1320.

MALLER, J. (1929). **Cooperation and competition: An experimental study in motivation.** New York: Teachers College, Columbia University.

MARKUS, H. (1978). The effect of mere presence on social facilitation: An unobtrusive test. **Journal of Experimental Social Psychology, 14,** 389–397.

MASQUD, M. (1980). Effects of personal lecture notes and teacher notes on recall of university students. **British Journal of Educational Psychology, 50,** 289–294.

MASTERS, B. (1979). Effects of social comparisons upon the imitation of neutral and altruistic behaviors by young children. **Child Development, 43,** 131–142.

MATTHEWS, B. (1979). Effects of fixed and alternated payoff inequity on dyadic competition. **The Psychological Record, 29,** 329–339.

MAY, M., & DOOB, L. (1937). **Competition and cooperation. Social Science Research Council Bulletin** (No. 25). New York: Social Science Research Council.

MAYER, A. (1903). Uber einzel und gesamtleistung des schul kindes. **Archiv fur die Gesamte Psychologie, 1,** 276–416.

MEAD, M. (Ed.), (1936). **Cooperation and competition among primitive peoples.** New York: McGraw-Hill.

MENGES, R. (1988). Research on teaching and learning: The relevant and the redundant. **The Review of Higher Education, 11**(3), 259–268.

MESCH, D., JOHNSON, D. W., & JOHNSON, R. (1988). Impact of positive interdependence and academic group contingencies on achievement. **Journal of Social Psychology, 128,** 345–352.

MESCH, D., LEW, M., JOHNSON, D. W., & JOHNSON, R. (1986). Isolated teenagers, cooperative learning and the training of social skills. **Journal of Psychology, 120,** 323–334.

MESCH, D., JOHNSON, D. W., & JOHNSON, R. (1988). Impact of positive interdependence and academic group contingencies on achievement. **Journal of Psychology, 138,** 345–352.

MILLER, L., & HAMBLIN, R. (1963). Interdependence, differential rewarding, and productivity. **American Sociological Review, 28,** 768–778.

VON MISES, L. (1949). **Human action: A treatise on economics.** New Haven, CT: Yale University Press.

MOEDE, W. (1927). Die richtlinien der leistungs-psycholgie. **Industrielle Psychotechnik, 4,** 193–207.

MONTAGU, A. (1965). **The human revolution.** New York: World Publishing Company.

MONTAGU, A. (1966). **On being human.** New York: Hawthorn Books.

MONTAGU, A. (1973). **Darwin, competition and cooperation.** Reprint, Westport, CN: Greenwood Press.

MOTLEY, M. (1988, January). Taking the terror out of talk. **Psychology Today, 22**(1), 46–49.

MURRAY, F. (1983). **Cognitive benefits of teaching on the teacher.** Paper presented at American Educational Research Association Annual Meeting, Montreal, Quebec.

MURRAY, H. (1985). Classroom teaching behaviors related to college teaching effectiveness. In J. G. Donald and A. M. Sullivan (Eds.), **Using research to improve teaching** (pp. 21–34). San Francisco: Jossey-Bass.

NATIONAL ASSOCIATION OF SECONDARY SCHOOL PRINCIPALS (1984). **The mood of American youth.** Reston, VA: Author.

NAUGHT, G., & NEWMAN, S. (1966). The effect of anxiety on motor steadiness in competitive and non-competitive conditions. **Psychonomic Science, 6,** 519–520.

NEER, M. (1987). The development of an instrument to measure classroom apprehension. **Communication Education, 36,** 154–166.

NELSON, L., & KAGAN, S. (1972). Competition: The star-spangled scramble. **Psychology Today, 6,** 53.

NESBITT, M. (1967). **A public school for tomorrow.** New York: Delta.

NIAS, J. (1984). Learing and acting the role: Inschool support for primary teachers. **Educational Review, 33,** 181–190.

NOEL, L. (1985). Increasing student retention: New challenges and potential. In L. Noel, R. Levitz, & D. Saluri (Eds.), **Increasing student retention: Effective programs and practices for reducing the dropout rate** (pp. 1–27). San Francisco: Jossey-Bass.

NOREM-HEBEISEN, A. (1976). A multi-dimensional construct of self-esteem. **Journal of Educational Psychology, 68,** 559–565.

NOREM-HEBEISEN, A., & JOHNSON, D. W. (1981). Relationships between cooperative, competitive, and individualistic attitudes and differentiated aspects of self-esteem. **Journal of Personality, 49,** 415–425.

OGILVIE, B., & TUTKO, T. (1971). Sport: If you want to build character, try something else. **Psychology Today, 5,** 60–63.

ORLICK, T. (1981). Positive socialization via cooperative games. **Developmental Psychology, 17**(4), 426–429.

ORLICK, T. (1982). **Second cooperative sports and games book.** New York: Pantheon.

PASCARELLA, E. (1980). Student-faculty informal contact and college outcomes. **Review of Educational Research, 50,** 545–595.

PATTERN, W. (1920). **The grand strategy of evolution: The social philosophy of a biologist.** Boston: Gorham Press.

PELZ, D., & ANDREWS, F. (1976). **Scientists in organizations: Productive climates for research and development.** Ann Arbor: Institute for Social Research, University of Michigan.

PENNER, J. (1984). **Why many college teachers cannot lecture.** Springfield, IL: Charles C. Thomas.

PEPITONE, E. (1980). **Children in cooperation and competition: Toward a developmental social psychology.** Lexington, MA: D. C. Heath.

PETTY, R., HARKINS, S., WILLIAMS, K., & LATANE, B. (1977). The effects of group size on cognitive effort and evaluation. **Personality and Social Psychology Bulletin, 3,** 575–578.

POSTMAN, N., & WEINGARTNER, C. (1969). **Teaching as a subversive activity.** New York: Delacorte Press.

PUTNAM, J., RYNDERS, J., JOHNSON, D. W., & JOHNSON, R. (1989). Collaborative skill instruction for promoting positive interactions between mentally handicapped and nonhandicapped children. **Exceptional Children, 55,** 550–557.

RATHBONE, C. (1970). **Open education and the teacher.** Unpublished doctoral dissertation, Harvard University.

REEVE, J., & DECI, E. (1996). Elements of the competitive situation that affect intrinsic motivation. **Personality and Social Psychology Bulletin, 22**(1), 24–33.

RENSBERGER, B. (1984). What made humans human? **New York Times Magazine,** 80–81, 89–95.

ROBERTS, G. (1980), Children in competition: A theoretical perspective and recommendations for practice. **Motor Skills: Theory into Practice, 4,** 37–50.

ROGERS, V. (1970). **Teaching in the British primary schools.** London: Macmillan.

ROSENSHINE, B. (1968, December). To explain: A review of research. **Educational Leadership, 26,** 303–309.

ROSENSHINE, B., & STEVENS, R. (1986). Teaching functions. In M. C. Wittrock (Ed.), **Handbook of research on teaching** (3rd ed.) (pp. 376–391). New York: Macmillan.

ROTTER, J. (1971). Generalized expectancies for interpersonal trust. **American Psychologist, 26,** 443–452.

RUGGIERO, V. (1988). **Teaching thinking across the curriculum.** New York: Harper & Row.

RUHL, K., HUGHES, C., & SCHLOSS, P. (1987). Using the pause procedure to enhance lecture recall. **Teacher Education and Special Education, 10**(1), 14–18.

SALOMON, G. (1981). Communication and education: Social and psychological interactions. **People & Communication, 13,** 9–271.

SANDERS, G., & BARON, R. (1975). The motivating effects of distraction on task performance. **Journal of Personality and Social Psychology, 32,** 956–963.

SCHOENFELD, A. (1985). **Mathematical problem solving.** Orlando: Academic Press.

SCHOENFELD, A. (1989). Ideas in the air: Speculations on small group learning, peer interactions, cognitive apprenticeship, quasi-Vygotskean notions of internalization, creativity, problem solving, and mathematical practice. **International Journal of Educational Research,** in press.

SELIGMAN, M. (1988). Boomer blues. **Psychology Today, 22,** 50–55.

SHALAWAY, L. (1985). Peer coaching . . . does it work? **R & D Notes, National Institute of Education,** 6–7.

SHARAN, S. (1980). Cooperative learning in teams: Recent methods and effects on achievement, attitudes, and ethnic relations. **Review of Educational Research, 50,** 241–272.

SHARAN, S., & HERTZ-LAZAROWITZ, R. (1980). **A group-investigation method of cooperative learning in the classroom.** Technical Report, University of Tel-Aviv, Tel-Aviv, Israel. (Review article).

SHARAN, S., & SHARAN, Y. (1976). **Small group teaching.** Englewood Cliffs, NJ: Educational Technology.

SHEINGOLD, K., HAWKINS, J., & CHAR, C. (1984). "I'm the thinkist, you're the typist": The interactions of technology and the social life of classrooms. **Journal of Social Issues, 40**(3), 49–61.

SHERIF, C. (1978). The social context of competition. In R. Martens (Ed.), **Joy and sadness in children's sports** (pp. 81–97). Champaign, IL: Human Kinetics.

SHERIF, M. (1966). **In common predicament.** Boston: Houghton Mifflin.

SHERIF, M., & HOVLAND, C. (1961). **Social judgement: Assimilation and contrast effects in communication and attitude change.** New Haven, CT: Yale University Press.

SILBERMAN, C. (1971). **Crisis in the classroom.** New York: Vintage Books.

SIMPSON, G. (1949). **The meaning of evolution.** New Haven: Yale University Press.

SKON, L., JOHNSON, D. W., & JOHNSON, R. (1981). Cooperative peer interaction versus individual competition and individualistic efforts: Effects on the acquisition of cognitive reasoning strategies. **Journal of Educational Psychology, 73**(1), 83–92.

SLAVIN, R. (1977). Classroom reward structure: An analytical and practical review. **Review of Educational Research, 47,** 633–650.

SLAVIN, R. (1980). Cooperative learning. **Review of Educational Research, 50,** 315–342.

SLAVIN, R. (1983). **Cooperative learning.** New York: Longman.

SLAVIN, R. (1991). Group rewards make groupwork work. **Educational Leadership, 5,** 89–91.

SLAVIN, R., LEAVEY, M., & MADDEN, N. (1982). **Team-assisted individualization: Mathematics teacher's manual.** Johns Hopkins University, Center for Social Organization of Schools.

SMITH, A. (1759). **The theory of moral sentiments.** Reprint. Edited by D. Raphael & A. Macfie (1976). Oxford: Clarendon.

SMITH, L., & LAND, M. (1981). Low-inference verbal behaviors related to teach clarity. **Journal of Classroom Interaction, 17,** 37–42.

SOBEL, D. (1995). **Longitude.** New York: Walker & Company.

SPILERMAN, S. (1971). Raising academic motivation in lower-class adolescents: A convergence of two research traditions. **Sociology of Education, 44,** 101–108.

SPURLIN, J., DANSEREAU, D., LARSON, C., & BOOKS, L. (1984). Cooperative learning strategies in processing descriptive text: Effects of role and activity level on the learner. **Cognition and Instruction, 1**(4), 451–463.

STARFIELD, A., SMITH, K., & BLELOCH, A. (1990). **How to model it: Problem solving for the computer age.** New York: McGraw-Hill.

STAUB, E. (1971). Helping a person in distress: The influence of implicit and explicit "rules" of conduct on children and adults. **Journal of Personality and Social Psychology, 17,** 137–144.

STENDLER, C., DAMRIN, D., & HAINES, A. (1951). Studies in cooperation and competition: 1. The effects of working for group and individual rewards on the social climate of children's groups. **Journal of Genetic Psychology, 79,** 173–197.

STEVENS, R., MADDEN, N., SLAVIN, R., AND FARNISH, A. (1987). Cooperative integrated reading and composition: Two field experiments. **Reading Research Quarterly, 22(4),** 433–454.

STEVENSON, H., & STIGLER, J. (1992). **The learning gap.** New York: Simon & Schuster.

STONES, E. (1970). Students' attitudes to the size of teaching groups. **Educational Review, 21**(2), 98–108.

STUART, J., & RUTHERFORD, R. (1978, September). Medical student concentration during lectures. **The Lancet, 2,** 514–516.

TERENZINI, P. (1986). **Retention research: Academic and social fit.** Paper presented at the meeting of the Southern Regional Office of the College of Entrance Examination Board, New Orleans.

THOMAS, D. (1957). Effects of facilitative role interdependence on group functioning. **Human Relations, 10,** 347–366.

TINTO, V. (1975). Dropout from higher education: A theoretical synthesis of recent research. **Review of Educational Research, 45**(1), 89–125.

TINTO, V. (1987). **Leaving college: Rethinking the causes and cures for student attrition.** Chicago: University of Chicago Press.

TJOSVOLD, D. (1986). **Working together to get things done.** Lexington, MA: D.C. Heath.

TJOSVOLD, D. (1991a). **The conflict-positive organization.** Reading, MA: Addison-Wesley.

TJOSVOLD, D. (1991b). **Team organization: An enduring competitive advantage.** New York: John Wiley.

TRIESMAN, P. (1985). A study of the mathematics performance of black students at the University of California, Berkeley (Ph.D. dissertation, University of California, Berkeley). **Dissertation Abstracts International, 47,** 1641-A.

TRIPLETT, N. (1988). The dynamogenic factors in pacemaking and competition. **American Journal on Psychology, 9,** 507–533.

TSENG, S. (1969). **An experimental study of the effect of three types of distribution of reward upon work efficiency and group dynamics.** Unpublished doctoral dissertation, Columbia University, New York.

VERNER, C., & DICKINSON, G. (1967). The lecture: An analysis and review of research. **Adult Education, 17,** 85–100.

VYGOTSKY, L. (1978). **Mind and society.** Cambridge, MA: Harvard University Press.

WALBERG, H., & THOMAS, S. (1971). **Characteristics of open education: Toward an operational definition.** Newton, MA: TDR Associates.

WALES, C., & SAGER, R. (1978). **The guided design approach.** Englewood Cliffs, NJ: Educational Technology Publications.

WALTON, M. (1986). **The Deming management method.** New York: Dodd, Mead, & Company.

WATSON, G., & JOHNSON, D. W. (1972). **Social psychology: Issues and insights**. Philadelphia: Lippincott.

WEBB, H. (1969). Professionalization of attitudes toward play among adolescents. In D. Kenyon (Ed.), **Aspects of contemporary sport sociology.** Chicago: The Athletic Institute.

WEBB, N., ENDER, P., & LEWIS, S. (1986). Problem-solving strategies and group processes in small group learning computer programming. **American Educational Research Journal, 23**(2), 243–261.

WILHELMS, F. (1970). Educational conditions essential to growth in individuality. In V. Howes (Ed.), **Individualization of instruction: A teaching strategy.** New York: Macmillan.

WILLIAMS, K. (1981). **The effects of group cohesiveness on social loafing.** Paper presented at the annual meeting of the Midwestern Psychological Association, Detroit.

WILLIAMS, K., HARKINS, S., & LATANE, B. (1981). Identifiability as a deterrent to social loafing. Two cheering experiments. **Journal of Personality and Social Psychology, 40,** 303–311.

WILSON, R. (1987). Toward excellence in teaching. In L. M. Aleamoni (Ed.), **Techniques for evaluating and improving instruction** (pp. 9–24). San Francisco: Jossey-Bass.

WITTROCK, M. (1990). Generative processes of comprehension. **Educational Psychologist, 24,** 345–376.

WULFF, D., NYQUIST, J., & ABBOTT, R. (1987). Students' perception of large classes. In M. E. Weimer (Ed.), **Teaching large classes well** (pp. 17–30). San Francisco: Jossey-Bass.

YAGER, S., JOHNSON, D., & JOHNSON, R. (1985). Oral discussion, group-to individual transfer, and achievement in cooperative learning groups. **Journal of Educational Psychology, 77,** 60–66.

ZAJONC, R. (1965). Social facilitation. **Science, 149,** 269–272.

Glossary

Acceptance: Communication of high regard for another person, for his or her contributions, and for his or her actions.

Additive tasks: Tasks for which group productivity represents the sum of individual member efforts.

Ad hoc decision-making groups: Faculty members listen to a recommendation, are assigned to small groups, meet to consider the recommendation, report to the entire faculty their decision, and then participate in a whole-faculty decision as to what the course of action should be.

Arbitration: The submission of a dispute to a disinterested third person who makes a final judgment as to how the conflict will be resolved. A form of third-party intervention in negotiations in which recommendations of the person intervening are binding on the parties involved.

Authentic assessment: Requiring students to demonstrate the desired procedure or skill in a "real life" context.

Base group: A long-term, heterogeneous cooperative learning group with stable membership whose primary purpose is for members to give each other the support, help, encouragement, and assistance each needs to progress academically.

Benchmarking: Establishing operating targets based on best known practices.

Bumping: A procedure used to ensure that competitors are evenly matched. It involves (a) ranking the competitive triads from the highest (the three highest achievers are members) to the lowest (the three lowest achievers are members), (b) moving the winner in each triad up to the next highest triad, and (c) moving the loser down to the next lowest triad.

Cohesiveness: All the forces (both positive and negative) that cause individuals to maintain their membership in specific groups. These include attraction to other group members and a close match between individuals' needs and the goals and activities of the group. The attractiveness that a group has for its members and that the members have for one another.

Colleagial teaching teams: Small cooperative groups (from two to five faculty members) whose purpose is to increase teachers' instructional expertise and success.

Communication: A message sent by a person to a receiver(s) with the conscious intent of affecting the receiver's behavior. The exchange of thoughts and feelings through symbols that represent approximately the same conceptual experience for everyone involved.

Communication networks: Representations of the acceptable paths of communication between persons in a group or organization.

Competition: A social situation in which the goals of the separate participants are so linked that there is a negative correlation among their goal attainments; when one student achieves his or her goal, all others with whom he or she is competitively linked fail to achieve their goals.

Competitive learning: The focusing of student effort on performing faster and more accurately than classmates.

Compliance: Behavior in accordance with a direct request. Behavioral change without internal acceptance.

Conceptual/adaptive approaches to cooperative learning: Teachers are trained in how to use a general conceptual framework to plan and tailor cooperative learning lessons specifically for their students, circumstances, curricula, and needs.

Conceptual conflict: When incompatible ideas exist simultaneously in a person's mind.

Conflict-of-interests: When the actions of one person attempting to maximize his or her needs and benefits prevent, block, interfere with, injure, or in some way make less effective the actions of another person attempting to maximize his or her needs and benefits.

Conformity: Changes in behavior that result from group influences. Yielding to group pressures when no direct request to comply is made.

Conjunctive tasks: Tasks for which group productivity is determined by the effort or ability of the weakest member.

Consensus: A collective opinion arrived at by a group of individuals working together under conditions that permit communications to be sufficiently open and the group climate to be sufficiently supportive for everyone in the group to feel that he or she has had a fair chance to influence the decision.

Continuous improvement: Ongoing search for changes that will increase the quality of the processes of learning, instructing, and assessing.

Controversy: When one person's ideas, information, conclusions, theories, and opinions are incompatible with those of another, and the two seek to reach an agreement.

Co-op Co-op: A complex cooperative learning script in which each group is assigned one part of a class learning unit, each group member is assigned part of the work and then presents it to the group, the group synthesizes the work of its members, and the group presents the completed project to the class.

Cooperation: Working together to accomplish shared goals and to maximize one's own and other's success. Individuals perceiving that they can reach their goals if and only if the other group members also do so.

Cooperation imperative: We desire and seek out opportunities to operate jointly with others to achieve mutual goals.

Cooperative curriculum package: Set of curriculum materials specifically designed to contain cooperative learning as well as academic content.

Cooperative Integrated Reading And Composition (CIRC): A set of curriculum materials to supplement basal readers in which students read, write, spell, and learn language mechanics in pairs and fours but are evaluated individualistically.

Cooperative learning: Students working together to accomplish shared learning goals and maximize their own and their groupmates' achievement.

Cooperative learning scripts: Standard content-free cooperative procedures for either conducting generic, repetitive lessons or managing classroom routines that prescribe students actions step-by-step.

Cooperative learning structures: See cooperative learning scripts.

Cooperative school: Team-based, high-performance organizational structure specifically applied to schools, characterized by cooperative learning in the classroom, colleagial teaching teams and school-based decision making in the building, and colleagial administrating teams and shared decision-making at the district level.

Criterion-referenced or categorical judgements: Judgements made comparing each student's performance against a fixed set of standards.

Decision making: Obtaining some agreement among group members as to which of several courses of action is most desirable for achieving the group's goals. The process through which groups identify problems in achieving the group's goals and attain solutions to them.

Delusion of individualism: Believing that (1) they are separate and apart from all other individuals and, therefore, (2) others' frustration, unhappiness, hunger, despair, and misery have no significant bearing on their own well-being.

Deutsch, Morton: Social psychologist who theorized about cooperative, competitive, and individualistic goal structures.

Developmental conflict: When a recurrent conflict cycles in and out of peak intensity as a child develops socially.

Direct/prescriptive approach to cooperative learning: Teachers are trained to use prepackaged lessons, curricula, strategies, and activities in a lock-step prescribed manner (step 1, step 2, step 3).

Disjunctive tasks: Tasks for which group performance is determined by the most competent or skilled member.

Distributed-actions theory of leadership: The performance of acts that help the group to complete its task and to maintain effective working relationships among its members.

Divisible task: A task that can be divided into subtasks that can be assigned to different people.

Effective communication: When the receiver interprets the sender's message in the same way the sender intended it.

Egocentrism: Embeddedness in one's own viewpoint to the extent that one is unaware of other points of view and of the limitations of one's perspectives.

Expert system: An understanding of a conceptual system that is used to engineer effective applications in the real world.

Expertise: A person's proficiency, adroitness, competence, and skill.

Feedback: Information that allows individuals to compare their actual performance with standards of performance.

Fermenting skills: Skills needed to engage in academic controversies to stimulate reconceptualization of the material being studied, cognitive conflict, the search for more information, and the communication of the rationale behind one's conclusions.

Formal cooperative learning: Cooperative groups that last from one class period to several weeks to complete any academic assignment or course requirement (such as solving a set of problems, completing a unit, writing a theme or report, conducting an experiment, or reading and comprehending a story, play, poem, chapter, or book). It ensures that students are actively involved in the intellectual work of organizing material, explaining it, summarizing it, and integrating it into existing conceptual structures.

Forming skills: Management skills directed toward organizing the group and establishing minimum norms for appropriate behavior.

Formulating skills: Skills directed toward providing the mental processes needed to build deeper level understanding of the material being studied, to stimulate the use of higher quality reasoning strategies, and to maximize mastery and retention of the assigned material.

Functioning skills: Skills directed toward managing the group's efforts to complete their tasks and maintain effective working relationships among members.

Genba: Where the action is.

Goal: A desired place toward which people are working, a state of affairs that people value.

Goal structure: The type of social interdependence structured among students as they strive to accomplish their learning goals.

Group: Two or more individuals in face-to-face interaction, each aware of his or her membership in the group, each aware of the others who belong to the group, and each aware of their positive interdependence as they strive to achieve mutual goals.

Group accountability: The overall performance of the group is assessed and the results are given back to all group members to compare against a standard of performance.

Group investigation: A complex cooperative learning script in which students form cooperative learning groups according to common interests in a topic, develop a division of labor in researching the topic, synthesizing the work of group members, and presenting the finished product to the class.

Group processing: Reflecting on a group session to (a) describe what member actions were helpful and unhelpful and (b) make decisions about what actions to continue or change.

Horizontal teams: A number of teachers from the same grade level or subject area are given responsibility for a number of students for one year or one semester.

Individual accountability: The measurement of whether or not each group member has achieved the group's goal. Assessing the quality and quantity of each member's contributions and giving the results to all group members.

Individualistic efforts: Individuals working alone to accomplish goals unrelated to and independent from the goals of the others.

Individualistic goal structure: No correlation among group members' goal attainments; when group members perceive that obtaining their goal is unrelated to the goal achievement of other members. Individuals working by themselves to accomplish goals unrelated to and independent from the goals of others.

Individualistic learning: Individuals working by themselves to ensure their own learning meets a preset criterion independently from the efforts of other students.

Informal cooperative learning: The use of temporary, ad hoc discussion groups that last for only one discussion or one class period, whose purposes are to (a) focus student attention on the material to be learned, (b) create an expectation set and mood conducive to learning, (c) help organize in advance the material to be covered in a class session, (d) ensure that students cognitively process the material being taught, and (e) provide closure to an instructional session.

Jigsaw: The work of a group is divided into separate parts that are completed by different members and taught to their groupmates.

Leadership: The process through which leaders exert their impact on other group members.

Learning goal: A desired future state of demonstrating competence or mastery in the subject area being studied, such as conceptual understanding of math processes, facility in the proper use of a language, or mastering the procedures of inquiry.

Lewin, Kurt: Father of group dynamics; social psychologist who originated field theory, experimental group dynamics, and applied group dynamics.

Maintenance of use: Continual, long-term use of cooperative learning over a period of years.

Maximizing task: Success is determined by quantity of performance.

Means interdependence: The actions required on the part of group members to achieve their mutual goals and rewards. There are three types of means interdependence: resource, task, and role.

Mediation: When a third person intervenes to help resolve a conflict between two or more people. A form of third-party intervention in negotiations in which a neutral person recommends a nonbinding agreement.

Motivation: A combination of the perceived likelihood of success and the perceived incentive for success. The greater the likelihood of success and the more important it is to succeed, the higher the motivation.

Negotiation: A process by which persons with shared and opposing interests who want to come to an agreement try to work out a settlement by exchanging proposals and counterproposals.

Norms: The rules or expectations that specify appropriate behavior in the group; the standards by which group members regulate their actions.

Optimizing task: Success is determined by quality of performance; a good performance is one that most closely approximates the optimum performance.

Outcome interdependence: When the goals and rewards directing individuals' actions are positively correlated; that is, if one person accomplishes his or her goal or receives a reward, all others with whom the person is cooperatively linked also achieve their goals or receive a reward. Learning goals may be actual, based on involvement in a fantasy situation, or based on overcoming an outside threat.

Paraphrasing: Restating the sender's message in one's own words.

Performance-based assessment: Requiring students to demonstrate what they can do with what they know by performing a procedure or skill.

Perspective taking: Ability to understand how a situation appears to another person and how that person is reacting cognitively and emotionally to the situation.

Positive environmental interdependence: When group members are bound together by the physical environment in some way.

Positive fantasy interdependence: When students imagine that they are in an emergency situation (such as surviving a ship wreck) or must deal with problems (such as ending air pollution in the world) that are compelling but unreal.

Positive goal interdependence: When students perceive that they can achieve their learning goals if, and only if, all other members of their group also attain their goals.

Positive identity interdependence: When the group establishes a mutual identity through a name, flag, motto, or song.

Positive interdependence: The perception that you are linked with others in a way so that you cannot succeed unless they do (and vice versa); that is, their work benefits you and your work benefits them.

Positive outside enemy interdependence: When groups are placed in competition with each other; group members then feel interdependent as they strive to beat the other groups.

Positive resource interdependence: When each member has only a portion of the information, resources, or materials necessary for the task to be completed and members' resources have to be combined in order for the group to achieve its goal. Thus, the resources of each group member are needed if the task is to be completed.

Positive reward interdependence: When each group member receives the same reward for achieving the goal.

Positive role interdependence: When each member is assigned complementary and interconnected roles that specify responsibilities that the group needs in order to complete a joint task.

Positive task interdependence: When a division of labor is created so that the actions of one group member have to be completed if the next team member is to complete his or her responsibilities. Dividing an overall task into subunits that must be performed in a set order is an example of task interdependence.

Procedural learning: Learning conceptually what the skill is, when it should be used, how to engage in the skill, practicing the skill while eliminating errors, until an automated level of mastery is attained.

Promotive interaction: Actions that assist, help, encourage, and support the achievement of each other's goals.

Roadblock: Hurdle that causes temporary difficulties in reaching a goal.

Role Interdependence: Interdependence created by assigning complementary and interconnected roles to each group member.

Roles: Prescription of what other groupmates expect from a member (and therefore what the student is obligated to do) and what that member has a right to expect from other group members who have complementary roles.

Routine-use level: Automatic use of a skill as a natural part of one's behavioral repertoire.

School-based decision-making: Task force considers a school problem and proposes a solution to the faculty as a whole, small ad hoc decision-making groups consider the proposal, the entire faculty decides what to do, the decision is implemented by the faculty, and the task force assesses whether or not the problem is solved.

Self-efficacy: The expectation of successfully obtaining valued outcomes through personal effort; expectation that if one exerts sufficient effort, one will be successful.

Self-regulation: Ability to act in socially approved ways in the absence of external monitors.

Small group processing: Each group member discusses how effectively they worked together and what could be improved.

Social dependence: When the outcomes of Person A are affected by Person B's actions, but the reverse is not true.

Social facilitation: The enhancement of well-learned responses in the presence of others. Effects on performance resulting from the presence of others.

Social independence: When individuals' outcomes are unaffected by each other's actions.

Social interaction: Patterns of mutual influence linking two or more persons.

Social interdependence: When each individuals' outcomes are affected by the actions of others.

Social loafing: A reduction of individual effort when working with others on an additive group task.

Social skills: The interpersonal and small group skills needed to interact effectively with other people.

Social skills training: A structured intervention designed to help participants to improve their interpersonal skills.

Social support: Significant others who collaboratively share a person's tasks and goals and provide resources (such as emotional concern, instrumental aid, information, and feedback) that enhance the individual's wellbeing and helps the individual mobilize his or her resources to deal with challenging and stressful situations.

Socioemotional activity: Behavior that focuses on interpersonal relations in the group.

Student management team: Three or four students plus the instructor who assume responsibility for the success of the class by meeting regularly and focusing on how to improve either the instructor's teaching or the content of the course.

Student Team Learning (STAD): A modification of TGT that is basically identical except that instead of playing an academic game, students take a weekly quiz. Teams receive recognition for the sum of the improvement scores of team members.

Sunburst Integrated Co-Op Learning Geometry Course: A combination of a geometry curriculum, an interactive computer program, discovery learning, and cooperative learning.

Superordinate goals: Goals that cannot be easily ignored by members of two antagonistic groups, but whose attainment is beyond the resources and efforts of either group alone; the two groups, therefore, must join in a cooperative effort in order to attain the goals.

Support: Communicating to another person that you recognize his or her strengths and believe he or she has the capabilities needed to productively manage the situation.

Synthesizing: Integrating a number of different positions containing diverse information and conclusions into a new, single, inclusive position that all group members can agree on and commit themselves to.

T-chart: Procedure to teach social skills by specifying the nonverbal actions and verbal phrases that operationalize the skill.

Team: A set of interpersonal relationships structured to achieve established goals.

Team-Assisted Individualization (TAI): A highly individualized math curriculum for grades 3 to 6 in which students work individualistically to complete math assignments using self-instructional (programmed learning) curriculum materials and have their answers checked, and help given, by groupmates.

Teams-Games-Tournaments (TGT): An instructional procedure in which cooperative groups learn specified content and then compete with each other in a tournament/game format to see which group learned the most.

Total quality learning: Continuous improvement of the process of students helping teammates learn can take place.

Transfer: Teachers take what they learn about cooperative learning in training sessions and use it in their classrooms.

Trust: Perception that a choice can lead to gains or losses, that whether you will gain or lose depends on the behavior of the other person, that the loss will be greater than the gain, and that the person will likely behave so that you will gain rather than lose.

Trusting behavior: Openness (sharing of information, ideas, thoughts, feelings, and reactions) and sharing (offering of one's resources to others in order to help them achieve their goals).

Trustworthy behavior: Expressing acceptance (communication of high regard for another person and his or her actions), support (communicating to another person that you recognize his or her strengths and believe he or she has the capabilities needed to productively manage the situation), and cooperative intentions (expectations that you are going to behave cooperatively and that everyone else will do likewise).

Unitary Task: Cannot be divided into subtasks; one person has to complete the entire task.

Vertical teams: A team of teachers representing several different subject areas are given responsibility for the same students for a number of years.

Index